MW00710871

Power

The Regenesis of Love, Faith, and Obedience

Dr. James C. Word

© Copyright 1996 — Dr. James C. Word

All rights reserved. This book is protected under the copyright laws of the United States of America. This book may not be copied or reprinted for commercial gain or profit. The use of short quotations or occasional page copying for personal or group study is permitted and encouraged. Permission will be granted upon request. Unless otherwise identified, Scripture quotations are from the King James Version of the Bible. Scripture quotations marked (NIV) are taken from the HOLY BIBLE, NEW INTERNATIONAL VERSION®. NIV®. Copyright © 1973, 1978, 1984 by International Bible Society. Used by permission of Zondervan Publishing House. All rights reserved. Emphasis within Scripture is the author's own.

Take note that the name satan and related names are not capitalized. We choose not to acknowledge him, even to the point of violating grammatical rules.

All poems in this book were written by the author.

Treasure House

An Imprint of
Destiny Image® Publishers, Inc.
P.O. Box 310
Shippensburg, PA 17257-0310

"For where your treasure is
there will your heart be also." Matthew 6:21

ISBN 1-56043-255-1

For Worldwide Distribution
Printed in the U.S.A.

Treasure House books are available through these fine distributors outside the United States:

Christian Growth, Inc.
Jalan Kilang-Timor, Singapore 0315

Rhema Ministries Trading
Randburg, South Africa

Salvation Book Centre
Petaling, Jaya, Malaysia

Successful Christian Living
Capetown, Rep. of South Africa

Vine Christian Centre
Mid Glamorgan, Wales, United Kingdom

Vision Resources
Ponsonby, Auckland, New Zealand

WA Buchanan Company
Geebung, Queensland, Australia

Word Alive
Niverville, Manitoba, Canada

Inside the U.S., call toll free to order:
1-800-722-6774
Or reach us on the Internet: **http://www.reapernet.com**

Contents

Preface

Many Christians believe that a book about "power" based on God's Word is a distortion of the purpose and the intent of the Bible. I believe just the opposite is true! The Bible, as much as anything else, is a book about *power*. Its basic theme is salvation, and it seeks to restore man to his original relationship with God. The goal in God's Word is to transform man from flesh and weakness to the Spirit and to strength. Nothing could be more empowering than that!

God equates restoration with power. Salvation is power. It takes supernatural power to fearlessly walk in the knowledge of eternal life and face every challenge with certainty! After all, the ultimate alignment with power is to have God on your side!

If salvation and restoration comprised all the Bible intended to portray about power in God's work with mankind, then even those two aspects of power would suffice for an entire book. However, God reveals many more aspects about power than just restoration and salvation in those pages! The Bible describes thousands of promises God has made to those who seek Him. Story after story describes the countless ways God has drawn people to Himself through His endless blessings and promises of personal power.

Although Adam's story illustrates the fall of human beings, the rest of the Bible is based on promises of God's power to uplift the human race. All of the patriarchs followed the promise God made to Abraham to make his descendants into a great nation, with no end to its prominence and power. It is out of the promise to Abraham that the rest of the Scriptures follow. The patriarchs, for example, were blessed as long as they followed the promise.

When calamity came, as it inevitably did when the promise was neglected, God set His people apart in a wilderness and made an eternal covenant with them. He specifically stated how He would fulfill all their needs, desires, and hopes—as long as they followed the original plan and promise.

The story of Israel after Sinai draws upon God's plan of restoration and the legal documents that set forth the terms and conditions for reaching that goal. Essentially, the history of Israel is nothing more than an instruction in power from on high! The theme never diminishes or changes through all of the trials of the judges, kings, prophets, and apostles. The promise set before them is always one of power. Ultimately the promise of power was a divine appointment for righteousness, but out of it flowed every other conceivable strength and blessing.

The purpose of this book is to detail the history, the promises, and the blessings of God as they relate to restoration in the broadest sense of the term. It demonstrates that the emphasis of power is clearly the central thrust of the Bible. This includes every possible type of power. It avoids dwelling on the subject of wealth, describing instead the basis for political power and personal advantage, as well as spiritual power and the enhancement of family and community.

This is an ambitious book, intended to be the blueprint for the power ministry God has given me. It reveals the basic principles in God's Word, and summarizes much of the biblical narrative. It confines its sources to the Scriptures with few exceptions. Each of its four major parts begins with a characterization of God and His Kingdom. I believe that *power* derives from the nature of God Himself, and from the structure of His government. Each of these parts parallels the perfect state of God with the imperfect state of the human species, contrasting God's nature and purpose with the fallen nature of the human race.

The first part, "Power Now!" demonstrates the urgency for power, and acknowledges its availability. The second and third parts, "The Power of Love" and "The Power of Faith," set out the prerequisites for acquiring power from on high. They examine the identity of the believer and the relationship between human beings and God. The fourth part, "The Power of Obedience," is the focal point of the work. It catalogs the blessings and promises found in God's Word and details the many types of power God promises His people. The fifth part, "The Power of the Word," describes the legal basis for God's promises of power, and the instruments available for wielding that power. The sixth part, "The Gift of Love," is an extension of part five that describes the ultimate form of empowerment, *the merger of the Holy Ghost with the human being*. The "Conclusion," part seven, shows how personal choice is part of God's plan to render absolute power to those who find love, faith and obedience.

I hope that through these pages you will be challenged to put God to the test. Either God is real and His promises are true, or He is false and they are all lies. I sincerely believe He has called us to *power*. It is His Great Commission. If you want it, you can have it. The Word of God is all about power. The Scriptures encourage it and point the way to it. Christ gives the Spirit for it. I pray that you, and everyone else who reads this book, will find power in your identity in God through Jesus Christ. May you grow in faith and vision by discovering the infinite strength of God that is available for you right now! May you rise to a new height in the Spirit and put on the power of God!

Holistic Healing and Deliverance

There is a "hidden concept" resident throughout this book on power. Called "Holistic Healing and Deliverance," it means that God's system is intended to strengthen *every part* of our lives, healing every sickness and wrong, and restoring all the life we've lost to sin. It simply means that God's system makes us "whole people." The most fundamental sources of healing are love, faith, and obedience. They often heal some of the worst spiritual and physical conditions of men, women, and angels. Godliness is the essence of healing power, since God is love, and loving itself makes us children of God (see 1 Jn. 4:7-8). When we fall short of perfect love, perfect faith, and perfect obedience, we are usually too far removed from God's healing power to receive His protection. That is when we must resort to principles and practices that close the gap, such as fasting and prayer. In the Old Testament, the Hebrew people also used diets, cleansing, and rest.

Spirituality, or righteousness, is the *primary* source of healing, however. The rituals of fasting, tithing, and praise are not intended to replace love, mercy, and faith (see Mt. 23:23). Yet when we fail to reach God's best, satan is sure to attack. At that point, the casting out of demons and the anointing of oil serve as remedies for sickness and affliction (see Jas. 5:13-15).

Holism says that the closer we come to God's perfect will, the more we will receive healing, deliverance, and power. Jesus, in the Sermon on the Mount, simply concluded, "Be ye therefore perfect, even as your Father which is in heaven is perfect" (Mt. 5:48).

Jesus taught the perfect way. In marriage, He taught no divorce (see Mt. 5:31-32). In personal affairs, He taught no worldly involvement (see Mt. 5:27-28). In civil affairs, He taught no judicial inquests (see Mt. 5:25-26). In financial affairs, He taught the treasures of Heaven (see Mt. 6:19-34). In dietary plans, He taught simplicity without waste (see Mt. 14:14-21; 15:30-38).

Somehow we have lost sight of the perfect way. Divorce is common. Lawsuits threaten to topple the courts. Every indulgence is incited to excess. The local churches are paralyzed by assaults on integrity and their press toward liberality.

Holistic healing looks back to Eden for the more simple and more perfect plans. Jesus said of divorce, "...but from the beginning it was not so" (Mt. 19:8). In the beginning, there was high holiness in speech and in comportment. Now the devil is in every part of our lives. Prayer, for example, has been outlawed from the schools while pornography is legally dispersed on the airways.

This book reminds us of the need to seek perfect love, perfect faith, and perfect obedience. It describes the diet in Eden and points to the perfect union of husband and wife. It lays out the perfect law of God contained in the Ten Commandments.

The Spirit of God through Jesus Christ has come into the believer, and He is the most radical healing strategy of God. God Himself has come into His creation to make us whole from within! The new covenant, of course, does not replace the old. The principles of love, faith, and obedience rest upon the premise that God's law is written by the Spirit in our hearts.

The indwelling Spirit merely fulfills the basic principles of God. The work of holistic healing and deliverance is brought to completion by the power and presence of the Almighty God.

Introduction

I remember crossing the plains of Kansas on my first trip to California. It seemed like the fields of golden wheat went on forever. I was always fascinated by the million miles of electrical power lines that stretched across the sky from Missouri to Colorado. I wondered, *Where do they all go? Where do they come from?*

No matter how often I saw the power lines that traced the roads from town to town, I never connected the towers and power lines to the source of the energy surging inside them or to their final destination. If I stopped overnight at a Motel Six and listened to the news on a local radio station or kept the lights on all night, I still didn't picture the electric wires or imagine the source of the electrical power.

So it is with our heavenly power Source. The gap between the light switch and the Power Plant seems too great for our minds to connect the two. Neither the golden wheat of Kansas nor the crisp blue sky of the midwestern plain can take the mind and senses back from the creation to the Source.

The connection between the gift and the Giver, and between the natural phenomenon and the Creator is somehow lost in the human part of things. Not even the celestial canvas that changes every moment with new and different divine artistry seems capable of carrying the distracted human mind to the heavenly hands that made it all possible.

Though most people agree that the very order of nature attests to the existence of God, many find it easier to believe that mankind is self-empowered than to trace nature's wonders back to their divine Source. However, I have found *a map to God*! It reveals every detail of our terrain with each strength, joy, and new burst of life and pain. Every created thing is linked to and empowered by the person and presence of God.

We might understand better if we could have been with Adam and Eve the day they were ejected from Paradise and barred from its pleasures and security by the fiery swords of cherubim. Were it not for the unfamiliar press of hunger and the now hostile terrain and animal life, the primal pair would have lingered near the gates, sobbing their lives away.

Few men were as holy and faithful as Adam, our earthly father who alone among us stood closest to the apex between divine power and human weakness. He could stretch out his arms and touch both the Source of life and the source of his own destruction. Adam saw both sides of Paradise. He clearly saw and felt the pain from the distance sin had made between God and His fallen creation.

Our task is to yield to the Holy Spirit as He patiently rebuilds, reconnects, and energizes the ancient pathways of power. At Calvary, our world regained the way to Paradise. It is up to us to open the door and enter in, but it can only be done with *power* from on high...

Part I

Power Now!

Behold the Lion.

Chapter 1

The Pathway to Power

There is a certain pathway that leads to power. It can be traced through the lives of apostles, prophets, and kings in the Bible. It is also revealed in the movements of the Hebrew children through the wilderness of sin, and it is fully exposed in the history of the early Church and the miraculous life of Jesus Christ. This pathway of God may even be seen in your life and mine!

The pathway to joy, peace, and fullness of life was laid down in the beginning by the hand and mind of the Creator. Somehow Heaven's pathway was lost again and again as the race of man wandered off the path of God and away from His power. But the pathway to power was never destroyed. It can still be found today, a living way open to every man, woman, and child. Yet, if there is a simple way that leads to power and abundant life, then why does it seem almost impossible to find? *Where did we go wrong?*

In the beginning, the main pathway to power was the one that led to the tree of life and away from the tree of the knowledge of good and evil. The pathway was open, clear, and direct because man *dwelt* with Power. Adam and Eve exercised dominion over all the earth in God's presence and with His approval. They could eat of the tree of life! There was only *one rule* in the earth in their day: "But of the tree of the knowledge of good and evil, thou shalt not eat of it: for in the day that thou eatest thereof thou shalt surely die" (Gen. 2:17). God established this rule to protect His created children from spiritual death. They didn't understand that disobedience would separate them from the eternal Spirit of God.

Once Adam and Eve sinned, they were separated from the immediate presence and *power* of God, so the Lord had to reveal the pathway to power He had ordained before the foundations of the earth. This way to power was more circuitous, but God was determined to bring Adam's children back to His garden of power and to the tree of life. The eternal Spirit of power would not return to intimately commune with the spirits of men and place them back on the pathway until Christ came, laid down His life, and poured out His Spirit on the Day of Pentecost (see Acts 1:8; Is. 32:13-15).

Our restoration has been incomplete. If the power at Pentecost was to set the course for our return to the power in Eden, then something is still missing! Jesus Christ has given us every necessary tool to clear the way, but someone in this generation has to lead. Someone has to say, "Rise up, mighty nation! Awaken the giant within you! Declare war against the enemy! The time for power is NOW!"

Again we have wandered from the pathway of power and followed the "road to weakness." We have passed through the seven cities mentioned in the Book of Revelation: Ephesus, Smyrna, Pergamos, Thyatira, Sardis, Philadelphia, and Laodicea (see Rev. 2–3). If these cities represent the universal Church in historical array, then, with few exceptions, the road to Laodicea has led us from strength to weakness!

Beginning in Ephesus, our great love for God was weakened from the start. Then it was shaken by tribulations at Smyrna, and compromised by evil infiltrations at Pergamos and Thyatira. The nearly dead church of Sardis saw a revival at Philadelphia, but the church at Laodicea is still remembered for its backslide to compromise for wealth and comfort.

Church history chronicles a gradual but continuous detour from the pathway of power to powerless apostasy interrupted only by God's sovereign acts of intervention and realignment. The miracles of the apostles slowly turned into pragmatic dogmas. The voices of the heavenly host gradually grew silent as we turned our hearts away and joined our voices with the noise of the world system. The visions of God have yielded to our flesh-bound desire for things that we can touch, see, or feel—and therefore accumulate and control.

The cry for power is timely and more urgent than ever! The sweeping hand of prophetic time has placed the world at the dawn of the third day after the death and resurrection of our Lord and Savior (see 2 Pet. 3:8). Many believe the restoration of God's Church and nation is not far into the future (see Jn. 2:19). There is a vital hope for renewed power in the congregation of the saints. Someone must put us back on the pathway of God.

This message gives voice to a promise—not a new promise, but an old and faithful one. It is the promise that says we can do all things through Him who called us. It is the promise of power to overcome despair and hopelessness and to live a full and abundant life. It is the promise of miracles in everyday life, and the power to ask what we will in Jesus' name and know that it will be done!

I speak of the power of God, the power He only gives to His people. It is the truth about God's pathway to that power and how we are to use it. This message is based on the things contained in the Word of God. It is based on the law, the prophets, the letters to the churches, and the Gospels. It is my humble attempt to sort out the basic concepts of the Scriptures within the overall framework of *power*.

Just before Jesus Christ ascended from the earth, His final words to His disciples revealed a divine order of priority and purpose for the Church:

> *And He said unto them, Go ye into all the world, and preach the gospel to every creature. He that believeth and is baptized shall be saved; but he that believeth not shall be damned. And these signs shall follow them that believe; In My name shall they cast out devils; they shall speak with new tongues; they shall take up serpents; and if they drink any deadly thing, it shall not hurt them; they shall lay hands on the sick, and they shall recover* (Mark 16:15-18).

These words stand in stark contrast to God's warning in Eden when He said, "For in the day that thou eatest thereof thou shalt surely die" (Gen. 2:17b). God's warning foretold the serpent's victory, but Christ's commandment foretold the serpent's defeat. One spoke of tasting death after willfully eating a deadly fruit; the other spoke of the power to overcome death after unknowingly drinking a deadly poison. One described the way to weakness, defeat, and death while the other described the way to power, victory, and life.

Joel prophesied under the Old Covenant that God would "pour out [His] Spirit upon all flesh" (Joel 2:28). Peter brought Joel's prophetic words to life in Acts 2:15-18, when he declared:

> *For these are not drunken, as ye suppose, seeing it is but the third hour of the day. But this is that which was spoken by the prophet Joel; and it shall come to pass in the last days, saith God, I will pour out of My Spirit upon all flesh: and your sons and your daughters shall prophesy, and your young men shall see visions, and your old men shall dream dreams: and on My servants and on My handmaidens I will pour out in those days of My Spirit; and they shall prophesy.*

If Peter considered his day to be "the last days," then our day 2,000 years later may be assumed to be the very last "hours and minutes"! Peter then added to his discussion of the second coming by saying this:

> *But, beloved, be not ignorant of this one thing, that one day is with the Lord as a thousand years, and a thousand years as one day. The Lord is not slack concerning His promise, as some men count slackness; but is long-suffering to us-ward, not willing that any should perish, but that all should come to repentance* (2 Peter 3:8-9).

Jesus Himself promised us, "...He that believeth on Me, the works that I do shall he do also; and greater works than these shall he do; because I go unto My Father" (Jn. 14:12). His promise is still true. He knew His disciples would touch more people than He could ever reach in His physical body. It also means that through undaunted faith, true believers have the power to change the world, even now! How? Faith touches and activates the power of God. Faith dispatches Heaven's angelic army by reaching directly to the throne room of the Almighty and the seat of the Captain of the host, Jesus Christ.

He personally intercedes to the Father for us, and we know that with God, "nothing shall be impossible" (Lk. 1:37)!

We need to get back to the basics of God and return to the pathway of God. This is synonymous with "getting back to the basics of power," and it challenges the position of weakness in which many believers seem content to live. God's call to return to His way of power presses us to the edge of practical faith. It brings together in one place the bounty of blessings for everyday life and the far-reaching miracles of the consecrated walk with God.

Why is the local church so weak, and why do the saints seem to be so defeated? Why is the power of God's Spirit that was revealed at Pentecost and throughout the Epistles conspicuously absent from congregations today? Most Christians live sickly lives full of failure. Where is the power Christ proclaimed? Surely "...the Lord's hand is not shortened, that it cannot save; neither His ear heavy, that it cannot hear" (Is. 59:1). God has promised us power and His promises are settled. We need to take heart and believe His Word: "God is not a man, that He should lie; neither the son of man, that He should repent: hath He said, and shall He not do it? or hath He spoken, and shall He not make it good?" (Num. 23:19)

I know thy works, that thou art neither cold nor hot: I would thou wert cold or hot. So then because thou art lukewarm, and neither cold nor hot, I will spue thee out of My mouth. Because thou sayest, I am rich, and increased with goods, and have need of nothing; and knowest not that thou art wretched, and miserable, and poor, and blind, and naked: I counsel thee to buy of Me gold tried in the fire, that thou mayest be rich; and white raiment, that thou mayest be clothed, and that the shame of thy nakedness do not appear; and anoint thine eyes with eyesalve, that thou mayest see. As many as I love, I rebuke and chasten: be zealous therefore, and repent (Revelation 3:15-19).

The last-day Church exemplified by the church at Laodicea is lukewarm, halfhearted, and full of compromise. Does it sound familiar? Is it any wonder this church is weak and ineffectual? Lukewarm water is generally worthless. It is unfit for consumption and useless as a cleaning agent. Most Christians today don't realize how closely we match this sad litany of Laodicea! We claim to be magnificent, but we are miserable. We rejoice that we are rich, but we are poor. We boast of our knowledge and vision, but we are blind. We parade in our Sunday best and boast of our righteousness, but we are naked. We need God's power.

Speaking through Hosea the prophet, God declared, "My people are destroyed for lack of knowledge.... As they were increased, so they sinned against Me: therefore will I change their glory into shame" (Hos. 4:6-7). Like Samson, who came from a barren womb with the calling of a Nazarite and judge of his nation, the modern Church was strong in spirit at first. Later on, a lust for pleasure and comfort permeated our ranks and weakened us. The evil and crippling force of compromise, apostasy, and apathy blinded our eyes and stripped away our strength. We are a laughingstock before our critics, a shadow of our potential, paraded before a jeering public like Samson before his mocking Philistine captors!

How could this happen? Delilah enticed Samson to tell her the condition of his Nazarite vow and reveal the secret of his great strength. She betrayed God's anointed for money and delivered him into the hands of a heathen power. Samson believed that his strength came from his vow not to cut his hair, though he might have toyed with the idea of being invincible without the vow. He suffered from the foolish delusion of the Laodiceans. He saw himself as increased in goods and having need of nothing. He did not know his life was about to be tried in the fire of adversity.

When Delilah learned of Samson's Nazarite vow, she had his head shaved and called in his enemies. The mighty champion of God was too weak to defend himself as his eyes were gouged out and as he was chained and cast into prison. As he passed each day at the mercy of his mockers, he once again remembered his vow to God. His promise was merely a vehicle of faith and obedience that put him in touch with the Source of all power in the universe. He finally began to understand that there was no magic in the strands of his hair or in his abstinence from wine. Only at the end of his life did his faith transcend the natural limits of his physical gifts. At last, he knew for certain that the Nazarite vow was just a pathway to the power that only God could provide!

Blind, poor, and wretched, Samson stood in the heathen temple of Dagon, the false god of the Philistines. While his enemies praised their idol for delivering Samson into their hands, his hair and his faith had begun to grow again. His own physical power was useless. He was chained, miserable, and lost, but out of the grips of his despair, Samson again called on the name of the Lord: "...remember me, I pray Thee, and strengthen me, I pray Thee, only this once, O God, that I may be at once avenged of the Philistines for my two eyes" (Judg. 16:28).

God responded to Samson's repentance by flooding his body with power from on high! Samson took hold of the two middle pillars of the temple and pulled down the roof of the building, killing more than 3,000 men and women in one act! By that act of faith, he killed more of Israel's enemies in his death than he had in the rest of his life. Through his faith, the worshipers of Dagon learned that Jehovah is the only true and living God.

The story of Samson is a prototype of the message in this book. He was a man born with a divine calling on his life and a promise of great power. When he remained on the pathway of power, he maintained his connection to the Source of his power and supernaturally fulfilled his calling. When he rejected the pathway and neglected the Source of the promise, he lost the power of his calling. Samson became weak long before the Philistine lords cut off his hair. He became lukewarm long before he told the secret of his vow. He was blind even before the Philistines put out his eyes, and he was wretched before Delilah and the Philistines began to tease and mock him for his weakness. *Samson lost his strength when he left the pathway of God.* He turned his eyes away from the empowering presence of God and became weak when he gave in to his lower passions and submitted to an evil force.

Samson is an Old Testament picture of the New Testament Laodicean church, and he is a type and shadow of the Church in our day! We are unaware of our sorry state of affairs because we are already blind, weak, poor, and miserable. We have left the pathway of God and have broken our connection with the Source of our increase. We are sick, and our spiritual eyes must be anointed with eyesalve so we can see our danger. The overcoming power of God is activated and preserved by a vow of surrender to God and by an unbroken relationship of love and commitment. We only have power when we follow the pathway of God, and that requires faith, obedience, and surrender.

Jesus Christ compares you and I to salt, a spice that was as valuable as money in His day. He said, "Ye are the salt of the earth: but if the salt have lost his savour, wherewith shall it be salted? it is thenceforth good for nothing, but to be cast out, and to be trodden under foot of men" (Mt. 5:13). He also compared the saints to light: "Ye are the light of the world. A city that is set on an hill cannot be hid. Neither do men light a candle, and put it under a bushel, but on a candlestick; and it giveth light unto all that are in the house" (Mt. 5:14-15).

The Laodicean church was like salt that has lost its savor. Like a dim and dying light, its power was almost gone because it had lost its zest and strength. God is out to wake up the drowsy disciples hidden in the congregation of saints. He wants to arouse the powerful giant inside each of us, and point the way back to His pathway. He calls us to be zealous and to repent so we can resist the enemy.

"For God hath not given us the spirit of fear; but of *power*..." (2 Tim. 1:7). "Behold, I give unto you *power* to tread on serpents and scorpions, and over all the power of the enemy: and nothing shall by any means hurt you" (Lk. 10:19). God made us to be filled with His power, and He is prepared to give it to us NOW. Something has gone terribly wrong; but, the answer and solution to restore us to power is only a choice away...

Part II

The Power of Love

All things were created by God, and all beings have their existence in God. All power in the universe is in God's hands. There is no power in any form that comes from any other source. God creates, sustains, and controls all power of every kind. God is the source of power.

God is the self-existent One. He depends on no one and nothing for His being, His continuation, or His strength. He is the essence and the fullness of power. Since God is the source of all life, every being outside of God requires the power of God to live, to grow, to build, and to relate.

Every created being gets its strength and its nourishment from its direct or indirect connection to the Source of all power, God Himself. The closer and more abiding the connection between a being and the Creator, the more power that being has at its command. The more distant and disconnected the being is from the Creator, the less power that being has at its command.

Chapter 2

The Dawn of Dissent

God has always governed the universe through the benevolent power of His love. From the beginning, He endowed man with intellect, spiritual power, and a moral imperative. All things were established and are maintained by God's strength and nurturing, but Adam and his descendants were subject to God solely by individual choice. Duress, force, coercion, or temptation were alien to the system of government created by the Omnipotent One. Pure love was the only basis for God's order. Then everything changed.

> *...every precious stone was thy covering, the sardius, topaz, and the diamond, the beryl, the onyx, and the jasper, the sapphire, the emerald, and the carbuncle, and gold: the workmanship of thy tabrets and of thy pipes was prepared in thee in the day that thou wast created. Thou art the anointed cherub that covereth; and I have set thee so: thou wast upon the holy mountain of God;*

thou hast walked up and down in the midst of the stones of fire. Thou wast perfect in thy ways from the day that thou wast created, till iniquity was found in thee. ...and thou hast sinned: therefore I will cast thee as profane out of the mountain of God: and I will destroy thee, O covering cherub, from the midst of the stones of fire (Ezekiel 28:13-16).

Lucifer was anointed a covering cherub for Jehovah God. At one time, he was full of wisdom and perfect in beauty. He walked on the holy mountain of God in the midst of stones of fire. He had every precious jewel as his covering, and his many voices were superior to all of the other voices of God's creations. His character was perfect from the day that he was made until pride and rebellion entered his heart.

Lucifer turned his heart from the majesty of his Maker and began to consider the perfect beauty and unusual intellect that he possessed in himself. Gradually the chief archangel, the morning star, began to think highly of himself. In his growing conceit and malevolent judgment, lucifer began to envy the power of God. More and more he had eyes and praise only for himself, until finally he exalted and magnified himself above the Creator: "I will overthrow the Kingdom of God and establish my own," he said in his heart.

...I will ascend into heaven, I will exalt my throne above the stars of God: I will sit also upon the mount of the congregation, in the sides of the north: I will ascend above the heights of the clouds; I will be like the most High (Isaiah 14:13-14).

It wasn't enough that lucifer had conceived such a wicked plan in his heart; he tried to persuade the other angels that God's government was unjust and tyrannical. He said that God wanted to subject "equally capable" beings to His rule to keep them from assuming their "rightful positions of equality" with God. (If this sounds familiar, it should be. Satan used the same lie on Eve in the garden, and he still tries it today on you and I!)

The ambitious covering cherub used the same strategy against God that he taught young Prince Absalom to use against his father, King David, eons later. Secretly, he began to spread the vicious lie that God was a self-possessed despot who was only using the angelic host for His own selfish purposes. He even said the Almighty was forcing worship through deception and delusion upon beings who were, at the very least, His "peers."

Lucifer's prideful lies triggered a brief rebellion and a would-be coup in Heaven. The Almighty God, in His infinite mercy, sought in every way to dissuade the covetous angel from his foolish blasphemy. He tolerated the wicked devices of this cherub (known as the "Day Star") for a time, but the moment came when He quelled the rising tide of rebellion in the twinkling of an eye and cast out the evil creature and all of his followers. Altogether, one-third of the angels believed the lies and joined satan's rebels. Michael the archangel and the hosts of Heaven threw lucifer and his rebels down to the earth. There, lucifer's light was extinguished and darkness prevailed. Now called "satan," he and his hordes continued in their rebellion by the same deception, preying upon human beings.

The power that God bestowed on those magnificent creatures was perverted by pride, and they quickly moved to lead Adam and Eve into conflict with their Creator, confusing the couple's purpose and identity. Soon the seed of Adam was wholly devoted to satan's paranoiac views of God and His Kingdom.

Satan and his angels worked tirelessly among the sons of Adam to establish a force in the earth to oppose the rule of God and the righteousness of His Kingdom. Though satan's corps of fallen angels were outnumbered two-to-one by the angels of God, they were bound by no "rules" or commitment to truth and free will. They did not have a fraction of the power of God or His legions of faithful spirits, but satan used all of the evil power at his disposal to misrepresent God and to deceive the lowly human. God, on His part, had sworn by His own name to remain true to His own nature and deal with man according to righteousness, truth, love, and justice.

The very accusations satan had hurled at his perfect Creator were in truth the blueprints and patterns he would follow in his own dominion of darkness. The evil lucifer, once forcibly removed from the light of the Almighty, became incredibly hideous and despotic. Now a self-possessed impostor who bullied his bitter angelic host to further his own selfish goals, satan demanded and even forced worship from his would-be peers through delusion, deception, fear, and manipulation. Satan's dark domain was founded upon coercion, disruption, and chaos; its chief virtues were hatred and envy, though for centuries he carefully hid the true character of his plan from fallen man. Satan promised to give his followers power, but from the beginning, his plan was to enslave them all to himself.

For a brief time, satan had access to the conventions of the sons of God (see the Book of Job). He spoke freely of the theoretical basis for his appealing counter-theory of the nature of man, and of the governance of God. Finally, after centuries of lies and broken and bitter schemes, satan's evil underside became apparent to all, and the Almighty banished the accuser of the brethren from Heaven. I can imagine the angels saying this:

If satan had the notion to resist,
Why couldn't he call up his own army to assist?
If there is no life in his hand
And no power in his plan,
Then he might as well shut up, cease, and desist!

Satan can neither give life nor take it away. He is absolutely at the mercy of God (see Job 1:12; 26:6-7). He cannot create even a single flower or a solitary blade of grass. After the Millennium, he will be challenged to create life, which he cannot do. In a last-ditch effort to overcome the Savior, he will raise up an army by deceiving the nations and attack the saints of the beloved city, Jerusalem. In an instant, however, God will command fire to fall from Heaven and destroy them (see Rev. 20:8-9).

Satan made a fatal error. God governs by neither force nor compulsion. His justice demands that all created spirit beings have moral choice. Just as the angelic host was allowed to choose between God and satan, so man is presented with the same decision. Ironically, God never ceased to love His fallen creatures. It was not in His nature to destroy His own creation, and for that reason He gave the heavenly hosts sufficient time to examine His character and come to their own conclusion. He gently discouraged the evil one from his fatal flight into hell, but to no avail.

Although all the forces of God's creation testified to His infinite love and affection, the devil refused to receive their counsel. In the end, God's justice compelled Him to distance Himself and His Kingdom from the evil in the rebels. Their very separation from the preserving and nurturing presence of God distorted their natures and they took on the character of vile wraiths and wretched, disenfranchised specters of darkness.

Earth became the hapless home of the fallen angels, and it became the "proving grounds" of the struggle between good and evil. The "garden of God" at Eden was created as a spiritual microcosm of Heaven, a place designed for the delight of its Creator. It was a precious paradise filled with every good and perfect gift from God. It was here that the dramatic conflict between God and His fallen cherub over the lives of Adam and Eve was to be played out.

The Garden of Eden possessed the fruits of both eternal life and eternal death. By divine design, God reproduced in real and symbolic form all the necessary elements of the forces present in the heavenly sphere. He endued one tree with life-giving power that was manifested in its delicious fruit. In another, He planted the knowledge of good and evil. Then He gave Adam authority over all created life, and He placed him in the garden with the command to dress and keep it (see Gen. 1:26; 2:15).

When the first humans lost sight of the character of their Creator, they, like satan before them, failed to appreciate the power and the love of God. As succeeding generations focused more and more upon their own attributes and wants, they dreamed of being as powerful and wise as their Creator. Man distorted worship by substituting deaf statues in human form in the place of God. He put material things before God, choosing to worship animals and inanimate objects. Ultimately, his chief object of worship and adoration was himself instead of God.

God refused to enslave His creation, although He saw the reenactment of the rebellion again and again. No wonder Samuel the prophet declared in King Saul's day, "For rebellion is as the sin of witchcraft, and stubbornness is as iniquity and idolatry" (1 Sam. 15:23a). This is true not only because of the ultimate consequences of good and evil, but also because of satan's persistent distortion of God's character. Satan repeatedly led humans to their own demise through lust and pride in their various forms. He is especially effective with the appetite for pleasure, love of wealth, love of beauty, and sexual excess. These things can quickly overthrow the strongest of earthly beings by usurping their God-given dominion over the earth and destroying their powerful relationship with God.

Chapter 3

The Twilight
of Dissent

Rebellion reigned on the earth until God Himself, in the form of Jesus Christ, came to rescue His creation and resolve the conflict between good and evil. Jesus the Messiah came to demonstrate the character of God framed in man. The Son of man and the Word of God, He was a living parable of God's nature and government, representing God's love and power in full measure. He embodied every instruction from the Father.

He fulfilled every Messianic prediction and clarified and confirmed the nature of the Godhead. As the Groom, He came with a mission of love and mercy for His Bride, providing a link between creature and Creator. Now fallen man can again taste joy and satisfy the transcendent urge to fulfill life's purpose by abiding in His plan. Jesus Christ revealed and illuminated the first element of power: *love*.

This Is No Accident!

Why?

Why did God make the rose so red,
Or the field of grain so golden?
Why did He make the grass so green—
If not to just behold them?
I can't recall a single tree,
Snowflake, raindrop, or grain of sand
Without perfect symmetry.
Why did God give the birds a song
Or make honey for the bee?
Why are the wondrous sounds of daybreak
All in harmony?
Why do the stars come out at night—
If not for you and me?

Just as the natural realm reflects the detailed will of God in all of its glory *by design*, so the Church reflects the beloved Bride of Christ! The love of Christ for the believer is greater than all other loves. God will withhold no good thing from His creation. "But my God shall supply all your need according to His riches in glory by Christ Jesus" (Phil. 4:19).

God wants to make "all things work together for good" in our lives (Rom. 8:28). He is deeply in love with His Church. We are like Him to the degree that we seek good for others. Miracles happen when our desires match His. When they don't, anything *but* the miraculous may occur! We will never allow God to make choices for us if we don't know and trust Him. We must love our Creator in order to receive His wisdom, blessings, and power. When we love Him, we learn He can "do exceeding abundantly above all that we ask or think, according to the *power* that worketh in us" (Eph. 3:20).

We all have *some* access to God's power, even if we hate Him or deny His existence! Natural laws affect all of us, and the sun, moon, and stars shine down on the just and the unjust alike. Yet, only those who meet His requirements have access to His greatest power. "...Eye hath not seen, nor ear heard, neither have entered into the heart of man, the things which God hath prepared for them that love Him" (1 Cor. 2:9).

The first requirement is love because a loving relationship with God destroys slavery to fear and prevents rebellion. Love of God reverses the curse of satan and sin. Love brings eternal peace. Any person who comes to love the Creator submits willingly to God. Love is the supreme solution to the spiritual and earthly conflict. Genuine love even benefits those who claim to hate God and oppose His system. God has always loved us unconditionally, but those who want to have eternal fellowship with Him must love Him in return and unite with Him. Jesus said that love of God is the first and greatest commandment of all (see Mt. 22:37).

Love bonds the universal family as an essential element of God's power. It releases God's unlimited blessings by literally ushering us into the family of the Creator. Love defines His community in Heaven and on earth. It is so important that John wrote, "For God is love" (1 Jn. 4:8b). Everything God thinks, feels, and does is an outpouring of His boundless, unconditional love for His creation—even His correction and chastisement in our lives.

God's love is the fruit and proof of His eternal interest in His creation. His love is the reason that He gave His Son to die for us (see Jn. 3:16). *Love holds dear and near.* By His love, God binds Himself to us by ceaselessly anticipating and considering human needs, desires, capacities, and limitations. He showers us with love because He made us in His own image and likeness (see Gen. 1:26).

Our make-up still bears the imprint of divine character. Parents still bond with their children by an intimate connection of love. The God/man, Jesus Christ, demonstrated His unity with man's mortality before entering eternity. God helps us conquer and overcome by the power of His love and the imprint of His character and Spirit.

We must voluntarily take on the mind and Spirit of God to gain complete access to His limitless love and blessings. We must return to our original state of innocence by voluntarily allowing God's Spirit to fill our bodies and minds with purity instead of evil and rebellion. *True love yields.*

Satan needs willing hosts to work his devious schemes. He won new power over the earth when Adam yielded control through disobedience. The devil ruled for centuries until Christ overcame him by giving up His life on the cross. Christ rose from the dead and rescued us from bondage to sin, restoring us to our original relationship to God.

The power of love helps us take on the mind of God in two ways. First, we *identify with God* by voluntarily surrendering to Christ and rejecting satan and sin. We cast satan out of our lives just like he was cast out of Heaven. We acknowledge God as the Lord of our lives. Second, we are given the *endowment of the Holy Ghost* (the presence of Christ in our lives and the seal of our inheritance) through Jesus.

"But as many as received Him, to them gave He power to become the sons of God, even to them that believe on His name" (Jn. 1:12). Jesus Christ restored man to his rightful place in God's family after sin marred our links to God—our character and identity. Adam was a created son modeled after Jesus, the only *begotten* Son of God. Had Adam not sinned, all of his descendants would have been children of God with all of Adam's characteristics (including eternal life). Each of us could have eaten from the tree of life and lived in eternal bliss (see Gen. 2:9,16).

Angels enjoy an everlasting station and order before God (see Eph. 1:19-21). We too were created to enjoy an eternal relationship with God (see Rom. 8:29-30)! Adam sinned, but God had already made provision for us in Himself. He could already see us at the marriage feast of the Lamb in the company of honored guests as old as time itself (see Rev. 19). Jesus likens us to His Bride, and declares that we are "members of His body, of His flesh, and of His bones" (Eph. 5:30). In marriage, the bride and groom become one. Jesus has bonded Himself to us as His Bride, the Church. We are destined to be forever united in love as one.

"For unto which of the angels said He at any time, Thou art My Son, this day have I begotten thee?" (Heb. 1:5a) This statement comparing Jesus the Son to angels now applies to us (see Gal. 3:26). "Behold, what manner of love the Father hath bestowed upon us, that we should be called the sons of God..." (1 Jn. 3:1). We are made higher than the angels, and have been restored to the intimate relationship Adam enjoyed with God before the fall. We are now God's children and heirs through Christ (see Gal. 4:7). God's love has lifted us up into His cradling arms.

For thousands of years, men served a God they could neither touch nor feel. The compassion and love of Jesus Christ fulfilled our deepest longing. Our reconciliation to God through Christ fulfilled the desire of Eve to be like God, but with humility and love instead of pride and lust. Eve had the image of God, but did not recognize it. We will have God's image, see it and be humbled by it through our love and submission to Christ (see 1 Cor. 13:9-13)! Jesus eradicated the pride of satan because He shared our pain and heartache and personally experienced our frustrations. He witnessed our failures, temptations, and triumphs; He tasted our hopes and faced our fears. He championed our need to be saved and gave us victory over the grave. *Love touches.*

Once, we wandered in darkness blinded and deluded by satan. Now, we have seen the light of Christ and walk in the brightness of His light (see Eph. 5:8), and we dare not return to the darkness (see Gal. 4:8-9). Christ came in the flesh to free us from ignorance and qualify us for adoption as sons (see Gal. 4:4-5). "But ye are a chosen generation, a royal priesthood, an holy nation, a peculiar people; that ye should shew forth the praises of Him who hath called you out of darkness into His marvellous light" (1 Pet. 2:9).

> *For ye have not received the spirit of bondage again to fear; but ye have received the Spirit of adoption, whereby we cry, Abba, Father. The Spirit itself beareth witness with our spirit, that we are the children of God: and if children, then heirs; heirs of God, and joint-heirs with Christ... (Romans 8:15-17).*

I believe when we receive our crowns in Heaven, the crowns of priestly kings (see Rev. 2:10; 20:6), we, like the 24 elders of Revelation 4:4, will cast them down before the throne of the One who is worthy to receive glory, honor, and power (see Rev. 4:10-11). We will be overwhelmed by the incredible power of God's love.

God's love is so strong that He put all the treasures of Heaven on the line for our souls. God spared nothing to ransom those He loved. What is our worth in His eyes if He sent His only begotten Son to die on the cross, and spared not His own blood? He sacrificed the prophets from Jeremiah to John the Baptist to bring our redemption to pass.

Think of the power of this love! It is deeper than the depths of the deepest ocean, and greater in height than any mountain! Nothing can match the depth and breadth and height of God's love for His people. Paul declares:

> *...neither death, nor life, nor angels, nor principalities, nor powers, nor things present, nor things to come, nor height, nor depth, nor any other creature, shall be able*

to separate us from the love of God, which is in Christ Jesus our Lord (Romans 8:38-39).

Christ has placed this God-sized love in our inner person, in the Holy Spirit of God, as the resident keeper of the house of our salvation. This is the second aspect of God's "love connection."

Christ said, "...Except a man be born of water and of the Spirit, he cannot enter into the kingdom of God" (Jn. 3:5). He consistently compared the Spirit to natural things that sustain life. He spoke of "living water" to the Samaritan woman (see Jn. 4:10-14), and of "living bread" to a multitude (see Jn. 6:51). The "living bread" Jesus described was a life-giving sustenance that had to be taken into the body. This was an image of the life-giving, life-sustaining Spirit of God Himself. *Love gives.*

In the beginning was the Word, and the Word was with God, and the Word was God. The same was in the beginning with God. All things were made by Him; and without Him was not any thing made that was made. In Him was life; and the life was the light of men. ... And the Word was made flesh, and dwelt among us, (and we beheld His glory, the glory as of the only begotten of the Father,) full of grace and truth (John 1:1-4,14).

Christ was and is the eternal God "made flesh" who dwelt among men. Christ the divine Spirit had to become flesh to make recompense for sin to recapture the power Adam had lost to satan. He paid the price for man's disobedience and fulfilled our duty to God. He showed that love is superior to hatred, envy, and pride. His example demonstrated that only the willing and only those with serious intentions should expect to come to God. The cruelty of His death at Calvary emphasized the high price of redemption and the gravity of our infraction against God, and it set the standard measure for God's love! We owe God our full and unrestrained love and devotion. The power of His love can overcome every negative influence in our lives!

Adam retained his body but submitted his will to satan and died spiritually in Eden, allowing sin to enter the bloodline of mankind. Jesus submitted His body to satan's agents of evil, but reserved His will and Spirit for total obedience to God. In the end, Jesus Christ died a sinless physical death and deposed the usurper, satan. He allowed the Spirit of God to enter the bloodline of man and empowered us once again to walk with God.

Wherefore when He cometh into the world, He saith, Sacrifice and offering Thou wouldest not, but a body hast Thou prepared Me: in burnt offerings and sacrifices for sin Thou hast had no pleasure. ... Then said He, Lo, I come to do Thy will, O God. He taketh away the first, that He may establish the second. By the which will we are sanctified through the offering of the body of Jesus Christ once for all. And every priest standeth daily ministering and offering oftentimes the same sacrifices, which can never take away sins: but this man, after He had offered one sacrifice for sins for ever, sat down on the right hand of God; from henceforth expecting till His enemies be made His footstool. For by one offering He hath perfected for ever them that are sanctified. Whereof the Holy Ghost also is a witness to us: for after that He had said before, this is the covenant that I will make with them after those days, saith the Lord, I will put My laws into their hearts, and in their minds will I write them (Hebrews 10:5-6,9-16).

The Holy Ghost is proof of our spiritual perfection through Christ. The Holy Ghost is the fulfillment of God's covenant with His people, the agent of Christ's promises, blessings, and hope. The Holy Ghost is simply the power of God's presence in our lives.

The power of God's love is manifested as the power of God Himself *in us*. Our vital relationship with God through the indwelling Spirit of God was made possible solely by Jesus Christ when He defeated satan with the power of the Almighty. He released the power of the Holy Spirit in the earth to help us walk in the light of God's Word. He reinstated us into the family and lineage of God with full rights and privileges. Now we possess the Spirit and mind of God, "for as many as are led by the Spirit of God, they are the sons of God" (Rom. 8:14).

Likewise the Spirit also helpeth our infirmities: for we know not what we should pray for as we ought: but the Spirit itself maketh intercession for us with groanings which cannot be uttered. And He that searcheth the hearts knoweth what is the mind of the Spirit, because He maketh intercession for the saints according to the will of God. And we know that all things work together for good to them that love God, to them who are the called according to His purpose. For whom He did foreknow, He also did predestinate to be conformed to the image of His Son, that He might be the firstborn among many brethren. Moreover whom He did predestinate, them He also called: and whom He called, them He also justified: and whom He justified, them He also glorified. What shall we then say to these things? If God be for us, who can be against us? He that spared not His own Son, but delivered Him up for us all, how shall He not with Him also freely give us all things? (Romans 8:26-32)

Love gives! Can you imagine it? God planned from the start to conform us to the image of His Son! He planned to freely give us all things because of love. Love is His source of power flowing through us. Love is this powerful weapon we have been given to overcome distress, pain, conflict, and destitution.

Who shall separate us from the love of Christ? shall tribulation, or distress, or persecution, or famine, or nakedness, or peril, or sword? ... Nay, in all these things we are more than conquerors through Him that loved us (Romans 8:35,37).

The Psalmist so beautifully symbolized the Father's love in his well-known image of the Good Shepherd. He pointed to the Spirit of God as his guiding and comforting rod and staff:

Yea, though I walk through the valley of the shadow of death, I will fear no evil: for Thou art with me; Thy rod and Thy staff they comfort me. Thou preparest a table before me in the presence of mine enemies: Thou anointest my head with oil; my cup runneth over. Surely goodness and mercy shall follow me all the days of my life: and I will dwell in the house of the Lord for ever (Psalm 23:4-6).

God's love compels goodness and mercy to follow us throughout our lives (see Deut. 5:10). If we surrender to Him like innocent lambs, He annoints our heads with the oil of the Spirit. He pours out such abundant blessings for us that we cannot help but to pass them on to others. We feast before our enemies, and are strengthened by God's love. He has declared:

When thou passest through the waters, I will be with thee; and through the rivers, they shall not overflow thee: when thou walkest through the fire, thou shalt not be burned; neither shall the flame kindle upon thee. ...

Since thou wast precious in My sight, thou hast been honourable, and I have loved thee... (Isaiah 43:2,4).

Love allows us to see God, especially as it is demonstrated by Jesus and is revealed in us through the Holy Spirit. It frees us, as children of God, from doubts about God's presence and His care. Love sweeps aside the questions doubt raises in the heart, allowing God to reveal Himself with fewer obstructions and partiality. The things of nature take on a new freshness and idealism in the light of love. The trees and the clouds in the sky are seen as a true testimony to the love of God within us. The world becomes a book we now read with enthusiasm because we know and love the Author! All of His works are full of interest for us because we love His hands, His mind, and His character in the earth.

Love always points us to the Father. Every day reveals more about how God wishes to lead us into goodness and into truth. Each day becomes a joyful passage into deeper conversation with the Lord as we find His message in the early morning light and close each day with thanks for all His love.

God's love draws wisdom near, too. Through love, we can better understand the nature of things around us because we accept the fact that He has made them all and we see them in God's light. Even the infinite complexities that surround us are revealed by the Holy Ghost (see 1 Jn. 2:27). We discern what science can never confirm or deny because love gives us wisdom, vision, and hope.

Love casts out fear, especially as we grow closer to God. Peter the fisherman knew the dangers of a stormy sea, yet when he saw Jesus walking on the water, he cast his fears aside!

...Lord, if it be Thou, bid me come unto Thee on the water. And He said, Come. And when Peter was come down out of the ship, he walked on the water, to go to

Jesus. But when he saw the wind boisterous, he was afraid; and beginning to sink, he cried, saying, Lord, save me (Matthew 14:28-30).

Peter loved the Lord. Despite all of his trials, failures, and confrontations, he held fast to Christ through the good and the bad. He knew that intimate relationship with Jesus was vital to the redeemed life. He wrote, "As newborn babes, desire the sincere milk of the word, that ye may grow thereby: if so be ye have tasted that the Lord is gracious" (1 Pet. 2:2-3). Our loving relationship with Jesus Christ sustains and increases the power of God in our lives.

Peter walked on the water as long as he kept his eyes on Jesus. He began to sink only when he looked away from Jesus to consider the boisterous sea and his own inability. Even then, the Lord gave Peter power to recover and returned him safely to the ship. Despite his failures and personality faults, Peter grew to be a giant among the apostles by abiding in the Lord. His love was perfected by the Spirit to the point that Peter was able to speak the Word of God with boldness, heal the sick, and even raise the dead (see Acts 3:1-9; 4:8-13; 5:14-16; 9:36-42). *Love stays.*

I am the true vine, and My Father is the husbandman. Every branch in Me that beareth not fruit He taketh away: and every branch that beareth fruit, He purgeth it, that it may bring forth more fruit. ... Abide in Me, and I in you....He that abideth in Me, and I in him, the same bringeth forth much fruit: for without Me ye can do nothing. ... If ye abide in Me, and My words abide in you, ye shall ask what ye will, and it shall be done unto you (John 15:1-2,4-5,7).

Our "love connection" to God empowers us to love one another supernaturally, according to John's epistle: "Beloved, let us love one another: for love is of God; and every one that loveth is born of God, and knoweth God. He that loveth not knoweth not God; for God is love" (1 Jn. 4:7-8).

We have no cause to neglect our neighbor if we truly abide in Christ. Because of His promise to us in John 15:7, we can freely give to others *without fear of want*. If we are certain of eternal life, then we can release the things most people believe bestow immortality—fame, wealth, and personal or political influence—even though we may possess them. If we are *completely* certain of eternal life, we can follow the footsteps of Jesus and give up our lives for those we love. Jesus said, "Greater love hath no man than this, that a man lay down his life for his friends" (Jn. 15:13). We say we love Jesus, but the Lord loved us first, when we weren't so lovable:

> *For when we were yet without strength, in due time Christ died for the ungodly. For scarcely for a righteous man will one die: yet peradventure for a good man some would even dare to die. But God commendeth His love toward us, in that, while we were yet sinners, Christ died for us* (Romans 5:6-8).

The Bible says the love of God is "shed abroad in our hearts by the Holy Ghost" (Rom. 5:5). God is the author of life itself, and His love gives force and power to every kindness that proceeds through us! He gives us reason to believe in ourselves and in our neighbors and He gives us identity and purpose through Jesus Christ. His gift of the Holy Ghost sets us free to love and live for things we cannot see. Because of His abiding presence, we are free to give. *Love gives!*

"We love Him, because He first loved us" (1 Jn. 4:19). Because God first loved us and placed His love in us, the love we have received from God possesses *the character* of God! His love in us is self-existent; it derives its force from the strength and power of God, independent of our purposes, our character, or our unique personalities.

Whenever we freely and obediently "give His love away" to others, God's love sustains *their* lives and empowers *them* with freedom and nourishment. The unconditional love of a grandmother for her granddaughter, for example, builds the character of the child and is not selfishly reserved for the grandparent. It frees the child and propels her to joyously reach for her highest potential. It fills the child with worth and direction without being forceful, coercive, or compromised. God's love lifts, lightens, and releases.

God's love also contains the character of God's governing order and His bond of love for mankind and the angels. It lends an eternal dimension to life and yields independent choice. God's love is full of power, purpose, and positive direction.

This love blossoms as the "unity of all" strengthens the "work of each."

For as the body is one, and hath many members, and all the members of that one body, being many, are one body: so also is Christ. For by one Spirit are we all baptized into one body, whether we be Jews or Gentiles, whether we be bond or free; and have been all made to drink into one Spirit. ... And whether one member suffer, all the members suffer with it; or one member be honoured, all the members rejoice with it (1 Corinthians 12:12-13,26).

Love is patient, love is kind. It does not envy, it does not boast, it is not proud. It is not rude, it is not self-seeking, it is not easily angered, it keeps no record of wrongs. Love does not delight in evil but rejoices with the truth. It always protects, always trusts, always hopes, always perseveres. Love never fails... (1 Corinthians 13:4-8 NIV).

The Twilight of Dissent

In the end of the beginning, the splendor of man's first home had died because the joy of relationship had been snatched away by the grip of sin. The first created humans walked with God in the cool of the morning in the flawless splendor of the Garden of Eden. That first generation had been crafted by the fingers of God, and represented the highest development of the human spirit, mind, and body.

The earth was a panoramic display of God's abundant love, care, and genius. This paradise had no hint of imperfection. There was no want, no pain, no sorrow, no sin, *and no death*. The fullness of life reigned in this place devoid of rain, snow, hail, cold, thunder, lightning, earthquakes, and floods. There were no volcanic eruptions or desert lands—no drought, famine, hunger, or fear. The earth was watered by a mist that rose from the ground and settled over all the terrain like a warm blanket in the waking hours of the morn. All of life was awakened to the melodious strains of the forest mixed with the sweet aromatic shades of the opening flowers and herbs.

It only took the rebellion of the devil and the sin of the first man to set the world on a crash course with destruction. With disobedience came the unlovely seeds of strife, hatred, and discord. Plants suddenly began to produce thistles with piercing needles and thorns under a sun that now scorched the earth, creating vast deserts, dust bowls, and wastelands. Many animals became carnivores and began to eat flesh to satisfy their ravenous taste for blood. Suffering and death had come to earth to stay.

With every passing generation, the human condition deteriorated and degraded from its first estate of perfection in

God's presence. Men became less and less able to resist the wiles of the devil as the earth became more tortured and battered in its cycles. The sun burst through the atmosphere and sent piercing death rays down to the earth, while misery, hunger, strife, and sadness settled in across the globe.

A glimmer of hope remained, as it always has. God the Creator still loved His creation, fallen though it was. The mind of God already had a redemption plan: "For God so loved the world, that He gave His only begotten Son, that whosoever believeth in Him should not perish, but have everlasting life" (Jn. 3:16).

For centuries though, the world lay in spiritual decay as God patiently dealt with a remnant of people descended from Abraham. Even this remnant was in its waning years when at last the Lord spoke through the Jewish prophet Joel, saying, "And it shall come to pass afterward, that I will pour out My spirit upon all flesh; and your sons and your daughters shall prophesy, your old men shall dream dreams, your young men shall see visions: and also upon the servants and upon the handmaids in those days will I pour out My spirit" (Joel 2:28-29).

Surely the time is fulfilled for the spiritual restoration of God's people. Jesus Christ has come, laid down His life, and risen again. Let us turn to the Lord with all our hearts and bask in His love. The love of God steadies the soul with the divine imprint of identity and purpose. Love lifts and carries; it sets the mind free. Love picked me up and set me higher. The love of God is the spark that lights a holy, unquenchable fire.

God's unconditional abiding love holds near and dear! Love gives! Love stays! Love touches! Love yields! Love never fails! In God's love we find identity, purpose, freedom of choice, vision, strength, wisdom, and courage!

Part III

The Power of Faith

God inhabits light unapproachable. He sits alone. His throne is high and lifted up. Above the throne are angels; each one has three pairs of wings. Two wings are to cover their faces. Two wings are to cover their feet. Two wings are to fly at His bidding. God is not reproved; neither is there contention with the Almighty. His thoughts are not our thoughts; and His ways are not our ways. As far as the heavens are above the earth, so far are His thoughts higher than our thoughts and His ways higher than our ways. God cannot be tempted with evil; neither tempts He any man with evil. He changes not. With Him there is no variableness. He cannot lie; neither is there shadow of turning in Him. He speaks and it must stand.

Chapter 4

The Origin
of Doubt and Faith

U nfortunately, any serious examination of the origin of doubt and faith requires a study of its unworthy author, satan, formerly known in the heavenlies as lucifer (the "shining one"). As we noted earlier, lucifer was a "covering cherub" assigned to the throne room of God. God exalted his station and made him magnificent in form and function. Over time, however, this created being wanted to be more. In his vanity he conceived a lie about God that has been repeated again and again. He said in his heart that God was not the final judge. He claimed that God was not just because He was untrue to His Word, and thus He could change.

In the Garden of Eden, lucifer (now called satan, the "hater and accuser") took the form of a serpent, one of the most beautiful of God's creatures at the time, and spoke to Eve.

Now the serpent was more subtil than any beast of the field which the Lord God had made. And he said unto the woman, Yea, hath God said, Ye shall not eat of every tree of the garden? And the woman said unto the serpent, We may eat of the fruit of the trees of the garden: but of the fruit of the tree which is in the midst of the garden, God hath said, Ye shall not eat of it, neither shall ye touch it, lest ye die. And the serpent said unto the woman, Ye shall not surely die: for God doth know that in the day ye eat thereof, then your eyes shall be opened, and ye shall be as gods, knowing good and evil (Genesis 3:1-5).

In the end, Eve ate some of the fruit from the tree of the knowlege of good and evil. She also gave her husband some of the forbidden fruit, and he ate it as well.

Oh, how the great trees are fallen down!
Their seed is scattered out into the garden and the field,
And the autumn gives no harvest now. The soil refuses yield.

Can we ever hope to reap before the barren earth is chilled?

Oh, how the great trees are fallen to the ground!
Scattered out!!
Seeds of doubt!!
And the shoots that have arisen,
Cynicism, skepticism, even atheism...

Oh, how the great trees are fallen down!

* * * * *

Satan is a liar and the father of lies (see Jn. 8:44). His snare is ancient and well-worn, but its bait excites the intellect and titillates the senses of man. His masterful temptation deeply touches our pride, causing the momentary impression that we are "missing something" that we should already have or should already know. It taunts us to "prove something" to ourselves and to others.

The devil's subtle lie provides a handy and "acceptable" excuse for his victims to convince themselves that they are "helping" or "extending" God's work by "reinterpreting" what God *really meant.*" This devilish snare induces momentary and voluntary forgetfulness of God's all-seeing eye and His all-powerful hands with thoughts like, "God certainly would not mind," or "This must be what He expects or intended." His deception blinds willing hearts to the blasphemy and the idolatry interwoven with the fruit of the lie.

The tempter is wise enough to "cover up" his continuous insults about the Creator, and he will even help us hide our own lust for a season. That is why he presents his favorite lie in a context of beauty, wisdom, and light. Many times those with little discernment or a weak relationship with God even believe that satan's whispers have come from God Himself! The fatal consequence of his prideful proposition is made to seem harmless. But Jesus Christ stripped away the sham and pretense for all time with this inspired revelation spoken to hostile accusers:

> *Ye are of your father the devil, and the lusts of your father ye will do. He was a murderer from the beginning, and abode not in the truth, because there is no truth in him. When he speaketh a lie, he speaketh of his own: for he is a liar, and the father of it* (John 8:44).

Although satan's temptation is extremely subtle, we do not have to yield or be fooled. God will not allow us to be tempted beyond our ability to resist, and He will always provide a route of escape (see 1 Cor. 10:13).

Eve was the first human being to yield to the lust of the flesh, the lust of the eyes, and the pride of life. Although these lusts were described by John in the New Testament (see 1 Jn. 2:16), they were birthed in the foul heart of satan in the Garden of Eden eons before John's day.

Eve "saw" that the tree was "good for food" for her flesh (see Gen. 3:6a). She recognized the pleasure it brought to her eyes (though it was forbidden). She believed satan's claim that the fruit would make her wise like God, and she desired that position. Although Adam ate the fruit knowingly—he was not deceived—he nonetheless yielded to the same temptations as Eve. The chief strength of the temptation Adam yielded to came from his relationship with Eve, not satan's subtle words. Perhaps it took Eve's beauty to beguile Adam. Whatever the cause, Adam placed his desire for the woman above his desire to obey God's direct command.

For all that is in the world, the lust of the flesh, and the lust of the eyes, and the pride of life, is not of the Father, but is of the world (1 John 2:16).

Vanity, lust, and pride are perhaps the most dangerous sins plaguing man. They all bear the mark of satan's active involvement in our affairs, and they make the most powerful impressions upon our flesh. They invoke strong passions and hungers that can quickly lure the spiritually debilitated into a false sense of self-confidence and cause them to divert their focus from the glory of God to themselves.

Eve's great temptation was to raise herself to the level of God and command her own destiny. Satan's ultimate goal all along was to trick man into wrongfully claiming the honor and glory that was rightfully due to God alone. This would ultimately require the children of Adam to put aside the true and living God and create a god in the image of man in His place. This is the basis for his lie. This is the origin of doubt.

His Name Is Cain

Cain and Abel were the first sons of Adam and Eve. Cain was a farmer, and Abel was a herdsman. Both brought offerings to God. Cain brought the "fruit of the ground," and Abel brought the firstfruits of his animals. Both sacrifices represented the products of their labors. God accepted Abel's offering, but He rejected Cain's grain offering. This angered Cain who, as the firstborn, felt he deserved honor for who he was in the family line and for what he had produced from the ground (even though the ground was cursed).

God was patient and loving to Cain as He explained to him the purpose of the offering. He reassured Cain that faithfulness has its sure reward, and admonished him to master every temptation. But Cain followed in the footsteps of his parents. He ignored God's counsel and yielded to his passions. His rage and envy led to his murder of Abel.

Cain was proud, self-possessed, and defiant. He wanted to substitute his own way for God's appointed way. Like Adam and Eve before him, Cain did not take God at His word. He placed *his* will above the will of God, and he and his seed were driven farther away from God as outcasts—just as his parents were driven from the garden of God years before.

Cain became a restless wanderer, the "firstborn" of all those who refuse to put their faith in the revealed Word of God. All who follow Cain's path of rebellion and selfish pursuits are exiles from the sure comforts and security of knowing God and trusting in His promises. They are doomed to wander outside of God's blessings until they repent or die.

Like his parents before him, Cain, by willfully sinning, produced a curse that affected everyone in his line. His beloved soil no longer yielded its bounty; he could harvest only thistles and thorns. His lack of faith and obedience made him both nonproductive and dispossessed. The ceaseless yearning of Cain's youth would never be satisfied. Every step only brought more uncertainty. There was no rest for his weary feet; he was cursed to wander for the rest of his days. He was a man without a home. Although he founded the city of Enoch, it was an unsuccessful attempt to "undo" the curse of God (see Gen. 4:17). His labors were in vain.

> *There is a man not satisfied with gain.*
> *Although he has the wealth of many men,*
> *He is lonesome just the same.*
> *Every new idea excites him,*
> *And he jumps on every train.*
> *But soon his steam runs out, and then,*
> *He's restless once again.*
> *That basic satisfaction in himself never came.*
> *Somehow, the joy of simple things is more than he*
> *can claim.*

> *His name is Cain.*

God Is Faithful

Faith is rooted in the character of God because God does not change. He is the constant from which all else receives its measure. He is the absolute value and the sure source of every power in the universe. All things have their being in God and continue to exist solely by His will. God cannot change. He is the essential proponent of all life, the "prime mover and first stroke," the beginning and most basic effect for every cause. He is perfect and complete, eternal and timely. He can do all things—except fail. He is ever-present, all-knowing, and always available. He neither slumbers nor sleeps. He is faithful.

God's faithfulness is written in the earth, the sun, the moon, and the stars. Their complex orbits and perpetual glow across the sky erase all questions of their presence. There is no failure of the sun's heat, light, or life-giving strength. Day after day, the heavenly bodies appear and disappear with a regularity that boggles the mind. Just as the seasons come and go and come again, there is the easy feeling that they have always been and always will be. The earth is one giant flower that always touches, feeds, shelters, and protects. Nothing is lacking and nothing is amiss. Nothing is untimely or in sharp discord with the rest.

The faithfulness of God is inscribed in the cycles of His creation. From century to century, the natural laws of God are openly revealed over and over again. The miracle of birth, the pattern of development, decline, and death move silently in pace with the eternal. Rain falls to the earth only to rise again in a vapor that softens the air. It forms the clouds and the atmosphere that create an invisible, ceaseless veil of life-giving moisture around our planet. The gaseous exchanges between plants and animals flow in and out like the ceaseless waves of the ocean tide. There is never a day that the sun does not rise, or a night that the moon does not glow. Birth, growth, and death follow the plan of God so faithfully that only the strongest deviations can shake our senses and renew our awareness that the rhythms of God go on. All of God's work is "insured and stamped" with the certainty of its innate and orderly self-perpetuation because of the character of its Author.

God's work reflects God's nature and glory. Even the simple, most elementary of His creations is crowned with a complexity and intricacy that staggers the imagination. Within every layer of life there lies another layer, and still another. Each level is equally diverse and elaborate. Animate or inanimate, each part of God's creation is woven with others to form an inextricable web of ordered and complicated clockwork. It is no wonder that the highest wisdom is the recognition of God. Seeing God's hand in the order of life is the beginning of understanding, and the intimate knowledge of God is sublime and transcendent revelation!

Enoch, the seventh son in line from Adam, had this intimate knowledge of God. He lived blameless before God. He was a total contrast to Cain; *Enoch* means "the consecrated one." Enoch prophesied that destruction would come to the wicked more than 950 years before the great flood of Noah's day. He yielded himself so completely to the will of God that he heard the voice of God and faithfully preached repentance and obedience for over 300 years.

Again, the world ignored the truth and grew darker and darker in its sin, yet the Lord found Enoch to be so faithful that He took him up to Heaven before he could taste the death that rebellion had brought to mankind. Because Enoch trusted the Lord, the story of his life became a perpetual reminder that when men dare to believe God, nothing shall be impossible.

Chapter 5

Faith Goes Beyond the Senses

Faith is a certainty that exceeds all of our human senses. Faith goes beyond what we can see, hear, touch, smell, or taste. Since faith cannot be fully understood by the mind or "probed" by the body's sensory system, theoretically we might reason and calculate for a thousand years only to find that faith would still elude our intellect! Faith defies all logic because it surpasses the finite realm. It stands outside the purely rational. Paul told the church at Corinth:

> *For the preaching of the cross is to them that perish foolishness; but unto us which are saved it is the power of God. For it is written, I will destroy the wisdom of the wise, and will bring to nothing the understanding of the prudent. Where is the wise? where is the scribe? where is the disputer of this world? hath not God made*

foolish the wisdom of this world? For after that in the wisdom of God the world by wisdom knew not God, it pleased God by the foolishness of preaching to save them that believe. For the Jews require a sign, and the Greeks seek after wisdom: but we preach Christ cruci-fied, unto the Jews a stumblingblock, and unto the Greeks foolishness; but unto them which are called, both Jews and Greeks, Christ the power of God, and the wisdom of God (1 Corinthians 1:18-24).

Paul bluntly told the Corinthians, "And my speech and my preaching was not with enticing words of man's wisdom, but in demonstration of the Spirit and of power: that your faith should not stand in the wisdom of men, but in the power of God" (1 Cor. 2:4-5). Faith is based on the power and presence of God. Paul warns us that we cannot understand God or the cross through mere human reasoning. Christ's death on the cross makes no sense to the human mind. Although it may appear to be melodramatic and sensational, there is still the spiritual importance. Many feel they can never take the gospel seriously precisely because they think God is incapable of "lowering" Himself to have a son or daughter as we perceive them (see Jn. 5:18), and they think He is incapable of experiencing death. The subtle spiritual connotations of Jesus' ministry are totally ignored by such logic.

Paul wrapped up his discussion of wisdom and foolishness by declaring, "But the natural man receiveth not the things of the Spirit of God: for they are foolishness unto him: neither can he know them, because they are spiritually discerned" (1 Cor. 2:14).

King Solomon, the wisest man who ever lived, advises us to "Trust in the Lord with all thine heart; and lean not unto thine own understanding. In all thy ways acknowledge Him, and He shall direct thy paths. Be not wise in thine own eyes: fear the Lord, and depart from evil" (Prov. 3:5-7). Paul preached the gospel with the demonstration of the power of the Spirit because faith is built upon *spiritual discernment.*

The Way of Faith

I will follow You, Lord,
Though the road be rough and long,
I will follow You, though the way may be unknown.
I will not ask You why You take a turn to left or right.
I will not make a fuss, though I must journey in the
night.
I will follow You, Lord,
Like a child behind his dad.
If I'm led into some danger,
I will not cease to move ahead.
Though the winds and rains may blind my path
And the road is washed away,
I will never turn my back on You,
And my course I pledge to stay.
'Cause I will follow You, Lord,
'Til my life will be no more,
For I will follow You
Until I reach the other shore.

Faith is not established by what is seen or felt. It does not rest upon signs and wonders, or come to us through the emotions. If faith were just a by-product of the miraculous, it would be lost as soon as the signs and wonders were gone. If it were based on human emotions, we would need a stopwatch with a second hand to measure its brief lifetime.

Miraculous signs simply reinforce the presuppositions you already have about God. If you already have doubts about the truth and the power of God, then signs and wonders will probably not shake your "negative faith." If you already believe, you need no sign. If you are searching, then God may well use a sign or wonder to capture your attention and draw you to Himself. Christ said that signs "follow" faith.

And these signs shall follow them that believe; In My name shall they cast out devils; they shall speak with new tongues; they shall take up serpents; and if they drink any deadly thing, it shall not hurt them; they shall lay hands on the sick, and they shall recover (Mark 16:17-18).

But if all prophesy, and there come in one that believeth not, or one unlearned, he is convinced of all, he is judged of all: and thus are the secrets of his heart made manifest; and so falling down on his face, he will worship God, and report that God is in you of a truth (1 Corinthians 14:24-25).

Signs are useless to people who have "made up their mind." The more skeptical Jewish leaders often asked Jesus for a sign of His authority *immediately after witnessing a miracle with their own eyes!* His many miracles didn't change them (see Mt. 12:38; Jn. 2:18; 6:30). Those who "request a sign" nearly always have wrong motives. Why would someone ask for a sign immediately after they have witnessed a miracle from God? These requests are not so much a search for faith as an indication of disbelief or a desire to set a snare.

In the case of the feeding of the 5,000, the request for a miracle indicated a lack of faith, an inability to recognize spiritual truth, and a selfish desire to satisfy the temporary needs of the flesh. They wanted more food, and they wanted Jesus to assume the authority of an earthly king over Israel and oppose the Romans. After Jesus had miraculously escaped a mob that wanted to make Him a military leader, He was found at Capernaum. (Jesus had walked upon the sea.) The people asked Him, "...Rabbi, when camest Thou hither?" (Jn. 6:25) He read their hearts and said:

> ...*Verily, verily, I say unto you, Ye seek Me, not because ye saw the miracles, but because ye did eat of the loaves, and were filled. Labour not for the meat which perisheth, but for that meat which endureth unto everlasting life, which the Son of man shall give unto you: for Him hath God the Father sealed* (John 6:26-27).

Basically those people were asking Jesus, "What can You do for us?" They had only received temporal food from Christ's ministry, totally unaware of the spiritual bounty He had laid before them! They wanted Christ to be the Roman-era equivalent of a "liberation theology" activist or social reform leader who could lead the masses in public demonstrations and overthrow the Roman government. "Feed us! Get the Romans off our backs! Oh yeah, and teach us to do miracles, too."

The Lord patiently and lovingly tried to touch their hearts with the truth. He offered them the priceless gift of salvation through faith, and warned them, "It is the spirit that quickeneth; the flesh profiteth nothing: the words that I speak unto you, they are spirit, and they are life" (Jn. 6:63).

The Basis of Faith

The ministry of Jesus to an unbelieving nation was in fulfillment of a prophecy given about 700 years before by Isaiah the prophet:

> ...*Go, and tell this people, Hear ye indeed, but understand not; and see ye indeed, but perceive not. Make the heart of this people fat, and make their ears heavy, and shut their eyes; lest they see with their eyes, and hear with their ears, and understand with their heart, and convert, and be healed* (Isaiah 6:9-10).

Most of the Jewish world, then and now, is deaf to the call of the Holy Spirit to receive and believe in Jesus Christ as the Messiah of the Torah. Jesus knew those who believed and those who disbelieved. He said by way of a parable, "I am the good shepherd, and know My sheep, and am known of Mine" (Jn. 10:14). He also said:

> *But ye believe not, because ye are not of My sheep, as I said unto you. My sheep hear My voice, and I know them, and they follow Me: and I give unto them eternal life; and they shall never perish, neither shall any man pluck them out of My hand. My Father, which gave them Me, is greater than all; and no man is able to pluck them out of My Father's hand* (John 10:26-29).

He told them, "No man can come to Me, except the Father which hath sent Me draw him: and I will raise him up at the last day" (Jn. 6:44). Faith is a gift from God. "For by grace are ye saved through faith; and that not of yourselves: it is the gift of God: not of works, lest any man should boast" (Eph. 2:8-9).

Jesus clearly taught that "It is the spirit that quickeneth..." (Jn. 6:63). The Spirit of God ministers inside each person, convicting them of sin and building up their faith. Jesus described the work of the Spirit this way:

> *...He will reprove the world of sin, and of righteousness, and of judgment; ... Howbeit when He, the Spirit of truth, is come, He will guide you into all truth: for He shall not speak of Himself; but whatsoever He shall hear, that shall He speak: and He will shew you things to come. He shall glorify Me: for He shall receive of Mine, and shall shew it unto you. All things that the Father hath are Mine: therefore said I, that He shall take of Mine, and shall shew it unto you* (John 16:8,13-15).

It takes faith to follow Jesus. When Jesus asked His disciples, "But whom say ye that I am?" Peter answered, "Thou art the Christ, the Son of the living God." To Peter, Jesus added, "Blessed art thou, Simon Barjona: for flesh and blood hath not revealed it unto thee, but My Father which is in heaven." (See Matthew 16:15-17.)

Faith cometh, therefore, by the Word of God and by the Spirit of God. In that sense, faith, like love, is an endowment of God. For God, through God, and by God are we empowered with faith. Paul reports in Roman 10:17, "So then faith cometh by hearing, and hearing by the word of God." Through the ministry of the word of Christ, the Holy Spirit is able to draw us to the Savior, instilling in our hearts trust in His redemptive power and faith in His abiding support and comfort. This faith is not one that requires reason, logic, or emotions. It is established and sustained by the indwelling Spirit. It is fed by the Word of God, on which we stand. By His Word and Spirit, we can rely on those characteristics of God we know and trust. By faith, then, we are confident of our place in the family of God. We cannot doubt and we cannot be moved. It is this position, a combination of the loving connection and mental condition of faith, that forms the basis of the power of the believer.

By faith we know that the worlds were formed by the word of God (see Heb. 11:3). By faith we know that God has called us to be His holy nation (see 1 Pet. 2:9). By faith we know that He will preserve us for all eternity (see 2 Tim. 1:12). By faith we know that He will provide every good thing according to His abundant love and grace (see Phil. 4:19).

God is omnipotent. Whether we know it or deny it, believe it or despise it, our response changes nothing. The extent to which we consider ourselves to be in control of our destiny is the exact extent to which we embrace delusion. Either we choose God and are faithful, or we deny Him and are unfaithful. There is no other ground upon which to stand.

Either God is all He claims to be or He is not. If He is who and what He says He is, then faith in God is the highest achievement any human being can have. Faith demands that men believe the invisible truth. Nothing stretches the human spirit more than the effort to reach beyond ourselves to grasp something most noble and sublime. Faith releases us from bondage to the earth and the flesh. It liberates our spirit to commune with the divine.

The Power of Faith

Faith has unlimited power. It can accomplish anything in the context of love, for nothing is impossible for those who believe (see 1 Cor. 13:2). God longs to shower His people with the full measure of His Spirit and power. He holds back nothing from those who love Him (see Ps. 34:9-10; 84:11). He will pour out the treasures of Heaven to establish the power of faith, and He invites us to prove Him at His word (see Mal. 3:10).

Jesus especially encouraged us to exercise our faith in prayer. He said, "...whatsoever ye shall ask in prayer, believing, ye shall receive" (Mt. 21:22). He also said, "...He that believeth on Me, the works that I do shall he do also; and greater works than these shall he do; because I go unto My Father" (Jn. 14:12). If we believe Jesus Christ, we can do the miracles He did! Just before He ascended to Heaven, Jesus gave His disciples the Great Commission and listed the kinds of power that would accompany their faith. (See Mark 16:15-18.) The list included the power to cast out devils, speak in tongues, and heal the sick. He said faith would even overcome death! What more could He have added to the list that would convince the world of the incredible power of faith in Him?

Faith unleashes the boundless power of God in ways most humans cannot really understand. The level of doubt in the world is so great that many people who call themselves Christians are really borderline agnostics. The attitudes and self-centered nature of the evil one has needlessly been allowed to pervade every area of our society. God is all powerful! God, in the person and presence of Jesus Christ, has all the power in Heaven and in the earth (see Mt. 28:18). Satan has been stripped of every vestige of true power by our Redeemer. Jesus made an astounding promise to every believer: "And, lo, I am with you alway, even unto the end of the world. Amen" (Mt. 28:20b).

Only God is patient enough to work with our doubting race. Even Jesus was frustrated at times as He attempted to arouse faith in His disciples. He often wept or grieved over the lack of faith He encountered (see Mt. 8:26; 14:31; 16:8; Mk. 4:39-40; Lk. 8:25).

> *...Have faith in God. For verily I say unto you, That whosoever shall say unto this mountain, Be thou removed, and be thou cast into the sea; and shall not doubt in his heart, but shall believe that those things which he saith shall come to pass; he shall have whatsoever he saith* (Mark 11:22-23).

Basically, if you and I had any faith at all—even if it were just one drop of faith—we would be dangerous. When the disciples failed to cast out a demon, Jesus completed what they started and told them why they had failed: "*...Because of your unbelief*: for verily I say unto you, If ye have faith as a grain of mustard seed...nothing shall be impossible unto you" (Mt. 17:20).

Faith that is founded upon the love of God taps the unlimited power of God. Faith opens up the miraculous and makes it an integral part of everyday life. The true believer cannot help but walk in the power of wonder-working faith! True believers should be known by their awesome and spellbinding faith. They know that God is real and that His Word is the centerpiece of all power in the universe. God cannot lie, and He has already promised us the power to do anything.

Faith literally unravels and destroys all the wicked work of the enemy! Faith is a rock-solid confidence in God that cannot be shaken (see Heb. 11:1), and it eternally forces satan back in his place of total submission to the power of God. God is in His Word and His people. Faith based on the love of God casts out satan with the same power and authority that unceremoniously removed him from God's presence eons ago! This is exactly what Jesus told the 70 disciples when they returned from field ministry:

> *And the seventy returned again with joy, saying, Lord, even the devils are subject unto us through Thy name. And He said unto them, I beheld Satan as lightning fall from heaven. Behold, I give unto you power to tread on serpents and scorpions, and over all the power of the enemy...* (Luke 10:17-19).

Faith takes away all the power of satan in our lives. It is a shield and an impenetrable barrier to every weapon of our defeated enemy. Paul listed faith as the single most important piece of armor we have in our battle against the wiles of the devil. He said, "Above all, taking the shield of faith, wherewith ye shall be able to quench all the fiery darts of the wicked" (Eph. 6:16). When Peter was in danger because satan wanted to "sift him like wheat," Jesus prayed a unique prayer for Peter: "But I have prayed for thee, that thy faith fail not: and when [not if] thou are converted [turned back], strengthen thy brethren" (Lk. 22:32).

Faith is indispensable to the Christian life because it establishes our eternal relationship with God. If doubt triggered the revolution in Heaven in the first place and was passed on to mankind, then faith is the only way to bring unity and obedience and to overcome division in God's ranks. Any breakdown in an army's code of allegiance raises questions for every soldier on the front line. Each one of us must confront and overcome doubt. Faith leads to a realignment of strength for committed participation in God's plan.

The battle lines are already drawn and the battlements are up; good and evil are at war. Once we are saved, faith goes on to establish righteousness in our lives through the process of loving correction. This is a natural outgrowth of our faith in God the Father, not a slavish attention to rules or regulations. Our commitment and devotion to God is more than what we have for our mothers, our spouses, our brothers, our sisters, our children, or even ourselves (see Mt. 10:37; Lk. 9:59-62). It is total commitment.

Believers are justified by faith through total commitment (see Rom. 3:28; 5:1). They are not justified by legalism, nationality, circumcision, or religious observances or rites. Salvation comes through faith working in the context of love (see Gal. 5:6). Jesus is the author and finisher of our faith because of His central role in our salvation. Faith is the power through Christ that makes us whole by healing all of our weaknesses and propelling us to our highest potential (see Mt. 9:22,29; 15:28; Mk. 5:34, 10:52; Lk. 7:50, 8:48, 17:19, 18:42).

Faith plants us in the strength of Jesus Christ and draws forth the unique virtue imparted by His blameless, victorious life and triumphant resurrection from the dead. Faith charges us with the overcoming power of the Holy Spirit. The Bible declares that Jesus is called "Faithful and True" in

Revelation 19:11. His faith overcame the world, and since we have been reborn in Him and dwell in union with our Creator, we too have the power by faith to overcome the world! (See First John 5:4.)

Chapter 6

The Champions of Faith

History proves that just a little faith will set the world on fire! The successes and failures of a rich legacy of champions demonstrate the power of faith in the volatile laboratory of human history.

Noah the Just Man

Two thousand years after God ejected Adam and Eve from the Garden of Eden, Noah lived in a generation in which "every imagination of the thoughts of his [man's] heart was only evil continually" (Gen. 6:5). God decided to destroy all mankind with the exception of Noah and his family. Noah was a just man in an ungodly generation. God told Noah to build an ark to preserve his family. Noah had probably never even seen a ship or conceived of a need for one. Nevertheless, he obeyed by faith.

For nearly 100 years, Noah preached repentance while building the ark. He did everything God asked, working in an atmosphere of derision and ridicule. When he was 600 years old, God told Noah to take his family into the ark with food, supplies, and a male and female of every species of animal. Then God personally closed the door of the ark and released rain and underground water sources for 40 days and nights, destroying all living things except those in the ark. Noah's faith saved him and his family from destruction. He preserved our race and saw the promises of God fulfilled.

Abraham the Father of Faith

Abraham left his father and homeland because he *believed* God. God said He would make him a great nation and bless the earth through him. By faith, Abraham received Canaan, the promised land, and even had a dream foretelling the 400 years of Egyptian captivity his descendants would endure. Abraham also trusted God for a son, though he was already 100 years old, and Sarah his wife was 90!

Isaac was born after years of patient waiting and occasional human tinkering. Later, Abraham *believed God* and took Isaac, his only son (see Gen. 22:2; Heb. 11:17), to Moriah to offer him as a burnt sacrifice! Abraham prepared to take Isaac's life in sacrifice to God because he believed God would provide a substitute or raise Isaac from the dead. As he raised the sharp knife in his wrinkled hand, God caught Abraham's hand and saved Isaac by providing a ram for the sacrifice. God blessed Abraham's faith with the greatest spoken blessing ever recorded in human history:

That in blessing I will bless thee, and in multiplying I will multiply thy seed as the stars of the heaven, and as the sand which is upon the sea shore; and thy seed shall possess the gate of his enemies; and in thy seed shall all the nations of the earth be blessed; because thou hast obeyed My voice (Genesis 22:17-18).

Abraham's servant said, "And the Lord hath blessed my master greatly; and he is become great: and he hath given him flocks, and herds, and silver, and gold, and menservants, and maidservants, and camels, and asses" (Gen. 24:35). Abraham lived in good health to the age of 175.

Isaac: Father of Two Nations

Abraham's son, Isaac, also sought the Lord's help by faith, and his barren wife, Rebekah, bore twin boys who became fathers of two nations. God blessed Isaac with great wealth and fame (see Gen. 26:12-16).

Jacob Becomes Israel (Ruling With God)

Jacob (the heel-catcher and supplanter) stole the paternal blessing of Isaac, his father, from his elder twin, Esau. His character flaws plagued him much of his life. While fleeing his brother's anger, Jacob had a vision of God's throne. When God promised Jacob prosperity and a great lineage, Jacob vowed to be faithful to God. By faith, Jacob was renamed *Israel* ("ruling with God"), became rich in goods, and fathered the 12 tribal heads of the nation of Israel (Gen. 35:9-26).

Joseph the Dreamer

Joseph was the son of Jacob's old age by Rachel and the envy of his older half-brothers. From an early age, he had the gift of interpreting dreams. He was already Jacob's favorite, and Joseph's brothers despised him even more when he shared a dream that he would rule over them! They promptly sold him to nomadic Ishmaelites, who re-sold him in Egypt.

Joseph still trusted the voice of God and won the favor of all who came to know him. He became overseer for the captain of the Egyptian guard, but was falsely accused when he refused the advances of his master's wife. He was thrown into prison but came to Pharaoh's attention by interpreting the dreams of the Pharaoh's baker and butler. He later interpreted Pharaoh's dream, accurately predicting a severe famine in Egypt. After Pharaoh made him governor over Egypt, Joseph devised a plan for the nation's survival, receiving great wealth in repayment.

Joseph knew his gift was from God, and he acknowledged it before Pharaoh: "It is not in me: God shall give Pharaoh an answer of peace" (Gen. 41:16b). Pharaoh later said, "...Can we find such a one as this is, a man in whom the Spirit of God is?" (Gen. 41:38) When Joseph's family came to Egypt for food during the great famine, Joseph showed mercy upon his brothers, who didn't recognize him. Israel and his sons moved to Egypt, survived the famine, and received the fertile land of Goshen.

Moses the Deliverer

When Egypt's Pharaoh ordered that all male Hebrew babies be thrown into the Nile River, the Lord delivered Moses by prompting his mother to hide him among the bulrushes where Pharaoh's daughter rescued him. She adopted him, unknowingly recruited his mother to nurse him, and raised him in the royal household.

Moses seemingly destroyed his destiny when he killed an Egyptian he saw beating a Hebrew man. He wanted to show allegiance to his people, but he was rejected by his fellow Jews and became an outlaw in Pharaoh's eyes. Moses fled to the land of Midian where he kept the sheep of a priest named Jethro, and married Jethro's daughter. Forty years later, God appeared to Moses in the form of a burning bush and commissioned Moses to deliver Israel. God showed him several miracles to strengthen his faith, and revealed His name, *I Am That I Am*. Moses was fearful, but he trusted God and obeyed His commands. By faith, Moses confronted Pharaoh with signs and wonders and eventually led the Jews out of slavery.

Moses was 120 years old when he encouraged the children of Israel at the Jordan River. He was the most humble and committed man on the face of the earth. He talked to God as a friend and had seen God write the holy Decalogue. He saw God open a highway through the sea, and he lived on heavenly manna for 40 years in the desert. He saw God win battles for His people against invincible odds; he saw Him produce water from a rock and send fiery serpents through the camp. His faith grew so much during the years he led Israel that he became an emblem of courage and faith. At the edge of Canaan, he spoke a litany of faith:

> *Be strong and of a good courage, fear not, nor be afraid of them* [the Canaanites]: *for the Lord thy God, He it is that doth go with thee; He will not fail thee, nor forsake thee* (Deuteronomy 31:6).

> *The eternal God is thy refuge, and underneath are the everlasting arms: and He shall thrust out the enemy from before thee...* (Deuteronomy 33:27).

Joshua the Possessor

Joshua was one of the 12 chiefs sent into Canaan as spies. Though God had already promised the land to Israel, only Joshua and Caleb brought a faithful report. They were the only adults who lived to set foot in the promised land. Joshua eventually succeeded Moses and led the Jews into Canaan. He fought the battle of Jericho and saw the walls of that fortified city fall to the ground *because he believed the report* of an angel and obeyed the word from God.

The Judges of Israel

After the death of Joshua, the Israelites forsook the Lord and adopted the idolatrous practices of the Canaanites, including child prostitution and infant sacrifice. Israel was dominated by several neighboring kingdoms until the Lord raised up "judges" to deliver Israel from bondage and administrate justice. Several of these judges exhibited extraordinary faith.

Othniel delivered Israel from the control of Mesopotamia and maintained peace for 40 years. The Bible says, "And the Spirit of the Lord came upon him, and he...went out to war..." (Judg. 3:10).

Barak was roused by the prophetess Deborah to pursue and defeat Jabin and Sisera. The Lord told Deborah that Barak should go up to Mount Tabor. Deborah said, "...Up; for this is the day in which the Lord hath delivered Sisera into thine hand: is not the Lord gone out before thee?..." (Judg. 4:14) Barak trusted the Lord and obeyed, to his ultimate success.

Gideon was perhaps the greatest judge of Israel. He obeyed the voice of God and tore down his own father's altar to the false god, Baal, offending an entire city in the process. When he called for recruits to battle the armies of the east, 32,000 men showed up, but God sifted them down to a little group of 300 hand-picked men. Gideon and his 300 men routed an army of 135,000 Midianites and, with the assistance of the tribe of Ephraim, killed 120,000 of them. Then he and his weary 300 men pursued the two remaining Midianite princes and their 15,000 troops, catching them by surprise. The Lord had revealed to Gideon that He must reduce the strength of the troops of Israel so no man could boast that deliverance had come from man instead of God (see Judg. 7:2). Gideon's victory came because he trusted the Lord and leaned on Him. When the people asked Gideon to rule over them, he said, "...I will not rule over you, neither shall my son rule over you: the Lord shall rule over you" (Judg. 8:23).

Samuel: "Here Am I"

Samuel was Hannah and Elkanah's miracle son of promise, the firstfruit of a barren womb and a rich prayer life. He was given to God even before his birth and raised as a Nazarite. As a young boy, he received a fearful commission from God to announce the doom of his mentor and spiritual model, Eli. Samuel trusted God rather than man and delivered God's prophecy of the destruction of the priestly family to Eli. "And Samuel grew, and the Lord was with him, and did let none of his words fall to the ground [fail]" (1 Sam. 3:19).

David: A Man After God's Own Heart

David, the son of Jesse, was from little Bethlehem in Judah. As the youngest son, he tended his father's sheep. In his youth, he slew Goliath the giant after declaring, "...You come against me with sword and spear and javelin, but I come against you in the name of the Lord Almighty, the God of the armies of Israel, whom you have defied" (1 Sam. 17:45 NIV). By faith, he prophesied to the giant, "All those gathered here will know that it is not by sword or spear that the Lord saves; for the battle is the Lord's, and He will give all of you into our hands" (1 Sam. 17:47 NIV). David killed Goliath, became a national hero, and triggered the lifelong envy of King Saul, who knew David would succeed him to the throne. David spent the next seven years avoiding King Saul's relentless campaign to kill him.

David succeeded Saul to the throne of Israel and became a great military leader. His military victories and personal defeats taught him to let God fight his battles for him. His songs and psalms of faith continue to inspire God's people. Perhaps none of these are as beloved as the famed "Twenty-third Psalm," which begins, "The Lord is my shepherd; I shall not want...."

Esther: A Humble Vessel of Deliverance

Esther was a beautiful orphan who was raised by her cousin, Mordecai, an officer of the king of Persia. Although she was a Jew, she was chosen to be the queen of Persia in place of the rebellious Queen Vashti. Esther demonstrated her faith in God by braving possible death to reveal a wicked plot to annihilate all the Jews in Persia. Although the king put away Vashti for her refusal to appear before the king and his guests, he showed Esther mercy when she broke his law with her daring intrusion into his court. Esther's faith won her the protection of the unseen hand of God and saved the Jewish nation from extermination. Jews around the world still commemorate this champion of faith in the Jewish festival of Purim.

Job: The Suffering of a Righteous Man

Job is the supreme Old Testament example of steadfast faith, a living testament that men are not to be obedient only to receive God's blessings. His life also reveals the diabolical tactics and hatred of satan toward God's human servants.

Job was blameless in all areas of his life and blessed with wealth, family, and prestige. Satan was allowed to test Job to see if his faith and obedience would vanish along with his material goods and earthly blessings. Job passed the test by holding on to his faith in God although he lost his wealth, his children, his health, and every hint of social standing. Even his three closest friends accused him of sin and falsehood. Still Job remained faithful to God.

Job eloquently declared the foundations of his faith to his critical friends in some of the most powerful passages in Scripture:

Though He slay me, yet will I trust in Him (Job 13:15a).

For I know that my redeemer liveth, and that He shall stand at the latter day upon the earth: and though after my skin worms destroy this body, yet in my flesh shall I see God (Job 19:25-26).

But He knoweth the way that I take: when He hath tried me, I shall come forth as gold (Job 23:10).

For what is the hope of the hypocrite, though he hath gained, when God taketh away his soul? Will God hear his cry when trouble cometh upon him? (Job 27:8-9)

Though he [the wicked] *heap up silver as the dust, and prepare raiment as the clay; he may prepare it, but the just shall put it on, and the innocent shall divide the silver* (Job 27:16-17).

I know that Thou canst do every thing, and that no thought can be withholden from Thee. ... I have heard of Thee by the hearing of the ear: but now mine eye seeth Thee (Job 42:2,5).

The Prophets of Faith

Old Testament prophets were judged by one standard alone—either the things they said came to pass or they didn't. In many cases, even if they were right, their enemies believed they could stop the prediction of doom if they killed the prophet who proclaimed it! Many of the great prophets declared God's word while Israel and Judah were in captivity, and many died martyrs' deaths because of their prophecies.

Nehemiah was a cupbearer to Artaxerxes Longimanus, king of Persia. He received permission to restore the walls of Jerusalem as governor of Judah and did it with remarkable speed and cunning, despite conspiratorial attempts by Sanballat and Tobiah to stop his work and even take his life. He declared, "...our God shall fight for us" (Neh. 4:20). Nehemiah repaired the temple, prohibited usury by the rich, reestablished Sabbath worship, and purified the priesthood.

Isaiah prophesied during the reigns of Azariah Uzziah, Jotham, Ahaz, and Hezekiah, repeatedly warning Judah and

Jerusalem that it would be judged for its wickedness. He is best known for his majestic Messianic prophecy foretelling a great restoration and the coming Savior. He paid a dear price for his prophecy; by order of Manasseh, he was sawn in two in the trunk of a carob tree. Isaiah described the Messiah in his prophetic vision:

> *...He hath no form nor comeliness; and when we shall see Him, there is no beauty that we should desire Him. He is despised and rejected of men; a man of sorrows, and acquainted with grief: and we hid as it were our faces from Him; He was despised, and we esteemed Him not. Surely He hath borne our griefs, and carried our sorrows: yet we did esteem Him stricken, smitten of God, and afflicted. But He was wounded for our transgressions, He was bruised for our iniquities: the chastisement of our peace was upon Him; and with His stripes we are healed. All we like sheep have gone astray; we have turned every one to his own way; and the Lord hath laid on Him the iniquity of us all* (Isaiah 53:2-6).

Jeremiah prophesied during the reigns of Josiah, Jehoahaz, Jehoiakim and Jehoiachin. Although he was despondent, pained, and dissatisfied because of the sorrow he saw in his visions, he remained undaunted and fearless in his duty to God. Often called "the weeping prophet," Jeremiah boldly opposed the enemies of God, but he was taken to Egypt after the death of Gedaliah. He continued to deliver God's stinging rebukes with even more power and authority in Egypt.

> *But the Lord is with me as a mighty terrible one: therefore my persecutors shall stumble, and they shall not prevail: they shall be greatly ashamed; for they shall*

not prosper: their everlasting confusion shall never be forgotten (Jeremiah 20:11).

Ezekiel was a priest who prophesied from the banks of the river Chebar for 22 years during the Babylonian exile. He was stern in his denunciations and solemn in his consolation. He prophesied against seven nations and was eventually murdered in Babylon and buried on the banks of the Euphrates River. He said, "The soul that sinneth, it shall die" (Ezek. 18:20a).

Daniel was a royal prince and a prophet who was among the captives taken to Babylon after Nebuchadnezzar's conquest of King Jehoiakin and Jerusalem. Daniel was chosen to enter the king's service and he supernaturally interpreted the king's dreams.

Daniel followed the path of faith and defied a ban on praying to anyone but the king, and therefore was cast into a den of lions. God shut the lions' mouths and "...no manner of hurt was found upon him, because he believed in his God" (Dan. 6:23). Because Daniel dared to believe God even in the face of certain death, Darius the Mede, successor to Nebuchadnezzar and the ruler of "the Medes and the Persians," assigned Daniel the highest civil post in the land just under the king himself.

Daniel's prolific prophetic ministry produced complex dreams and prophecies of far-reaching importance, encompassing everything from changing world empires to the second coming of Jesus Christ. He summed up the whole of human history when he declared to King Nebuchadnezzar, "...the most High ruleth in the kingdom of men, and giveth it to whomsoever He will" (Dan. 4:25).

* * * * *

As the "fullness of time" approached and God invaded the earth in the form of a man, a new breed of man emerged that was even more intimately connected to the Messiah. Their focus was devoted to one man, one ministry, and one purpose—to proclaim the good news of the Messiah, Jesus Christ.

John the Baptist: Forerunner of the King

John the Baptist was born six months before Jesus Christ. His Levite parents were "well stricken in years" when an angel appeared to Zacharias the priest and told him that his barren wife, Elisabeth, would bear him a son (see Lk. 1:7,13). John was filled with the Spirit of God from the very start of his life and was ordained to be a Nazarite from his birth. He was prepared for his divinely appointed mission by a solitary life in the wild where he lived on locusts and honey.

He finally emerged from the wilderness "in the spirit and power of Elias" (see Lk. 1:17), calling for repentance from sins and baptism with water. He pointed to Jesus Christ and proclaimed, "Behold the Lamb of God, which taketh away the sin of the world" (Jn. 1:29b). At Jesus' request, John baptized Him in the Jordan River and saw the Spirit descend from Heaven and abide on Him. Later, John was imprisoned and beheaded for reproving the adulterous marriage of Herod Antipas to Herodias, his brother's wife. Christ said of him, "Verily I say unto you, Among them that are born of women there hath not risen a greater than John the Baptist" (Mt. 11:11a).

Peter the Rock

Peter the apostle stood before a noisy crowd on the Day of Pentecost and proclaimed that Jesus was the Messiah with a new self-confidence and absolute devotion to Christ. He had reached a higher level of maturity, and now could boldly defend the actions of the 120 persons who had been filled with the Holy Spirit and spoke in tongues giving praise to the Lord. He bluntly exposed the wicked and senseless killing of the benevolent Savior, pointing to the prophets as evidence of Christ's divinity.

Peter later confirmed the converts at Samaria, personally visited the churches in Asia, and defended the baptism of Gentiles. His imprisonment by Herod was thwarted through the miraculous visitation of an angel. By faith, Peter healed the sick and ministered to those lost in sin. Church history and tradition indicates that he worked in the Christian community in Palestine before his visit to Rome where he was imprisoned and later crucified by Nero. Peter said of temptation:

> ...now for a season, if need be, ye are in heaviness through manifold temptations: that the trial of your faith, being much more precious than of gold that perisheth, though it be tried with fire, might be found unto praise and honour and glory at the appearing of Jesus Christ (1 Peter 1:6-7).

James the Evangelist

James the evangelist was the elder brother of John the beloved and one of the first men called to discipleship by Jesus. James joined Peter and John at the Lord's transfiguration and during His agony in Gethsemane. According to Acts 12:2, he was killed by Herod in an effort to stop the growth of the Church.

John the Beloved

John was known as "the disciple whom Jesus loved" (see Jn. 13:23). The younger brother of James the evangelist, John was in the council chamber with Peter when Jesus was accused before Caiaphas. He witnessed the crucifixion and received Jesus's charge to care for His mother. He was the first of the 12 disciples to see the open tomb after Jesus' resurrection, and the first to recognize Jesus when He appeared on the shore of the Sea of Galilee (see Jn. 21:7). Church tradition claims that John remained in Jerusalem after the Day of Pentecost and was imprisoned in Rome by Domitian. He miraculously survived immersion in boiling oil and was exiled to the isle of Patmos where he received the divine Revelation of Jesus Christ. He later returned to Ephesus where he died.

The author of the fourth Gospel, John characterizes the nature and person of Christ and reveals the meaning of faith in Him. He wrote, "But these are written, that ye might believe that Jesus is the Christ, the Son of God; and that believing ye might have life through His name" (Jn. 20:31).

Paul: The Apostle to the Gentiles

This powerful man of God, originally called Saul, was born a Benjamite and a Roman citizen. He pursued a rigorous study of the ancient Scriptures under the personal tutelage of Gamaliel, Israel's premiere sage and teacher of the law. He zealously orchestrated the persecution and murder of Christians from Jewish synagogues—even in other countries. This highly educated and well-spoken Pharisee from Tarsus of Cilicia pursued success by fulfilling the will of the Sanhedrin until he was blinded by a bright light and heard the voice of Jesus on the road to Damascus.

The Lord Jesus Himself commissioned Saul to bear His name "before the Gentiles, and kings, and the children of Israel" (Acts 9:15). After he declared that Jesus was the Messiah to Jews in Damascus, Paul fled the city to escape assassins. He went into the Arabian desert for a time where he received divine revelations from the Lord, and then he returned again to Damascus before he met the apostles at the church in Jerusalem. Soon after he began ministering with Barnabas, he changed his name from *Saul*, which means "desired," to the humble name of *Paul*, meaning "small or little" (see Acts 13:9).

Paul founded churches throughout Asia Minor during three missionary journeys. He set up elders in each city to oversee the congregations and wrote 14 letters to instruct, encourage, comfort, challenge, and correct his charges. After two imprisonments in Rome, Paul was beheaded by Nero around A.D. 67 or 68. Even as he faced death, Paul declared in faith:

> *For I am now ready to be offered, and the time of my departure is at hand. I have fought a good fight, I have finished my course, I have kept the faith: henceforth there is laid up for me a crown of righteousness, which the Lord, the righteous judge, shall give me at that day: and not to me only, but unto all them also that love His appearing* (2 Timothy 4:6-8).

Jesus Christ: The Lamb of God, the Messiah Himself

Jesus Christ, born in Bethlehem of Judea, is more than a hero of faith; He is the *object* of faith. His Father is God Himself. His mother was the Virgin Mary. Like John the Baptist, His birth was announced by the angel Gabriel. His beginnings were humble. Born in a livestock manger, He was destined to turn the world upside down and establish an "upside-down" set of values that focused on the heart, not the outward appearance. At the age of 12, His knowledge of the law and the prophets astonished the doctors of the law who had gathered around Him for three days in the great temple of Herod in Jerusalem during the Feast of Passover (see Lk. 2:46-47).

Jesus began His public ministry at the age of 30, after being baptized by John the Baptist and enduring 40 days of fasting and temptation in the wilderness. He defined His ministry with a passage from the Book of Isaiah (see Lk. 4:18-19; Is. 61:1-2), and performed countless miracles of healing, miraculous provision, exorcism, and resurrections of the dead. Jesus preached unconditional love, total commitment by faith, the baptism and power of the Holy Ghost, and a radical separation from worldly concerns.

Jesus endured constant resistance and the continual threat of death. His people, the Jews, were under the domination of Augustus Caesar and the Roman Empire, and the local authority of the appointed king of Judah, Herod Antipas. Heavy taxes and onerous laws made many Jews hope for a military leader to overthrow Rome. Likewise, the religious leaders of Israel hoped for a military leader—so long as they could retain their powerful positions in the governing system.

The Romans feared insurrections and revolution. The ministry of Jesus fueled the fears of the Romans but satisfied none of the hopes of the Jews. Ultimately, the Jews themselves brought charges of blasphemy and treason against their own Savior, and after a mock trial, pressed the Roman leaders into crucifying Him. Three days later, Jesus rose from the grave and made 11 appearances to His disciples over a period of 40 days. He baptized His followers with the Holy Ghost and commissioned them to preach the good news of salvation through faith in His name. He ascended to Heaven from the Mount of Olives and promised to return for the saints of God who would dwell with Him for eternity.

Jesus Christ was fully human and fully divine. His life was sinless. He resisted the most subtle and tempting advances of satan with no inclination to fall. His Spirit is ever with us to defend us from the enemy, deliver us from sin, and bring us victoriously through every confrontation between good and evil.

Chapter 7

The Failures of Faith

We learn as much from failure as we do from success. The Bible records some of the most monumental "failures of faith" in human history, and in every case the failures were costly or fatal.

Destruction at Sodom

When Abram and his nephew, Lot, returned to Canaan from Egypt, they brought great riches and large herds of cattle. When a dispute occurred between their herdsmen over limited forage land, Abram suggested they part ways and allowed Lot to choose where he would settle.

Lot decided the lush and fertile plains of Jordan were superior to the hills of Bethel, so he moved to the area beside the city of Sodom, known for its idolatry and wicked sensuality. In contrast, Abram dwelt in the peace and quiet of rolling hills and pastureland.

Lot became caught in the middle of a feud between four kings and was captured, but Abram came to his rescue with armed servants. While the Lord was set to destroy Sodom and Gomorrah, Lot had become a leader in the city! God mercifully sent angels to warn Lot of the coming judgment, but his weak faith and compromising ways caused him to doubt the warning of the holy messengers and he hesitated to leave. Finally, the angels intervened and carried Lot and his family away from Sodom just before fire rained down on the city. The angels had warned everyone in Lot's family not to look back at the city, but Lot's wife was so enamored with Sodom that she turned around to see the destruction and instantly became a pillar of salt. Lot's lack of faith nearly cost him his life and his family.

The Golden Calf at Sinai

While the finger of God Almighty carved the Decalogue and established the covenant with Israel at Sinai in the presence of Moses, satan was working in the hearts of faithless people to undermine and overcome the effects of the law and the covenant. Satan knew the power of the law because it was the same law he had broken in Heaven. He began to stir up the Israelites to impatience and rebellion. They told Aaron, "Up, make us gods, which shall go before us" (Ex. 32:1). Apparently the people had not thrown out Jehovah, but had decided they wanted to *see* Him and know Him *with the senses*. They wanted to leave spiritual worship rooted in faith in favor of the sensual worship of the man-made works of the flesh. (Even as they made their plans, God was giving Moses the plans for a tabernacle or "dwelling place" as a symbol of His abiding presence with His people.)

God demands that His people walk by faith, not by sight (see 2 Cor. 5:7). The Israelites demanded to have a god made by their own hands that they could see and manipulate. Aaron, the brother of Moses and his right-hand man, had been left in charge while Moses climbed the mountain to commune with the Almighty. Aaron felt his faith waver under the pressure of public impatience, and finally he caved in to their sinful demands. Aaron collected the gold trinkets the people had collected from their Egyptian captors (gold that was meant to be reserved unto God and His people), and fashioned a golden calf. Then in Exodus 32:5 Aaron built an altar and proclaimed "a feast to the Lord" (but which "lord"?).

The open disobedience of the multitude and the compromising weakness of Aaron had broken the covenant with God because the covenant required faith and obedience. As Moses descended the mountain with the Decalogue written by the finger of God, he saw that the people had corrupted themselves and were dancing and singing in the heat of idolatry. In his anger, Moses threw down the stone tables of the law and broke them at the foot of the mountain. This was symbolic of the fact that those laws had already been broken in the hearts of the people.

Murmuring in the Wilderness

The Lord helped Moses choose elders to help him lead the people and judge their disputes. He gave the elders the spirit of prophecy as a sign of their anointing. Aaron the high priest, and his sister Miriam the prophetess, questioned the supremacy of Moses as leader and prophet of the Most High. Like lucifer who challenged God in the heavenly realm, these leaders impugned the authority and the name of the highest prophet of God. They wanted to make *their* words and spiritual revelations superior to those of Moses. Faith fails when it is mixed in unholy union with wrong motives or pride.

Miriam tried to justify her actions and obscure the real issues by criticizing Moses for his interracial marriage to an Ethiopian woman. The Lord immediately called a conference with the three leaders to kill the sin of pride at the root, before it infected the entire camp and destroyed God's established lines of authority.

The Bible says the meekness of Moses was greater than that of all the other men on the earth (see Num. 12:3). Faith requires submission to God, and the Most High God delights in using the lowly of spirit. He reaffirmed the high calling of Moses and told them that while prophets know God by visions, Moses spoke to Him mouth to mouth. In consequence for her murmuring against Moses, Miriam was struck with leprosy. She was only allowed to return to the camp after Moses interceded on her behalf, and after a seven-day quarantine period. Aaron was not punished directly, perhaps because his role was secondary, or perhaps because the leprosy would have been a more far-reaching offense to the office of high priest. The seven-day delay focused all attention on God's judgment and His forgiveness. Unfortunately, even this wasn't enough to prevent the next tragedy and failure of faith!

The Unfaithful Spies

At the command of the Lord, Moses sent one man from every tribe of Israel to spy out the land of Canaan. The spies were to bring back samples of the fruit in the land to show the people the bounty God had given them, and give a report about the people and their cities.

All the spies returned with the same report: The land was fruitful, the cities were strongholds, and the people were of great stature. From the brook of Eshcol, they brought a cluster of grapes so large it had to be carried upon a staff between two men. They also brought figs and pomegranates that were large and impressive. Everyone agreed that Canaan was a land "flowing with milk and honey." The disagreement came in their interpretations of what they had seen.

Ten spies yielded to doubt and said it would be impossible to subdue the Canaanites because they were bigger and stronger than the Israelites. They described giant sons of

Anak and portrayed themselves as insects by comparison. They said that the walled cities were virtually impenetrable. Their evil report destroyed faith and sent a wave of doubt throughout the camp, discrediting the revealed word of God and weakening the trust of His people.

> *And all the congregation lifted up their voice, and cried; and the people wept that night. And all the children of Israel murmured against Moses and against Aaron: and the whole congregation said unto them, Would God that we had died in the land of Egypt! or would God we had died in this wilderness! And wherefore hath the Lord brought us unto this land, to fall by the sword, that our wives and our children should be a prey? were it not better for us to return into Egypt? And they said one to another, Let us make a captain, and let us return into Egypt* (Numbers 14:1-4).

God was so angry about the faithlessness of the people that He decided to destroy them all and raise up a new and greater nation from Moses! Only Moses' strong intercession persuaded Him to pardon the people. God forgave the faithless people, but He declared that no one who was 20 years old or over who murmured against Him would ever enter into the promised land! "...Your carcases, they shall fall in this wilderness. And your children shall wander in the wilderness forty years, and bear your whoredoms..." (Num. 14:32-33). Then God sent a plague through the camp that killed the ten unfaithful spies.

Achan's Sin Nullifies Faith

Joshua's victory over Jericho was a splendid display of God's power and of faith's reward. Yet, Israel quickly suffered an embarrassing defeat by a small force from the city of Ai. Joshua's scouts had told him, "...Let not all the people go up; but let about two or three thousand men go up and smite Ai;

and make not all the people to labour thither; for they are but few" (Josh. 7:3). So Joshua took only 3,000 men from Jericho to Ai, confident they would be successful. The Israelites' confidence faded and their "hearts melted and became like water" (see Josh. 7:5) after the men of Ai chased them from the gate of the city as far as the stone quarries, killing 36 of them! Something was terribly wrong.

Joshua was confused and distraught. He tore his clothes, fell face down before God, and remained in prayer until evening. The Lord told Joshua that Israel had sinned by taking objects of conquest out of Jericho. He said He would not be with Joshua unless the thing was destroyed.

The next morning, Joshua brought all the people before the Lord to narrow down the culprit by tribe, by clan, by family, and then by man. The lot finally fell on Achan, the son of Carmi, the son of Zimri, the son of Zerah of the tribe of Judah. Once he was exposed, Achan confessed to taking a "Babylonish" garment plus some silver and gold and hiding them in his tent. Because of his disobedience, Achan and his family were stoned, and his possessions were burned.

Saul's Disobedience Voided Faith

Saul had already disobeyed God by sparing the life of the Amalekite king, Agag, and by holding back some livestock that should have been destroyed. Samuel the prophet told Saul that his kingdom would be given to someone better than him and secretly anointed David as Saul's replacement (see 1 Sam. 15:28; 16:1-13). Saul wasn't sure how his kingdom would be taken, but he believed the prophecies from God and lived in perpetual doubt and fear. The Bible says, "But the Spirit of the Lord departed from Saul, and an evil spirit from the Lord troubled him" (1 Sam. 16:14).

When the Philistine army assembled at Shunem, Saul feared the prophecy was unfolding. Terror struck him because he knew he couldn't win without God's help. "And when Saul inquired of the Lord, the Lord answered him not, neither by dreams, nor by Urim, nor by prophets" (1 Sam. 28:6). Desperate and misguided, the king defied God's eternal command to never consult with diviners, witches, or wizards. Saul sent his servants to find a woman with a familiar spirit so he could get a reading from her.

Saul's servants sent him to the witch of Endor who was said to call forth spirits of the dead. Saul disguised himself and asked the woman to speak to the spirit of Samuel. "And when the woman saw Samuel, she cried with a loud voice: and the woman spake to Saul, saying, Why hast thou deceived me? for thou art Saul" (1 Sam. 28:12). Saul asked her what she saw, and once he was satisfied it was Samuel, he asked Samuel what to do. Samuel sealed Saul's doom by prophesying that David would have his throne, that the following day he and his sons would die, and Israel would be defeated by the Philistines.

Solomon's Unholy Marriages Banished Faith

Solomon was David's youngest son and the only living son of Bathsheba (1 Chron. 3:5). He was not David's successor in the eyes of the nation, but he was the chosen of the Lord. After the death of Absalom and the defeat of Adonijah, Solomon was the uncontested heir to the throne. In his last words to his son, David advised Solomon to "keep the charge of the Lord thy God, to walk in His ways, to keep His statutes, and His commandments, and His judgments, and His testimonies, as it is written in the law of Moses..." (1 Kings 2:3).

Solomon remained faithful to the Lord in the early years of his 40-year reign. When the Lord appeared to him in a dream at Gibeon and offered him whatever he asked, young Solomon asked for an understanding heart to judge God's people and to discern between good and evil. God was so pleased with his request that He also gave him riches, honor, and a long life with one condition: *"And if thou wilt walk in My ways,*

to keep My statutes and My commandments, as thy father
David did walk, then I will lengthen thy days" (1 Kings 3:14).

According to the Bible, "And Solomon's wisdom excelled
the wisdom of all the children of the east country, and all the
wisdom of Egypt. For he was wiser than all men..." (1 Kings
4:30-31). He was richer and wiser than all the other kings of
the earth, and "the whole world sought audience with Solomon to hear the wisdom God had put in his heart" (1 Kings
10:24 NIV). Solomon completed the temple of God in the elev-
enth year of his reign, and he also built himself a magnificent
and imposing palace that was 13 years in the making (see
1 Kings 7:1). Despite his accomplishments and wisdom, one
sin was left untouched and, in the end, it brought about his
downfall.

*But king Solomon loved many strange women, together
with the daughter of Pharaoh, women of the Moabites,
Ammonites, Edomites, Zidonians, and Hittites; of the
nations concerning which the Lord said unto the children of Israel, Ye shall not go in to them, neither shall
they come in unto you: for surely they will turn away
your heart after their gods: Solomon clave unto these in
love. And he had seven hundred wives, princesses, and
three hundred concubines: and his wives turned away
his heart. For it came to pass, when Solomon was old,
that his wives turned away his heart after other gods:
and his heart was not perfect with the Lord his God, as
was the heart of David his father. For Solomon went after Ashtoreth the goddess of the Zidonians, and after
Milcom the abomination of the Ammorites. And Solomon did evil in the sight of the Lord, and went not fully
after the Lord, as did David his father. Then did Solomon build an high place for Chemosh, the abomination
of Moab, in the hill that is before Jerusalem, and for
Molech, the abomination of the children of Ammon.*

And likewise did he for all his strange wives, which burnt incense and sacrificed unto their gods. And the Lord was angry with Solomon, because his heart was turned from the Lord God of Israel, which had appeared unto him twice (1 Kings 11:1-9).

Perhaps Solomon's "open mind" caused insensitivity to the impurity of these forms of worship. Curiosity might have led to temptation, and then to attraction. Nonetheless, the Lord divided Israel into two kingdoms because of Solomon's sin. Upon Solomon's death, ten tribes passed to Jeroboam, the son of Nebat, an Ephraimite, leaving only the tribes of Judah and Benjamin to Rehoboam, the son of Solomon (see 1 Kings 11:29-36).

Judas' Greed Betrays His Faith

Judas Iscariot was one of the 12 disciples of our Lord. Although he was handpicked by Jesus, the Savior knew that Judas was a devil (see Jn. 6:70). The demon that ultimately possessed him could probably have been cast out, but Judas gave way to its evil sway instead. Judas may have been chosen for his skill at managing funds. He accounted for the ministry funds and dispensed them (see Jn. 12:6; 13:29), and it was in this area that he began to manifest greed, unfaithfulness, and theft. Eventually his greed led to his open betrayal of our Lord for 30 pieces of silver (see Mt. 26:14-16). Even though he returned the money to the priests, Judas never sincerely repented for his sin, and in the end, he hanged himself (see Mt. 27:3-10). Had he found the faith to believe the teachings of our merciful Savior, perhaps he would have gained both repentance and salvation.

The Lie of Ananias and Sapphira Brings Death

After the Holy Ghost had been poured out on the Day of Pentecost in Jerusalem, the new Church experienced radical revival and growth. A supernatural spirit of giving and sharing characterized this first century Church:

And the multitude of them that believed were of one heart and of one soul: neither said any of them that aught of the things which he possessed was his own; but they had all things in common. ... Neither was there any among them that lacked: for as many as were possessors of lands or houses sold them, and brought the prices of the things that were sold, and laid them down at the apostles' feet: and distribution was made unto every man according as he had need (Acts 4:32,34-35).

Ananias and Sapphira pledged to give God the money from the sale of their property. They privately schemed to hold back part of the proceeds for their own use, while presenting the remainder as though it were the full amount received for the property. Peter confronted them individually and said, "...why hath Satan filled thine heart to lie to the Holy Ghost, and to keep back part of the price of the land? ...thou hast not lied unto men, but unto God" (Acts 5:3-4; see also 5:9). Both the husband and wife in turn fell dead before his feet, and were carried out.

Simon's Wrong Motives Diverted His Faith

Simon was a sorcerer who came to the Lord through Philip's ministry in Samaria. When he saw converts receive the Holy Ghost after Peter and John prayed for them, he offered money to the apostles, "saying, Give me also this power, that on whomsoever I lay hands, he may receive the Holy Ghost" (Acts 8:19). Peter rebuked him. "...Thy money perish with thee, because thou hast thought that the gift of God may be purchased with money" (Acts 8:20). Simon's request was rooted in avarice, not faith; he was just trying to enlarge his bag of magic tricks.

Chapter 8

The Practice of Faith

Would you endure years of study to become a medical doctor and then not *practice* medicine? What a waste of knowledge and power! Mere *knowledge about faith* is useless if you do not *practice faith*. Here are eight practical steps from God's Word to help us build and *practice* faith.

Step 1: Set Your Sights on God, and Nothing Less.

You won't catch a whale if you are fishing in a pond. The only Source for the power of God is God Himself. Christians should believe that the farthest star is within reach and the most difficult problem can be solved! "For with God nothing shall be impossible" (Lk. 1:37). We must be fully persuaded that He is able to perform everything He has promised (see Rom. 4:21).

God made the heavens and set the course of the stars. He laid the foundations of the earth and the boundaries of the oceans. Jehovah strung the beautiful Pleiades and loosed the cords of Orion. Job described God's countless wonders in the Book of Job, chapters 38 and 39. God can do anything but fail!

By faith, Peter set his eyes on Christ and walked on the sea (see Mt. 14:26-31). When he looked away from his Source, he instantly lost the power to stand on the supernatural, and began to sink, crying "Lord, save me!" Jesus rescued him, saying, "O thou of little faith, wherefore didst thou doubt?" (See Matthew 14:30-31.)

Even the Magi Believed

The wise men from the East (Magi) dared to follow a star to find the King of the Jews. They kept their sights on God's sign and discovered the origin and foundation of all faith (see Mt. 2:1-12)! These astrologers, philosophers, and stargazers knew the Messianic prophecies, probably from the writings of Daniel who had served Babylonian and Medo-Persian kings in the east. He predicted the coming of our Lord in his prophecy of "seventy weeks" five centuries before Jesus was born. Hundreds and perhaps thousands of Jewish scholars also *knew* the Messianic prophecies, but they didn't *believe* them enough to act. Knowledge and faith are two different things. The actions of the Magi speak more of faith than of mere knowledge considering the gifts and worship they offered the infant Savior.

These foreign wise men were able to find the Savior before the doubting Jews did because their eyes were fixed on the heavens. The Jews had the law, the prophets, and the oracles, and were the seed of Abraham, but only faith could lead them to the Lord. Our guiding light is the Holy Spirit who is commissioned to lead us into all truth. We must believe in heavenly things more than in things we see.

Step 2: Expect Miracles and Don't Be Surprised When They Come!

Expectation is essential to faith. It builds the hope we need to expel doubt and confirm the reality of our belief. If you say someone is taking you to the airport, I expect to see you packed for the trip. If you aren't packed, I won't believe you're going. Expectation builds enthusiasm and propels faith. On the other hand, if you act surprised when your ride shows up, I'll wonder if you really expected them. Faith requires expectation and anticipation—the greater the expectation, the greater the faith.

Abraham's Trial of Faith

Abraham is called the "father of faith" because he exercised it. He did not hesitate to obey God's command to sacrifice Isaac because he had *faith* in God's ability to raise him from the dead. He did not understand the circumstances, but he chose to trust God more than the situation (see Gen. 15:4; 21:12), even though Isaac was born when Abraham was 100 and Sarah was 90, and was their only son. Abraham based his expectation on the word he received from God (see Heb. 11:17-19).

The Fiery Furnace of Faith

Another extraordinary example of faith is the fiery trial of the three Hebrew princes, Hananiah, Mishael, and Azariah. When King Nebuchadnezzar made a giant statue of gold and ordered his subjects to worship it or be thrown into a fiery furnace, the three princes said:

If we are thrown into the blazing furnace, the God we serve is able to save us from it, and He will rescue us from your hand, O king. But even if He does not, we want you to know, O king, that we will not serve your gods or worship the image of gold you have set up (Daniel 3:17-18 NIV).

These princes set their faith on God. If we approach our fiery trials today with a firm conviction of faith in Christ, then no fire in hell can destroy our holy hope! The faith of these princes was vindicated when Christ Himself (the "fourth man") met them in the furnace and delivered them from the burning flames (see Dan. 3:25).

The Trial of Bereavement

Faith must carry us through certain trials we cannot avoid in this life, such as death. Jesus had to overcome the grief of Mary and Martha, as well as the unbelief of the mourners at the grave of Lazarus. Jesus purposely delayed two days before going to see His friend, and when the disciples learned that Lazarus was dead, they reluctantly followed Jesus to the tomb halfway expecting Him to be killed by those who sought the Lord's life (see Jn. 11:16). Martha and Mary both told Jesus that Lazarus would not have died if Jesus had been there. Jesus was troubled by their weeping, but He called the dead man back to life anyway, causing many to believe after the fact (see Jn. 11:32-45).

Bereavement can challenge the faith of even the strongest believer. Regardless of what we face in life, we must deepen our hope and push aside every negative thought by recalling God's promises. Take a stand with the Hebrew princes and Abraham. Build your hope upon God's Word. Set your sights on God Almighty and expect to see a miracle from His hand.

Step 3: See God at Every Step; Praise Him Every Day.

"The steps of a good man are ordered by the Lord" (Ps. 37:23a). God has promised us that "there shall no evil befall thee, neither shall any plague come nigh thy dwelling" (Ps. 91:10). He is our "strong habitation, fortress, and rock of defense" (see Ps. 71:3). His chosen people will not stumble, nor will they fall. He is their shepherd, their comfort, and their safety (see Ps. 23:1). He will gather them up in His arms like lambs, and gently lead those with little ones (see Is. 40:11).

He orders our steps and He paves our way with love. We have the assurance that we are guided from above, but we must sharpen our perception and perceive each step as a fulfillment of God's plan. From creation, you were already in the mind of the Lord. He has chosen and called *you* for Himself from all the people in the world (see Is. 41:9)! Be humble, servile, and grateful. God "needs" no one to fulfill His plans, yet He chose you and I in His mercy and love. He loves us though He knows us! Despite our sin, He has pardoned us and called us His own.

Faith requires a vital, ongoing knowledge of God's presence. His Spirit and power always surround us, but we must be accustomed to the company of God. We should punctuate every action with thoughts of Jesus. "What does He think? What would He do? What is He saying to me now?" Our life should resemble continuous prayer. His praises should continually be on our lips, and His work should be on our minds.

Step 4: Never Look Back! Never Countenance Defeat! Never Give Place to Doubt! Persevere!

Lot's wife is a picture of "salvation lost." She disobeyed the angel of God and "looked back" to the very thing from which she had been delivered! Sometimes we do the same thing! Jesus warned a young man, "...No man, having put his hand to the plough, and looking back, is fit for the kingdom of God" (Lk. 9:62). *Never look back!*

Jesus said the last days would be like the days of Noah with people marrying, eating, and drinking with no thought of the coming destruction. They will be unprepared for the things of God. "In that day, he which shall be upon the housetop, and his stuff in the house, let him not come down to take it away: and he that is in the field, let him likewise not return back" (Lk. 17:31). *Never look back!*

Faith takes us beyond the flesh to the spirit, from the earth to heavenly realms. Lucifer fell from Heaven for *lack of faith*, but Jesus ascended to Heaven *because of His faith.* Faith in Jesus Christ breaks the barrier between "the impossible" on earth and the "possible" in Heaven.

Once you choose the path of faith, God will lead you into the impossible! He knows that if you cannot face the impossible, you cannot see the power of God. Those of little faith abandon the course when the odds seem insurmountable. The weak give up hope when there is no way out. Yet, it is the impossibilities of man that introduce the power of God. We can handle anything less than the impossible—*it is only in the face of the impossible that we can see God!*

Even after we receive Jesus Christ as Lord and Savior and set our hopes on His promises, the sins of the past return to haunt us again. The people we used to know come to take us back to the old ways and life. We may feel trapped and search in panic for a way out. When we find nothing, it is as if we have landed back in Exodus 14!

> *...They are entangled in the land, the wilderness hath shut them in. ... And when Pharaoh drew nigh, the children of Israel lifted up their eyes, and, behold, the Egyptians marched after them; and they were sore afraid...* (Exodus 14:3,10).

When we are surrounded by barricades on every side, we know the Lord has led us into an impossible situation. We face mountains of impossibility on two sides, and a sea of uncertainty to the front. Our "Egyptian" bondages and failures are closing in from the past. What can we do? We have three choices.

We can *turn back*. This is the first impulse of weak believers when they can see no other alternative. They give up hope, accept defeat, and may even turn their bitterness and blame toward their Deliverer like the children of Israel:

...Was it because there were no graves in Egypt that you brought us to the desert to die? What have you done to us by bringing us out of Egypt? Didn't we say to you in Egypt, "Leave us alone; let us serve the Egyptians"? It would have been better for us to serve the Egyptians than to die in the desert! (Exodus 14:11-12 NIV)

Generally these situations are so major that our entire Christian life is on the line. When you cannot see any way out except to give in, then nothing short of a miracle can save you! Most of us will "throw in the towel" for much less dramatic reasons. "God won't mind. This is my thorn in the flesh. Aren't we saved by grace?"

Moses declared the will of God for these situations: "...Fear ye not, stand still, and see the salvation of the Lord, which He will shew to you today: for the Egyptians whom ye have seen today, ye shall see them again no more for ever" (Ex. 14:13).

Our second choice is to *stand still*! This is a godly choice—for a time. Moses refused to look back. He gave no hint of doubt. He expected a miracle from God. Moses knew he was operating in the center of God's will.

Moses could not look back for the same reason many of us today cannot look back—he had received a special invitation and revelation from God. The flame of God's fire in the midst of the burning bush opened his eyes to a new power and a whole new world, and from that point on he could not turn back! He could never return to the ignorance of the days before he received the living word from God! He had heard the promises of God and seen His light. He was forever changed and sealed by God's Word and by His flaming presence in the Holy Spirit!

God wants all of His children to expand their faith! That goes for all of us, from the feeble to the mighty. That is why

God gave Moses a shocking third alternative: "And the Lord said unto Moses, Wherefore criest thou unto Me? speak unto the children of Israel, that they go forward" (Ex. 14:15).

God says, *"Go forward!"* He wants us to know that He is God. "I will open rivers in high places, and fountains in the midst of the valleys: I will make the wilderness a pool of water, and the dry land springs of water" (Is. 41:18). *Go forward* and see the hand of God that goes before you. Divide the sea, and see the children of Israel pass on dry ground!

Faith demands that we act, even in the face of impossibility! Faith requires an impossible challenge, and the perseverance to overcome it in God's strength. The gates of hell cannot prevail against this kind of faith (see Mt. 16:18). Satan's joyless gates and the very strongholds of hell must give way before us like the vast stretches of the Red Sea. We always emerge on the other shore fully washed in the waters of God's salvation. Faith is the strength of our salvation, if we just do not look back!

God will take us through many things before we can stand up to the enemy, and some of these things are not pleasant. The desert is not pleasant when you are on foot. The open seas can be disheartening, and satan will always be there to taunt us and constantly remind us that the road to God is rough, narrow, and dangerous. So what? Satan is the only real obstacle, and he is already defeated.

If we must look back, we should look back at the mighty works of God and the triumph of Jesus on the cross. Jesus paved the way with the greatest act of faith of all time on Calvary. His "trial" before the Sanhedrin and Pilate was like no other, and the passion of Jesus Christ, the Son of God, as He carried the cross through the streets of Jerusalem is unequalled (see Mt. 27; Mk. 15). At Golgotha, the Hill of the Skull, He was brutally crucified with two thieves.

Those who passed by hurled insults at Him, shaking their heads and saying, "You who are going to destroy the temple and build it in three days, save Yourself! Come down from the cross, if You are the Son of God!" In the same way the chief priests, the teachers of the law and the elders mocked Him. "He saved others," they said, "but He can't save Himself! He's the King of Israel! Let Him come down now from the cross, and we will believe in Him. He trusts in God. Let God rescue Him now if He wants Him, for He said, 'I am the Son of God.'" In the same way the robbers who were crucified with Him also heaped insults on Him (Matthew 27:39-44 NIV).

Jesus came to die that we might live. At any moment on the cross, if He had chosen to live, you and I would have to die in our sins. Jesus could have said, "You committed the offense. You pay the price." Praise God, Jesus did not say that! He refused to turn back!

Those who scoffed at Jesus on Calvary took their taunts from the script satan used to tempt Jesus in the wilderness: "If You are the Son of God, save Yourself" (see Mt. 4:3,6). Christ is the origin and issue of life. He sustained life and gave breath to each of those mocking voices, but He could have revoked their breath in a moment and watched each one strangle and choke to death (see Job 12:10; 34:14-15). Yet Jesus refused to look away from "the joy that was set before Him" (Heb. 12:2).

When Peter drew his sword to defend Jesus from His captors in the garden, Jesus reminded Peter of the word and will of God:

...Put up again thy sword into his place: for all they that take the sword shall perish with the sword. Thinkest thou that I cannot now pray to My Father,

and He shall presently give Me more than twelve le-gions of angels? But how then shall the scriptures be fulfilled...? (Matthew 26:52-54)

All faith depended on Jesus. His faith is the key to the promises of God; His faith is the key to salvation's door. If Christ had turned back and given up hope, if He had come down from the cross, faith would have died forever. Our foun-tain of hope, our way through the deserts and stormy seas of life, was bound to that cross. He is "the author and finisher of our faith" (Heb. 12:2). We must *never look back, never give up!* Christ stands beside you; He has confirmed His Word with His life.

Step 5: Speak to Your Victory With a Vocabulary of Hope.

Our victory through faith is beyond speculation. God's faithfulness was such a certainty to Jesus that He often had to clarify His words for groups of people! When He prayed before the tomb of Lazarus, He thanked God for hearing His prayer, but added, "I knew that You always hear Me, but I said this for the benefit of the people standing here, that they may believe that You sent Me" (Jn. 11:42 NIV).

Jesus publicly thanked His Father for hearing His prayer, but He was careful not to imply that God *might not* hear and answer Him. Under no circumstance would He imply doubt! Outside the temple of Herod, Jesus prayed out loud, "Father, glorify Thy name." "...Then came there a voice from heaven, saying, I have both glorified it, and will glorify it again" (Jn. 12:28). Jesus again clarified to the crowd that the voice was not for Him, but for them (see Jn. 12:30).

We should be just as careful about the words that we use and never speak defeat into our lives through words of uncer-tainty. Always speak God's victory in your circumstances with words of hope and faith. Rather than pray, "Oh Lord, we hope and pray that You will go before us and abide with us," we should pray, "I thank You, Lord, that You are ever by my side. Your Word declares that You hear me always. You answer me even before I call upon Your name." We should shout like Joshua before the seemingly impenetrable walls of Jericho, "The Lord hath given us the city!" (See Joshua 6:16.)

God is not hard of hearing, and His memory is not faulty; yet Christ asked Peter three times, "Dost thou love Me more than these?" (see Jn. 21:14-17). Peter had insisted that he loved Christ enough to die for Him (see Jn. 13:34-37). His pride had hidden the weakness of his flesh from his mind, and that weakness caused him to deny the Lord three times! Each denial was "washed away" by Peter's proclamation of love on the beach. The subtle influence of "doubting words" upon our flesh is something we rarely appreciate until we have fallen. The practice of faith demands that we feed our minds and spirits with victory.

We should not listen to music that casts a shadow over the high spirit of hope and obedience to God. Many supposedly spiritual tunes do not flow from the Word of God. Some are borrowed from worldly influences, and many of them actually darken the spirit. Believers should never imitate the world's vocabulary and sound because they carry the world's sin and doubt into the redeemed spirit.

God will never fail us, so we should speak personalized words of power to ourselves from His Word: We will "be strong and of good courage, for the Lord God will be with us; He will not fail us, nor forsake us, until we have finished all the work He has given us" (see 1 Chron. 28:20). We say boldly, "The Lord is my helper, and I will not fear what man shall do unto me" (see Heb. 13:6). (See also Deuteronomy 31:6,8 and Joshua 1:5.) "I know with all my heart and soul that not one of all the good promises the Lord my God gave me has failed. Every promise has been fulfilled; not one has failed" (see Josh. 23:14).

We should make it a habit to repeat God's words of victory. My "victory passage" is Isaiah 41:8-16, because my name is derived from the name Jacob. Declare the truths of First Kings 8:56 or Psalm 118:6. Adopt Job's powerful testimony in Job 19:14-27 as your own! He says, in essence, that all of his family and friends have failed him, and his flesh has come to nothing, but...

> *...I know that my redeemer liveth, and that He shall stand at the latter day upon the earth...yet in my flesh shall I see God: whom I shall see for myself, and mine eyes shall behold, and not another; though my reins be consumed within me* (Job 19:25-27).

There is no end to God's power. "...The Lord is the everlasting God, the Creator of the ends of the earth. He will not grow tired or weary, and His understanding no one can fathom" (Is. 40:28 NIV). "And this is the victory that overcometh the world, even our faith" (1 Jn. 5:4b).

Step 6: Make Your Petitions Known to God; Pray.

Peter answered Jesus, "Lord, Thou knowest all things" (Jn. 21:17). He was right; God is all-knowing. That is why prayer is a faith-builder! When we pray, we strengthen our convictions and humble ourselves before the Lord. We should do this every moment of every day.

Prayer brings us into the presence of God. His Spirit overshadows our spirit in the sanctity of prayer as both the mind and the body come into the realm of the supernatural. The moment you close your eyes in prayer, you may discover you have been taken in the Spirit to a quiet place where hovering angels attend with rapt anticipation. At other times, the Spirit may confirm your communion with a gentle "blanket" of God's approval and tangible presence. Once you know God in an intimate way, you will be able to sense His presence as surely as you would recognize a friend nearby. This intimate spiritual communion with God is the primary element of prayer's faith-building potential.

Prayer also *prepares the soul to do God's bidding*. Our all-knowing God does not need "information"; He is interested in the depth of our surrender and commitment. He already knows what we need, and He has already promised it. Prayer deepens our submission to His will and our allegiance to His Word. Prayer aligns the soul with God's purposes and prepares the rich soil of the heart for the planting, watering, weeding, pruning, and sowing of God's Word. Prayer softens and sweetens the heart of the penitent, and moves the reluctant mind to subjection. Prayer motivates us by planting the word of faith in every part of our conscious life. Prayer fortifies our faith, and since faith is built on the Word of God, prayer braces the foundations of faith in the mind.

Prayer washes the human mind in the power of God's Word. Like a living creed, prayer plants the basic principles of God's Word in the spirit, stabilizing the soul with God's assurances! Prayer establishes a godly life by moving God's Word from the mind to the heart. It protects our character by elevating the purpose and activities of life to a high and holy footing with eternal foundations. Prayer settles, seasons, and centers our faith through communion with God, allowing us to walk with divine purpose and direction each day.

Prayer ushers God's Word into the earthly affairs of men! The spoken Word is power, and prayer harnesses the unlimited power of faith and the Holy Spirit with God's Word to fulfill God's will. Prayer in the name of Jesus Christ calls into being the things that we pray for. It quickens the objects of our faith and releases the Holy Spirit to render God's grace in every situation.

Finally, the Holy Spirit of God literally prays through our spirit! Prayer "in the Holy Ghost" is like an unction or holy anointing that covers the mind and the body like an oil, bringing divine healing, instruction, protection, and warmth. This miracle has to be experienced to be fully appreciated. At times you may sense the voice of the Spirit in prayer or meditation. He may prophesy, direct, preach, counsel, or simply make His sweet presence known. He gladdens, deepens, and lightens simply with His presence, awakening the mind to the things around you and guiding you to wiser decisions. The Spirit touches the heart with a holy compassion, severs every entangling confusion, banishes every distraction, and delights to expose the nature of the indwelling Christ in you and those around you!

Step 7: Walk in the Vision.

God always reveals His purposes to those who seek Him. This may happen in night visions, dreams, or prophecy; but most of the time His Spirit will speak to us through the Word of God and our circumstances. Faith only works when Christians acknowledge the work of God in their lives and take the initiative to live out His purpose and plan. The apostle Paul knew his calling on the road to Damascus, but he perfected that purpose in his life day by day. We are all called to walk in submission to God's will by *daily* sacrificing our lives to His will (see Rom. 12:1-2). Faith demands sacrifice but yields great rewards.

Obstacles to the fulfillment of purpose should never stop us. As with Abraham, faith may demand that we walk north, south, east, or west to follow the vision of God's plan for us (see Gen. 13:14-18), but we must always pitch our tents in the center of His will to appropriate the power of His purpose.

Elijah Walked in the Vision

"Elijah the Tishbite" suddenly appeared out of nowhere in an impossible situation to prophesy three years of drought over Israel as punishment for the apostasy of Ahab and Jezebel. These incredibly violent rulers had already killed countless prophets of God. Elijah retreated to the brook Cherith where he was miraculously fed by ravens, and later moved to Zarephath where a widow kept him for nearly two years through God's miraculous provision of meal and oil. Elijah also raised the widow's son from the dead.

Elijah emerged from obscurity again to challenge King Ahab's chosen prophets of Baal in a death-defying contest in front of all the people of Israel! He called down the fire of God from Heaven, killed 850 false prophets of Baal, and boldly told King Ahab that rain was on its way again after three years of total drought!

Elijah again fled to the wilderness to escape the vengeance of Jezebel and was fed by an angel of God. He journeyed 40 days and nights to Mount Horeb where he received a vision from Jehovah. Later, he anointed Elisha as prophet in his place, predicted the demise of Ahab and Jezebel, and was taken to Heaven in a whirlwind when the Lord chose to bring divinity into time.

The Whirlwind of God

Elijah himself; Elisha, his assistant; and the entire school of the prophets knew the day that Elijah would be taken by God. Only God knew exactly when and where. It was the voice of God that led Elijah to the spot where the miraculous would happen. Therefore Elijah had to walk in the counsel of the Almighty God with an audience of 50 prophets gazing from afar.

Elijah tried to leave Elisha to walk alone from Gilgal to the city of Bethel, but Elisha refused to leave him, knowing he would soon go to meet God. When the "sons of the prophets" told Elisha, "Knowest thou that the Lord will take away thy master from thy head today?" he told them, "Yea, I know it; hold ye your peace" (2 Kings 2:3). Basically he was saying, "The Lord has spoken; the rest is silence. Walk in the vision!" So the two of them walked to Bethel.

Elijah asked Elisha to stay in Bethel while he travelled to Jericho, but Elisha would not stay. So they walked from Bethel to Jericho where the sons of the prophets again asked Elisha if he knew that the Lord would take away his master that day. He answered, "Yea, I know it; hold ye your peace" (2 Kings 2:5). Essentially he repeated, "The Lord has spoken; the rest is silence. Walk!" So Elijah and Elisha walked from Bethel to Jericho.

In Jericho, Elijah tried a third time to have Elisha stay behind so that he could face the challenge alone. But Elisha would not stay. He was determined to follow the prophet of God and see the Lord's miraculous purpose fulfilled in his life as much as in Elijah's. So the two men walked from Jericho to the Jordan River. There Elijah divided the water so the two of them could pass on dry ground. *Walk in the vision! Walk!*

After Elisha steadfastly walked at Elijah's side, the old prophet finally said to Elisha, "...Ask what I shall do for thee, before I be taken away from thee. And Elisha said, I pray thee, let a double portion of thy spirit be upon me" (2 Kings 2:9). Elijah responded, "...Thou hast asked a hard thing: nevertheless, if thou see me when I am taken from thee, it shall be so unto thee; but if not, it shall not be so" (2 Kings 2:10). As they walked and talked, there appeared a chariot of fire and horses of fire that separated the two and took Elijah up into Heaven on a whirlwind. Elisha saw it and cried aloud, "...My father, my father, the chariot of Israel, and the horsemen thereof" (2 Kings 2:12a).

WALK in the knowledge of the miraculous!
WALK in the power of His Word!
WALK in the center of His purpose!
WALK in the vision of His call!

Step 8: Claim the Power of Faith!

Elisha was quick to claim the power of God passed down through the spirit of Elijah. He didn't hide the gift of God; he immediately took the mantle of Elijah and struck the Jordan River, then crossed over on dry ground (see 2 Kings 2:14). This was only the first of a steady string of miracles in his ministry. He purified the springs of Jericho, prophesied the presence of water in the wilderness of Edom and foretold the defeat of the Moabites, multiplied a widow's oil, predicted the birth of a son to a kindly Shunammite woman, and raised that son from the dead! (See 2 Kings 2–4.) He fed 100 men with 20 loaves, cured Naaman of leprosy, caused iron to float, struck the Syrian army with blindness, and predicted the death of King Benhadad of Syria (see 2 Kings 4–6; 8:10). Even after his death, Elisha's bones restored a man to life in Second Kings 13:21! Elisha was a type of Christ, since Jesus followed the revival of John who "came in the spirit of Elijah" (see Lk. 1:17).

How often do we receive a word from God and fail to charge forward with a vengeance? How many times has God given us a word of promise, but we fail to claim its fulfillment? More commonly, how often do we simply doubt the voice of the Spirit and ignore His counsel and instructions? We must always claim the power of prayer, of fasting, and of the word of hope as much as that of visions, miracles, and prophecy. With every ounce of additional faith, there is an ocean of new power and strength from God.

In the story of the widow's oil, we have an example of the unlimited power of faith. In Second Kings 4, the wife of a deceased prophet was on the verge of losing her two sons to indentured servitude for failure to pay her husband's debt. She went to Elisha for a petition to God, saying, "Your servant my husband is dead, and you know that he revered the Lord..." (2 Kings 4:1b NIV). The prophet asked the woman what she had in her house, to which she responded, "Nothing except a little oil" (see 2 Kings 4:2). So the prophet told her to borrow as many jars as she could find, shut herself in her house, and fill them all from the oil she started with. The widow borrowed all the jars in town, and the oil never stopped flowing until the last of the jars was full!

God's supply is as large as our faith; and as our faith grows, so does His bountiful supply! Little faith yields little power; great faith yields great power. Claim the power of faith! The power of faith in the end is the badge of our salvation. Only the faithful will inherit the riches of God. Only those who have unshakeable faith will overcome the great trials of our day and be ready when Jesus comes. Make sure your lamps are trimmed and that you have oil to spare for the Bridegroom (see Mt. 25:1-13).

Chapter 9

The End of Doubt

Agreat war between good and evil has been waged since the dawn of man's existence. The battle lines are clearly drawn; there is no demilitarized zone. Everyone is involved. This battle is the overriding concern of all creation until Jesus comes. Every act, every thought, and every word is a practice round in the engagement. Nothing can be labeled "neutral." Every aspect of art, science, work, recreation, or social interaction, whether harmonious or antagonistic, is a part of the struggle. No worthwhile expenditure of human effort or energy can be separated from the controversy, for it is the all-consuming reality of every other reality.

The full attention of the spirit realm is focused on the earth to see the outcome of satan's rebellion. Every angel and demon is fully committed to the struggle. Whether good or evil, each is armed and goes forth to independently attack the enemy's spiritual posts and to assist in the parallel conflict in the physical world.

God's full battle plans have not been revealed, although chapter 20 of the Book of Revelation describes the second coming of Christ and His final destruction of satan's works. Yet the Savior Himself said, "But of that day and hour knoweth no man, no, not the angels of heaven, but My Father only" (Mt. 24:36).

Christ's return will catch satan by surprise for the *second time*. Paul said the mystery of salvation and the cross, especially as it pertained to the Gentiles, surprised satan and even the angels of Heaven!

> *...By revelation He made known unto me the mystery...* **which in other ages was not made known unto the sons of men,** *as it is now revealed unto His holy apostles and prophets by the Spirit; that the Gentiles should be fellowheirs, and of the same body and partakers of His promise in Christ by the gospel: ...this grace [was] given, that I should preach among the Gentiles the unsearchable riches of Christ; and to make all men see what is the fellowship of the mystery,* **which from the beginning of the world hath been hid in God,** *who created all things by Jesus Christ: to the intent* **that now unto the principalities and powers in heavenly places might be known** *by the church the manifold wisdom of God, according to the eternal purpose which He purposed in Christ Jesus our Lord* (Ephesians 3:3,5-6,8-11).

According to Peter, the prophets of old wrote under the guidance of the Holy Ghost, but they did not fully comprehend the exact meaning of their revelation or to whom the messages were addressed. They did not know how Christ was to come or when and how He was to suffer and die. They believed God, though they did not fully understand the nature of salvation.

(See Second Peter 1:10-12.) Peter also says the angels did not know these mysteries:

> *...unto us they did minister the things, which are now reported unto you by them that have preached the gospel unto you with the Holy Ghost sent down from heaven;* **which things the angels desire to look into** *(1 Peter 1:12).*

God has revealed Himself through men and angels, and His Word speaks of a time when doubts about Christ will be no more. "For now we see through a glass, darkly; but then face to face: now I know in part; but then shall I know even as also I am known" (1 Cor. 13:12). The apostle John sealed the question with his revelation:

> *...Jesus Christ, who is the faithful witness, and the first begotten of the dead, and the prince of the kings of the earth.... Behold, He cometh with clouds* [of angels]*; and every eye shall see Him, and they also which pierced Him: and all kindreds of the earth shall wail because of Him...* (Revelation 1:5,7).

The fact that Christ will descend to the earth again is no mystery. As He ascended to Heaven, the Book of Acts tells us, "and while they looked stedfastly toward heaven as He went up, behold, two men stood by them in white apparel; which also said, Ye men of Galilee, why stand ye gazing up into heaven? this same Jesus, which is taken up from you into heaven, shall so come in like manner as ye have seen Him go into heaven" (Acts 1:10-11).

The apostle Paul also prophesied of His return:

> *For the Lord Himself shall descend from heaven with a shout, with the voice of the archangel, and with the trump of God: and the dead in Christ shall rise first:*

then we which are alive and remain shall be caught up together with them in the clouds, to meet the Lord in the air: and so shall we ever be with the Lord (1 Thessalonians 4:16-17).

The apostle John adds in Revelation 1:5-7 that *everyone* would see Jesus come again. The prophecies of John and Paul and the "two men in white" indicate that everyone alive, along with the dead in Christ and those who pierced Him, will witness His second coming.

Despite the fact that Christ will come again, the doubts that satan has carefully planted among men concerning the Lord's sovereignty, justice, and love continue to persist. The fact is that every man and woman will face a judgment. Paul warned the church at Rome, "...we shall all stand before the judgment seat of Christ. For it is written, As I live, saith the Lord, every knee shall bow to Me, and every tongue shall confess to God" (Rom. 14:10-11).

Jesus Christ declared, "All power is given unto Me in heaven and in earth" (Mt. 28:18b). Concerning the "judgment," He said:

When the Son of man shall come in His glory, and all the holy angels with Him, then shall He sit upon the throne of His glory: and before Him shall be gathered all nations: and He shall separate them one from another, as a shepherd divideth his sheep from the goats: and He shall set the sheep on His right hand, but the goats on the left. Then shall the King say unto them on His right hand, Come, ye blessed of My Father, inherit the kingdom prepared for you from the foundation of the world: ... Then shall He say also unto them on the left hand, Depart from Me, ye cursed, into everlasting fire, prepared for the devil and his angels (Matthew 25:31-34,41).

Wherefore God also hath highly exalted Him, and given Him a name which is above every name: that at the name of Jesus every knee should bow, of things in heaven, and things in earth, and things under the earth; and that every tongue should confess that Jesus Christ is Lord, to the glory of God the Father (Philippians 2:9-11).

And He said unto me, It is done. I am Alpha and Omega, the beginning and the end. I will give unto him that is athirst of the fountain of the water of life freely. He that overcometh shall inherit all things; and I will be his God, and he shall be My son. But the fearful, and unbelieving...shall have their part in the lake which burneth with fire and brimstone: which is the second death (Revelation 21:6-8).

According to the Book of Revelation, satan will be bound for a thousand years while the earth has a period of rest. Christ will reign as the king of the earth with the martyrs and those who do not fall to the antichrist (see Rev. 20:1-4). After the thousand years are passed, satan and his followers will be cast into the lake of fire and brimstone (see Rev. 20:7-10). Then the great war will be ended.

The destruction and judgment will come because "all men have not faith" (2 Thess. 3:2).

But ye, brethren, are not in darkness, that that day should overtake you as a thief. Ye are all the children of light, and the children of the day: we are not of the night, nor of darkness. Therefore let us not sleep, as do others; but let us watch and be sober. For they that sleep sleep in the night; and they that be drunken are drunken in the night. But let us, who are of the day, be sober, putting on the breastplate of faith and love; and for an helmet, the hope of salvation (1 Thessalonians 5:4-8).

Faith Is the Key That Unlocks the Door

This is the passageway through life
That we are fortunate to share.
We cannot say why we are chosen ones;
We know not when we go, nor where.

We see the beauty all around us.
There is perfection in our midst,
But in the time we spend, we cannot comprehend
The smallest part of what exists.

Without the gift of God inside us,
Life, at best, would seem to spite us.
But with the plan of grace and then a promised place,
The hope of glory should excite us.

Faith is the only way to soar.
It is the vision and the revelation of
*   what life must have in store.*
Faith takes the plain and simple things around us,
*   and puts them in perspective.*
And if we ever hope for more,
Faith is the key that unlocks the door.

Chapter 10

Personal Power and Little Green Apples

When I was a little boy, I had a recurring dream in which I had to eat little green apples. These hard, sour crab apples drew in my cheeks and sent bitter chills up into my ears and temples. More than a few times, my childish fantasies turned to the same odd situation: "Here they are, the little green apples. Eat them." I would ask the Lord in my dreams, "Why, Lord, do I have to eat these little green apples when everybody else is able to eat the plump red ones that look so sweet and so delicious?" His response was always the same: "You are not like the rest."

The Power to Be Different

God openly declares His desire for a *peculiar* or "private, enclosed jewel" of a people, reserved solely for Himself in Exodus 19:5, Deuteronomy 14:2, Titus 2:14, and First Peter 2:9. A clear pattern can be seen in the Chronicles, the Book of Exodus, the Book of Judges, and in the prophets—God often pulled His people away from their homeland to lands of His own choosing, and *every time they lapsed into sin by conform-ing* to the people around them! As soon as they adopted the sinful ways of nearby nations, He allowed them to be sent into captivity in a strange land, among strange customs and foreign practices.

We usually consider the captivity of God's people simply as punishment for their sins, but they also represent God's attempts to separate His people from the alluring sin of neighbors and co-nationals. The Canaanites worshiped Baal and Asherah with impure practices that went far beyond idolatry through animal sacrifice. The worship of these demonic deities also involved male and female prostitution, and human sacrifices! (See Judges 3:7; 6:25; First Kings 18:19; and Hosea 2:13; 4:13-14.)

The wild orgies, drinking, and debauchery of the heathen nations were far removed from the holy restraints and the ordered rituals of the worship God had ordained. There is little wonder that the children of Israel quickly broke the covenant at Sinai by declaring Yahweh to be "one of several gods" who had delivered them from the Egyptians. The lure of sexuality and drunkenness, especially when sanctioned as part of an organized religion, was nearly irresistible to people who chose to follow "social" norms (we should learn from this in our day). Israel quickly returned to idol worship and the revelry that went with it (see Ex. 32:1-8).

A modern equivalent is the current "social norm" of sexual involvement outside of marriage as a prelude to engagement. Civil (or uncivil) law has given official sanction to unrestrained indulgence between consenting adults, making biblical restrictions appear archaic and narrow-minded. Even the most dedicated believer may find it difficult to imagine marriage without previous sexual experimentation by the couple. The social normalization of these practices seems to give young believers few, if any, opportunities for finding a suitable partner among the general population of this country.

God sees beyond the boundaries of the earth and ever-changing social norms. He has not hesitated to call out His chosen vessels from among the peoples of the earth: "Wherefore come out from among them, and be ye separate, saith the Lord, and touch not the unclean thing; and I will receive you" (2 Cor. 6:17).

If the children of Israel had obeyed the Lord's command to cleanse the land of the Canaanites, the risk of contamination from their evil idolatry could have been reduced or eliminated. The Israelites failed to obey God, and once the temptations of the Canaanite practices captured their eyes, ears, and mind, the flesh itself was not far behind the surrender of the senses. The bodies and the souls of the Israelites were rapidly and thoroughly polluted by the very first taste of compromise, and their minds slowly became anesthetized to the horrible atrocities done in the name of religion.

Separation becomes the only way to find a point of objectivity in these situations involving peers and social acceptance. The power of God's love inside us includes the power of the renewed mind (see Rom. 12:2). The mind must see beyond "social" conformity by peering beyond what we hear and see in the natural, to perceive a new reality. God's reality clashes with the things we have learned from friends and family. God invites us into clarity of vision by washing away the sick and weakly bonds of conformity to our past and to our compromised surroundings.

God calls us to be visionaries with a superior understanding of the things we experience, know, and are. To reach for the arm of the invisible and infinite God, we must go beyond our families, our churches, our social traditions, our governments, and even our friends' expectations. The power of personal choice must take us into a strength that few can ever hope to see or to achieve.

God has given us the power of choice and the courage to use it. Now we can confront our blemishes and discern the falsities disguising life's snares laid by satan and triggered by sin. God still calls us out of our "comfort zones," just as He called Abram out of the land of his father (see Gen. 12:1). He longs to see us "arm ourselves" with the mind of Christ Himself!

Forasmuch then as Christ hath suffered for us in the flesh, **arm yourselves likewise with the same mind***: for he that hath suffered in the flesh hath ceased from sin; that he no longer should live the rest of his time in the flesh to the lusts of men, but to the will of God* (1 Peter 4:1-2).

There is infinite power through faith and obedience to the mind of Christ. The power of "freeing the mind" becomes the power to engage and commune with the God who cannot change, the God who knows all things, and the God of tomorrow and eternity.

The fact is that this personal power, this courage, this freedom, this vision, *is not easy to achieve.* It is like the little green apples the Lord offered to me in my dream. They were bitter and hard, and I felt they made me look foolish to everyone around me. Even when I could bear to chew them with a few small reluctant bites, I was always afraid that an aching stomach and a queasy sickness might follow. Fear of the unknown can quickly lead us back to the old and familiar, and we can always count on the disapproving crowd to come to take us back into our past. It is difficult to forge ahead to the new when the negative forces of adversity, fear, and peer pressure join forces with our own lack of clear direction and uncertainty!

Consider the pressures we faced as virgin teenagers standing outside the popular crowd of kids who sported cars, fashionable clothes, and plenty of company. Sixteen years just did not seem to provide enough preparation for us to resist and overcome the challenges of growing maturity, with all the subtle but alluring temptations of wine, sex, and songs! We could hardly resist the fads, the hairstyles, and the brand names sold to us by popular recording artists and TV and movie stars who sported lifestyles that did not deserve our emulation!

If we survived high school intact, college and university life introduced us to secret societies and Greek fraternities and sororities with initiation rites and hazing that seemed to imitate all of the impure rituals of the ancient Canaanites! (With the rising abortion rates among college coeds, it seems that even the cruel sacrifice of infants has been added to this wholehearted embrace of Canaanite religious practices.)

The power to turn away from "social activities" that seem so innocent calls for divine intervention in the life of many a plebe. How many of our teenage idols have been sacrificed to the consuming gods of sex, drugs, and fast lifestyles? The list of the dead includes Marilyn Monroe, Jimi Hendrix, Janis Joplin, Elvis Presley, Rock Hudson, Liberace, and River Phoenix to name just a few. Few of us can claim ingratitude for the simple fact that we survived our teenage years in one piece.

Some of us somehow avoided many of the mistakes that plagued the lives of our parents. Having seen the full consequences of alcohol and greed, for example, perhaps we chose a better way because personal experience and objectivity had already opened our eyes. When we stand as objective observers watching a failing marriage or co-dependency, God speaks to us just as if He had called us to be separate and apart from a situation or temptation. I've said many times, "If I ever get my own family, I will never argue with my spouse or rail against my children."

I believe that my childhood disputes were enough for two or three full lifetimes. Today, I refuse to get into another argument with anyone. I think that I would rather give in than listen to some loud and angry confrontation. My mind has set itself in line with peace and harmony. Though I no longer count the cost, I have found the path to peace by simple understanding through blessed objectivity!

It is usually easier to *see* a problem or obstacle clearly than to actually overcome it. Many of our social norms seem to go to the core of our emotions. The "accepted way" often wins that distinction by being the "easy way"! It is human nature to avoid difficulty and hardship. God commands us to remain sexually pure until we marry, but our hormones and our society say, "If it feels good, do it." God will lead each of us into absolute truth if, by faith, we give Him leave to be our Guide.

God's plan doesn't include our "traipsing into Heaven" without focus or direction. Those who keep their old confinements and avoid total transformation "because it is painful" are like ancient bottles taking in new wine. They cannot bear the requirements of their new identity, divine purpose, and heavenly citizenship. They will inevitably burst. They usually turn back again as they are drawn away by the cares of the world. God offers and requires us to live in overcoming power, the power to separate.

Even though Christians are endued with the power to overcome the traps satan scatters throughout life, the whole process can really test the soul. Abram suffered genuine emotional pain when he had to leave Haran and forever leave his family, friends, and familiar faces. Abram must have spent many a night in solitude, weighed down with lonely thoughts of all the kinfolk he left behind and the little babies he would never see grow up—not to mention all the old Chaldean customs he had abandoned that marked holidays, birthdays, and new births. He was 75 years old, and he had recently lost his father. His new life in Canaan required major adjustments in language, food, clothing, and social customs. Later on, he faced threats in Egypt because of Canaan's droughts and famine, and the loss of Lot and Ishmael set him on an even narrower course with his invisible God. Learning through great leaps of faith and headlong plunges into doubt, Abram found that God knows best. He came to love God first and foremost, even before his very flesh and bones—this is the essence of the power of love.

You learn to use your "power to overcome" in the same way a bird learns to fly. When you try to leave the comfort of the nest for the first time, fear grips your heart and locks the very muscles you need to take flight. The nest is safe, but looking down reinforces your growing need for frequent reassurance. The first leap seems like a death-defying plunge into a whole new way of life! Nearly all of us seem to "land on our heads" that first time, only to rise and nurse our broken feathers and splintered pride.

The process starts all over again and repeats itself until we can navigate the "lower corridors of air" close to the ground. Unfortunately, we encounter more obstacles at ground level than in any other area! Your friends and family often stand solidly against any plans that "set your mind apart" from them or the lifestyle they have agreed upon and practiced for generations. You may become the object of caustic ridicule intended to send you back into the nest. Your low-to-the-ground flight path requires you to stay alert for trees, poles, wires, and countless other natural and man-made objects. Every now and then, you will take a stunning blow to the head due to some momentary inattention to the rough and cluttered terrain, just as Abram was staggered by adversity in Egypt.

Maturity brings wisdom and greater ability to soar *above* rooftops, treetops, and the hills of the countryside. Your vision begins to broaden, and your courage has brought expanded understanding and perception. Few of your old buddies will perceive the world as you do. You now see things far in the distance and you plan with a knowledge unknown to your peers. God gives us vision to perceive the future by His Spirit and His holy Word. God gave Abram a vision that guided his entire life (see Gen. 12:7). So it will be with each one of us who takes the plunge and withstands the ridicule that comes from opposition.

As we continue to walk with God, we will learn to soar among the clouds and have mountaintop experiences. We begin to commune with heavenly beings and are less attached to earthbound things. Courage has given us vision, freedom, and spiritual revelation. This revelation comes only as we fly from our natural nest into the Kingdom and presence of God. He said, "If you have raced with men on foot and they have worn you out, how can you compete with horses?" (Jer. 12:5a NIV) "I have spoken to you of earthly things and you do not believe; how then will you believe if I speak of heavenly things?" (Jn. 3:12 NIV)

The personal power to overcome can only come from God. Only God fully understands where we came from, where we are going, and the tools we have been given for the task. Any path other than God's way leads into traps. God takes each of us on a *personal* voyage to freedom, and He gives each of us a vision of destiny! This reminds me of Abram in Canaan, Isaac in Egypt, Jacob with Laban, Joseph in Egypt, Moses in the land of Midian, and Saul (who became Paul) in Arabia. Each of us must allow God to take us to a solitary place where He can take us out of our old mind-sets and out of ourselves and bring us into the full identity of His purpose!

Psychology cannot do this. I have seen a thousand attempts by psychotherapists to give identity and purpose to their clients, but their best efforts only produced limited success. Psychologists often teach their own biases, which amounts to substituting one set of "social norms" for another. A therapist might look into your mind and pull out random pieces of information to build a sense of character, but this idea of "character" is usually based upon negative labels, like the personality descriptions used for psychiatric diagnoses.

Individuals under psychological treatment generally leave with either an incomplete transformation or some random characterizations based upon the particular therapist and school of thought, or the latest popular mode of treatment. I shutter to think of the potential negative effects of psychotropic medication in therapy. It is beyond debate that very few positive acquisitions can be associated with tranquilizers and chemical mood stabilizers.

God knows all things. Unlike third-party therapists and psychiatrists, He approaches us individually and works with a full and complete understanding of life and of our unique composition. His knowledge, perception, and wisdom infinitely outstrip that of the hypnotist I consulted about anxiety one time. He asked me "what suggestions I needed" in my psyche to help rebuild confidence and restore relaxation. The Holy Spirit told me that same night, "Don't return; he'll scramble up your mind which I have ordered to My purposes." I cancelled the appointment the next morning.

God transforms the human mind supernaturally with positive suggestions through His Word and indwelling Spirit. He can "write upon the psyche of man with perfect penmanship" since He is the only *author* of our lives! The mind is His.

It was only after years of following Jesus and in the wake of His ascension that Peter finally realized on the shore of Lake Tiberias that *Christ knew him better than he knew himself!* The personal power to overcome adversity only comes through faith that rests on the love of God. The strength to overcome is a positive force contained in God Himself. Nothing else in all the earth can be substituted for this spiritual power. Every supposed "alternative" is steeped in compromise.

We must move quickly into line with God. He is waiting to empower us with the courage and vision to overcome all of life's obstacles—social expectations, political traps, entanglements of our background, erroneous dogmas of organized religions, and the unceasing pressure to conform to what is clearly unproductive and ungodly!

I invite the lovely secretary who sends flowers to herself in the name of fictitious lovers to *overcome!* I invite the man who makes up stories about his sexual exploits to apologize to the innocent victims of his misdirected ego. *Overcome!* I invite alcoholics who are so frozen by their fears that they are unable to attack life head-on because all the challenges seem so overwhelming: *Overcome!* I invite the child who has learned to curse and hangs out with bullies because he doesn't see himself as strong and able: *Overcome!*

I invite the aging female who is losing hair while wrinkles settle into her sun-blotched skin and despair quietly takes up residence in her color-washed eyes: *Overcome!* I invite the empty wives and husbands who live a lie pretending to be married to each other, while they settle into separate worlds with secret families in other places: *Overcome!* I invite the sexual deviant who is hiding behind the facades of drugs and alcohol, or social, political, and religious associations, to disguise the lonely, empty, alienated, and confused person within: *Overcome!*

I invite the girl who manufactures a new past to hide her poor upbringing, and who learned to play a seduction game to find some reassuring wealth: *Overcome!* I invite the many millions who measure their worth by television network standards, who think they must become stars and symbols of sexuality to avoid wasted lives: *Overcome!* I invite the crying elderly who put more energy into dying than they ever gave to living: *Overcome!*

The little green apples of my childhood memories are symbols of the difference God can make. He asked me if I would dare to be adventurous and follow Him where He leads me. *He asked if I would dare to be different.* I knew the little green apples would make me stand out from the rest, but He never told me that these little green apples would also build courage, freedom, and vision. Now I see it. The personal power of God to overcome the world begins with a simple bite into a little green apple!

Words of Wisdom From the Street

I was walking from the National Archives subway entrance in downtown Washington, D.C. to the Post Office when I had to move around some bleachers set up for the inauguration of the newly-elected president. Suddenly I saw a homeless man approaching me. He was a gentle-looking, portly blond man of about 50 years of age. He was pushing a cart that contained a large green garbage bag that appeared to contain all of his earthly possessions. He seemed to be focused on the skyline as he came within ten feet of me. Just as we met, he said out loud to no one in particular, *"It is all based on faith."* He didn't even break his stride as he walked past me that damp winter morning.

I was so astounded by what the man had said that I stopped in my tracks! If I passed him on my return trip, I decided I would ask him to repeat what he'd said. Was he talking to me? I really believed the message was for me, and I was fairly sure of why he said it. I just wanted to be certain.

The revelations I have received from God have always stood out from the rest of life. They always seem to grab me by the gut. I saw the man on the other side of the street as I returned, but I completely forgot that I had planned to ask him something. The message apparently needed no confirmation. The Master said to me in that encounter, "I am with you always."

The man was absolutely right. *It is all based on faith.* Love is based on faith. Obedience is based on faith. Power is based on faith. Faith is the foundation of our relationship with God, and the source of our confidence and hope. It is almost synonymous with obedience, and it is indispensable to the love of God. Without faith, the power of the invisible God can only be "written off" as capricious acts of nature, fate, or coincidence. Without faith even this encounter would appear random or accidental! No one can come to God unless they first *believe* that He exists.

Faith is *beyond intellect*! It is *beyond the senses*! Faith even reaches *beyond signs and wonders*! Faith is beyond the earth!

> *Set your sights on Heaven.*
> *Expect miracles.*
> *See God at every step.*
> *Never look back, never doubt.*
> *Speak victory.*
> *Pray.*
> *Walk in the vision.*
> *Claim the power!*

Part IV

The Power of Obedience

In the beginning there was good and evil. Good was a vital loving impulse; evil was a long fatal plunge away from good. God stood above good and evil with the power to give life and take life. He could form the end and the beginning. He separated the blessings of love, joy, faith, peace, meekness, gentleness, and justice out of good. He set apart the evil fatal plunge, putting away hate, doubt, fear, want, misery, and inequity. God knew that willful created beings would come to see and try the evil fatal plunge. Hence, God made a plan to restore the coming breach. The sacrifice would equalize. Mercy and goodness would justify.

God made the negative force subject to the positive force. One would serve the other. Hate would follow love and depend on it for its strength and endurance; and doubt would follow faith and depend on it for its strength and its endurance. Disbelief would grow out of belief, and not the reverse. Hate would grow out of love, and not the reverse. Injustice would grow out of justice, and not the reverse (see *Rom. 4:15*). One was superior; one was inferior. One was first, and one was last. Without belief, there can be no disbelief. Without love, there can be no hate. Thus the evil fatal plunge grows out of the vital loving impulse. The evil fatal plunge is the weaker force, for it cannot create. The vital loving impulse can neither destroy nor disappear, yet the evil fatal plunge is doomed to destroy itself.

Chapter 11

Distinguishing Faith and Obedience

U nder the law, every crime is known by two essential aspects: the *mens rea* and the *actus reus*. *Mens rea* literally means "guilty mind," and it refers to the criminal intent behind a crime. *Actus reus* refers to the criminal act or the physical motions—especially the final motion—necessary to complete a crime. Some crimes are intentional (like murder), but many acts may be criminal though they are *unintentional*. Both aspects must be analyzed to know whether a crime has been committed.

The "law of Moses" makes a distinction between intentional and unintentional acts of wrongdoing in the Book of Leviticus, chapter 4, and in Numbers 15:24-31. Intentional acts done with a "high hand" are punished more severely than those done unintentionally (see Num. 15:28-31). This distinction and more severe punishments for intentional crimes are virtually universal in every social and legal system in human society.

Faith is related to obedience in the same way *mens rea* is related to *actus reus*. Faith is the *mental state* that accompanies the *physical act* of obedience. You may have your mind set on God, and you may *purpose* to obey Him—but belief must produce obedience. Believing is the beginning of power. "For God so loved the world, that He gave His only begotten Son, that whosoever believeth in Him should not perish, but have everlasting life" (Jn. 3:16).

It is practically impossible to imagine an act of obedience or righteousness that is not a product of faith, yet there are such acts. Satan often imitates God to deceive those who do not know the true worship of God. Satan may also "speak words of truth" in a context or manner that will mislead the unwary or uninformed. These "right actions" are done with evil intent.

Paul, Silas, and Timothy, for example, encountered a young demon-possessed woman on the streets of Philippi who made her living by soothsaying. For days, this lady followed them through the city crying out, "...These men are the servants of the most high God, which shew unto us the way of salvation" (Acts 16:17). This apparent "display of faith" was actually a ploy of the enemy designed to cast doubt on the apostles by associating them with a sorcerer who was known to be demon-possessed. The woman's words were absolutely true, but they were spoken out of absolute faithlessness. Her *true* words were spoken with *evil intent* in total opposition to God!

Paul revealed that even acts of benevolence count for nothing if they are done without love! The motive must match the act. "And though I bestow all my goods to feed the poor, and though I give my body to be burned, and have not charity, it profiteth me nothing" (1 Cor. 13:3). So it is with faith. Jesus made a clear and unmistakable connection between inward intent and outward acts:

Beware of false prophets, which come to you in sheep's clothing, but inwardly they are ravening wolves. Ye shall know them by their fruits.... Not every one that saith unto Me, Lord, Lord, shall enter into the kingdom of heaven; but he that doeth the will of My Father which is in heaven. Many will say to Me in that day, Lord, Lord, have we not prophesied in Thy name? and in Thy name have cast out devils? and in Thy name done many wonderful works? And then will I profess unto them, I never knew you: depart from Me, ye that work iniquity (Matthew 7:15-16,21-23).

Jesus also denounced the scribes and Pharisees who kept the law of tithing, but had no faith:

Woe unto you, scribes and Pharisees, hypocrites! for ye pay tithe of mint and anise and cummin, and have omitted the weightier matters of the law, judgment, mercy, and faith: these ought ye to have done, and not to leave the other undone. Ye blind guides, which strain at a gnat, and swallow a camel. Woe unto you, scribes and Pharisees, hypocrites! for ye make clean the outside of the cup and of the platter, but within they are full of extortion and excess (Matthew 23:23-25).

Jesus clearly denounces obedience without faith. Tithing is said to be necessary and it should not be left undone, but our Savior considers faith, mercy, and judgment to be more important aspects of obedience.

God does not reward acts of obedience done as a show to gain the praise of men. Jesus warned His disciples:

Take heed that ye do not your alms before men, to be seen of them: otherwise ye have no reward of your Father which is in heaven. Therefore when thou doest thine alms, do not sound a trumpet before thee, as the hypocrites do in the synagogues and in the streets, that they may have glory of men. Verily I say unto you, they have their reward. ... And when thou prayest, thou shalt not be as the hypocrites are: for they love to pray standing in the synagogues and in the corners of the streets, that they may be seen of men. Verily I say unto you, they have their reward. But thou, when thou prayest, enter into thy closet, and when thou hast shut thy door, pray to thy Father which is in secret; and thy Father which seeth in secret shall reward thee openly (Matthew 6:1-3,5-6).

Acts of obedience that are done under coercion, duress, or obligation are not acts of faith either! Many believers force their children to attend church, to pray, and to pay tithes. These parents, who themselves may be sincere believers, are usually shocked when their "obedient" children promptly leave the church as soon as they become independent!

In Jesus' time, an Israelite could be compelled to carry a load for a Roman citizen for up to a mile without compensation. Going the first mile would, therefore, be obligatory, not an act of love or obedience. That is why Jesus told His Jewish followers, "And whosoever shall compel thee to go a mile, go with him twain [two]" (Mt. 5:41). Only the second mile of service would be out of love or mercy. The measure of obedience, then, is the liberality of the heart.

This is the reason Paul told the Corinthians:

...He which soweth sparingly shall reap also sparingly; and he which soweth bountifully shall reap also bountifully. Every man according as he purposeth in his heart, so let him give; not grudgingly, or of necessity: for God loveth a cheerful giver (2 Corinthians 9:6-7).

The other side of this dichotomy is faith without obedience. James put faith in perspective when he declared:

Thou believest that there is one God; thou doest well: the devils also believe, and tremble. But wilt thou know, O vain man, that faith without works is dead? (James 2:19-20)

Many people believe that there is a God and that His Word is true, but they do not want to obey that Word or get to know God. According to James, any "faith" that consists of empty words is empty faith!

What doth it profit, my brethren, though a man say he hath faith, and have not works? can faith save him? If a brother or sister be naked, and destitute of daily food, and one of you say unto them, Depart in peace, be ye warmed and filled; notwithstanding ye give them not those things which are needful to the body; what doth it profit? Even so faith, if it hath not works, is dead, being alone (James 2:14-17).

Faith is more than merely an assent of the intellect. Any intellectual decision that does not produce obedience in behavior and deed is also dead faith. Many people obey man's law to avoid going to jail, but they freely disobey God's law because they don't see any *immediate consequences* for their actions. A person who would never consider killing anyone because of the prospect of going to prison, might commit adultery without a conscious sense of wrong because man's law declares adultery legal between consenting adults. God says both are sins.

Peter urged Christians to lay aside "...all malice, and all guile, and hypocrisies, and envies, and all evil speakings" (1 Pet. 2:1). Peter was concerned about *sins that cannot be seen.* He knew the new believer might be tempted by a pharisaical faith that could never really touch the deeper layers of conviction and restraint.

Faith and sin both originate in the mind. Jesus said, "...whosoever looketh on a woman to lust after her hath committed adultery with her already in his heart" (Mt. 5:28). He also warned that "whosoever is angry with his brother without a cause shall be in danger of the judgment..." (Mt. 5:22). Jesus saw lust as the basis for adultery and anger as the root cause of murder.

Faith and obedience must go hand in hand. They must both spring from the heartfelt conviction that God is real, and every word of His law is true. They work together to help us take an uncompromising stand against the godless ways and standards of the world. They forge a strength and determination in our being that doesn't permit a quiver or falter in our fulfillment of God's purposes, principles, and plan. Faith and obedience speak of discipleship.

> *...As they went in the way, a certain man said unto Him, Lord, I will follow Thee whithersoever Thou goest. And Jesus said unto him, Foxes have holes, and birds of the air have nests; but the Son of man hath not where to lay His head. And He said unto another, Follow Me. But he said, Lord, suffer me first to go and bury my father. Jesus said unto him, Let the dead bury their dead: but go thou and preach the kingdom of God. And another also said, Lord, I will follow Thee; but let me first go bid them farewell, which are at home at my house. And Jesus said unto him, No man, having put his hand to the plough, and looking back, is fit for the kingdom of God* (Luke 9:57-62).

Men may see the acts of men, but God reads the very hearts of men! He knows our innermost thoughts and secret musings. Though we may speak words meant to deceive, He weighs the intents of the heart.

But the Lord said unto Samuel, Look not on his countenance, or on the height of his stature; because I have refused him: for the Lord seeth not as man seeth; for man looketh on the outward appearance, but the Lord looketh on the heart (1 Samuel 16:7).

The wisdom of Solomon in the Book of Proverbs declares:

The preparations of the heart in man, and the answer of the tongue, is from the Lord. All the ways of a man are clean in his own eyes; but the Lord weigheth the spirits. Commit thy works unto the Lord, and thy thoughts shall be established (Proverbs 16:1-3).

Paul described the process of reformation and transformation to the believers in Rome: "And be not conformed to this world: but be ye transformed by the renewing of your mind, that ye may prove what is that good, and acceptable, and perfect, will of God" (Rom. 12:2).

The Ordered Life: Power by Design

Everyone I have ever known has had a hidden passion to fly—without airplanes, rockets, helicopters, or hot air balloons. We all long to fly like a bird on the wing. We secretly long to stretch out our arms and leap into the air to soar among the clouds and skim over the trees into the valleys, high above the sparkling streams and ponds and rolling hills. It is a universal dream.

Like the mythological Icarus, who dreamed of escaping imprisonment by taking flight on artificial wings, we watch in wonder as God's winged creatures somehow capture the strength of a breeze and harness its hidden power to lift their forms above the pull of gravity. The very thought of flying free creates the urge to soar above the earth. Even the development of modern aircraft, with all of their speed and convenience, has not diminished this urge.

The success of Orville and Wilbur Wright propelled more than just an aircraft. They demonstrated the transcendent power of design. Drawing from nature's patterns provided by the omniscient God, these men framed those patterns into a form that was fit for heavier earthbound creatures with a desire to fly. Their design lifted earthly creatures up and brought them closer to the divine. The aerodynamics of flight are just one example of the revelation of the blueprints of our God.

Every artist, scientist, and creature of curiosity gazes into the infinite wisdom of God each time they investigate the most basic lines in nature. Every wonder of nature leads back to God. God's creation gives man nearly endless clues to the mind of the Creator. Nature beckons us to reach up to a higher plateau to discover the foundations of beauty and truth.

More basic than the bird, however, are the patterns found in chemical elements. Scientists have discovered many of the fundamental arrangements of atoms. They have calculated the number of electrons and the weight of the atoms for these elements, hoping to uncover the very structure of our universe. This minute atomic and subatomic structure defines the strength and the utility of every known element of life in our universe. We also have learned that by changing these atoms in certain ways, we can unleash enormous power. The power that energizes atomic bombs and nuclear reactors, for example, is a power that is inherent in all matter. Its potential power is clearly defined by a certain order of nature...a *power by design.*

The nearly weightless feathers of a bird and a heavy block of solid lead have something in common! Both are composed of tiny particles called "atoms," and even smaller particles called "quarks." Every atom, and every quark in an atom, is governed by God's physical laws. These particles never move or act in contradiction to these laws unless they are tampered with, and then certain consequences always follow (hence, the atomic and nuclear bombs, and nuclear fusion). Apart from the tinkering of man, these elements never trespass the boundaries established by this ordered storehouse of knowledge and physical laws, for their individual strength, characteristics, and purpose are rooted in the laws that order their existence.

The structure and function of a bird's wing feathers are governed by the natural and physical laws of God. Every feather has its own purpose and place within the general task of manipulating the air to maneuver and transport the rest of the bird's body. Each individual feather finds its full purpose and power only in the ordered and concerted actions of all the parts of a bird assisting in flight.

God is a God of order. *Purpose and power are products of design.* The order of this design comes from God. Although this book focuses on the conflict between good and evil, somehow the words "good" and "evil" create an image that is quite different from the eternal issues before God. The ultimate concerns in Heaven and on earth relate to *order* and *disorder*. Good and evil should not be seen merely as "helping versus hurting," or "unselfishness versus selfishness," and "trust versus distrust." The deepest issues refer to order versus chaos, and God versus godlessness.

Consider the "original sin" in the Garden of Eden. The "evil" of eating the forbidden fruit wasn't a matter of "helping versus hurting," nor "selfishness versus unselfishness." Honestly, under most circumstances, eating a piece of fruit could hardly be considered bad at all! Even in Eden, eating fruit was not wrong. The problem was that God told them *not* to eat this *one type of fruit* from *one tree* in the garden. God had forbidden the act. Unlike rape, for example, the "evil" in Eden did not depend on whether Adam and Eve hurt someone. The original sin simply involved *obeying or disobeying God!*

The terms *good* and *bad* are really vague words disguising the real issue: *obedience to God* versus *rejection of God*. In other words, the issue is this: Will you choose God's plan or not? The ultimate issues have to do with order versus disorder, God's design versus chaos.

Of the ten great commandments in the Decalogue, none of the first four commandments involve "hurting other people" at all. They explicitly direct individuals to choose Jehovah God over everything and everyone else. The first three forbid having other gods before Jehovah God, making and worshiping images of things as god, and taking God's name in vain. The fourth commandment sets aside a day to honor God as Creator of the universe. The other six laws prohibit actions that hurt other people, but they also implicitly direct individuals to *choose God's order* rather than merely to follow a rule. (The Ten Commandments are not blanket instructions for every situation. They are general guidelines to be applied to individual situations, but are subordinated to instructions from God.)

Killing was wrongful for Cain, but not for David *as a military leader protecting his nation.* Stealing was wrongful for Achan and Saul, but the children of Israel were commanded to occupy (or *take and possess*) Canaan by God. Questions of "hurt" or "selfishness" are not the critical issues. The most important issues concern the plan of God as opposed to the instructions of self or others.

The Ten Commandments provide only a basic structure to adapt ourselves and our society to God's heavenly order. Advanced two-way communication and understanding comes with the indwelling Spirit who personally helps us center our lives in the will of God through Christ. Both the law and the Spirit promote the system of God's Kingdom. These two things bring Heaven to earth in the form of godly principles and order.

In his ill-fated rebellion against God, satan immediately broke four of the last five commandments with his lying, robbing, lust, and envy toward the holy Father. The killing came later when the devil incited Cain to spill his brother's innocent blood in the world's first murder. God gave Moses the ten prohibitions as *barricades* to prevent satan's infiltration into the lives of men. The ultimate organization of God is in radical opposition to the disorganization and deadly chaos of sin and satan. The first four commandments call us to God, while the last six halt the enemy. Righteousness hinges on the position we take in relation to God and satan.

Wisdom demands that first and foremost, we obey God rather than satan, aligning ourselves with God's dictates and principles. According to the Bible, this is the beginning of wisdom (see Prov. 9:10). It is also the beginning of power. God's order and design is our only avenue to find true power and the way to direct that power into our lives. Since the created realm comes from God the Creator, then God's system establishes the formula for tapping into the Designer's ultimate plan for optimizing creation! It directs and conveys the inherent "meaning of life" into the ordinary practices of people. God longs to "fine tune" and maximize the purpose and destiny of our individual functions so we will match the thrust of God's entire universe. Only God the Omnipotent and Omniscient is wise enough and powerful enough to subordinate and fit together the functions of the parts into the whole.

When we fail to align with God, we become like birds with clipped wing feathers or a broken wing. The altered "feathers and wings" in our lives may be sufficient for "hopping or short-term gliding," but they will never allow us to soar into the heights! The ideal in the mind of our Creator is for every "feather" in our lives to be developed to its fullest and used for the proficient execution of flight. He longs to see us fulfill in ourselves the ordered purposes He has established for us. With God, even the most insignificant of birds may reach and even exceed its natural aeronautical limits!

The ordered life is appointed, established, fit, structured, and patterned within the highest will of God. This "highest will" is found in God's Word and by His Spirit. It is only in God's plan and purpose that God's creation can reach its maximum potential for power. Our manifest destiny as God's people will only reach our fullest development as we remain in the very center and heart of God's will!

Salvation unto eternal life is nothing less than total assent to God's order! Love for God is acknowledging His sovereignty. Faith is engaging His presence. Obedience is walking in His will.

"Salvation" consists of more than giving to the needy to look "good" in the eyes of other people. The power of salvation is only released when you position yourself within God's plan. Our strongest defense against corruption is the alignment of our lives with and *by* God! Sin in the life of individuals presses them toward disorder while pushing God's whole creation toward chaos. To this degree, the salvation of the individual person contributes to the salvation of the whole of God's system and order. The ordered life, by evoking God's design and principles, participates in God's divine purpose of saving the universe.

Order defines "right" behavior by adding a vital purpose to our actions. Order marks the activities of our lives as negative or positive according to their ability to connect us with God. This particular "elemental balance" comes from *personal choice. Order either values our life for its alignment with its eternal* purposes in God, or it charges our life with everlasting *separation and distinction* from God. God's order prevents destruction.

When we become immersed in His will and influence, our intentions become purer, our resolve and effectiveness become more durable, our conviction becomes more steadfast, and our spiritual condition becomes more secure. The true power of *God-ordained* self-assurance is found in *the ordered life*.

The ordered life must be a priority. Some fear the discipline of the ordered life and warn of the risk that we might revert to man's "order" and become modern Pharisees and hypocrites. God's order is designed to conform flawed men to a perfect image. His order has the power to restore our allegiance to God. It explicitly acknowledges the sovereignty of God, and it bestows upon us the powers inherent to godliness.

Once your life is submitted to God's will, He supernaturally incorporates the power of *parallel design* into your life! Aircraft have *parallel design* with birds. Science, in general, has parallel design with the physical universe because our formal knowledge was gathered through observation of God's creation. Our products, from pharmaceuticals to new polymers to the martial arts—all seem to imitate nature in some way. There is power in God's blueprint. The creation reflects God's beauty and truth. God's order contains divine power to transcend.

Our common dream of flying is more than just a desire to do what birds do. These dreams reveal our profound desire to overcome the obstacles of life and be liberated from earthly limits. We long to be changed by metamorphosis into something *greater*. We are caterpillars longing to become butterflies.

God empowers us and fulfills these deep longings through Jesus Christ. Obedience releases the hand of God to work through us, and it fulfills our urge to *take flight*! The longings come from our eternal bond with our Creator, who wants to complete the work He began. Ultimately, we will be changed in a moment, in the twinkling of an eye, as our corruptible form puts on the incorruptible.

For the Lord Himself shall descend from heaven with a shout, with the voice of the archangel, and with the trump of God: and the dead in Christ shall rise first: then we which are alive and remain shall be caught up together with them in the clouds, to meet the Lord in the air: and so shall we ever be with the Lord (1 Thessalonians 4:16-17).

On the first day of the new creation, we will fly! This is my prayer:

My Prayer

Nothing less than all I am,
And all I come to be,
I give to You, Who gave to me,
To give to others freely.

Here's my body and my soul
That one time I tried to hold.
I give You control of the parts and whole.
Please forgive the years I stole.

Take my hands and feed the poor.
Teach them strength, so they'll endure,
Use my lips to bless, show them gentleness,
And the doubting ones assure.

Move my feet in paths of peace,
Finding pardon and release.
Let my arms embrace mercy, truth, and grace.
Every day my love increase.

Show my eyes the good in man.
Teach my heart to understand.

Give me words of cheer and a listening ear,
Even though I have no plan.

Use my time howe'er You please,
For the pains that I might ease,
But when things get tough and I've done enough,
Draw me nearer on my knees.

Use my mind to spread Thy Word
To the ones who have not heard.
Tell me what to say when they come my way.
Leave no blessing long deferred.

Nothing less than all I am,
And all I come to be,
I give to You, Who gave to me,
To give to others freely.

The Intrinsic Benefit of Obedience

Every act of obedience is a tiny Christmas present because "wrapped inside" of the act itself is a reward to the actor. The Bible describes it this way: "...to him that soweth righteousness shall be a sure reward" (Prov. 11:18). When you obey, you empower yourself in God! Every obedient act is a reward in and of itself; and every disobedient act is a detriment in and of itself. Moses said of the Lord's law, "Behold, I set before you this day a blessing and a curse; a blessing, if ye obey...and a curse, if ye will not obey..." (Deut. 11:26-28).

"And the Lord God commanded the man, saying, Of every tree of the garden thou mayest freely eat: but of the tree of the knowledge of good and evil, thou shalt not eat of it: for in the day that thou eatest thereof thou shalt surely die... (Gen. 2:16-17). Here is a command that is a warning. To eat of the tree of the knowledge of good and evil is both to disobey and to die; to eat of the tree of life is both to obey and to live. From the very beginning, *obedience* was paired with a blessing, and *disobedience* was paired with a curse! And from the very beginning, *man was free to make the choice.*

Partaking of the Divine Nature

The perfect state in Eden before sin entered the world will only be regained when Jesus comes. Faith and love are the primary ingredients of a cure for sin that only Jesus has provided. But along with these, a third component must be added to "fulfill all righteousness" (in the words of Jesus to John the Baptist before He was baptized). This third component is obedience.

Second Peter 1:3-11 (NIV) says:

His divine power has given us everything we need for life and godliness through our knowledge of Him who called us by His own glory and goodness. Through these He has given us His very great and precious promises, so that through them you may participate in the divine nature and escape the corruption in the world caused by evil desires. For this very reason, make every effort to add to your faith goodness; and to goodness, knowledge; and to knowledge, self-control; and to self-control, perseverence; and to perseverence, godliness; and to godliness, brotherly kindness; and to brotherly kindness, love. For if you possess these qualities in increasing measure, they will keep you from being ineffective and unproductive in your knowledge of our Lord Jesus Christ. But if any one does not have them, he is nearsighted and blind, and has forgotten that he has been cleansed from his past sins. Therefore, my brothers, be all the more eager to make your calling and election sure. For if you do these things, you will never fall, and you will receive a rich welcome into the eternal kingdom of our Lord and Savior Jesus Christ.

In this passage, Peter teaches that godly behavior actually develops faith. But he also acknowledges that it keeps the believer from corruption in the world and allows him to participate in the divine nature.

Indeed, obedience allows God to occupy and use the lives of His people. Rebellion opposes the plans of God. Rebellion opposes God's efforts to heal mankind. Obedience, however, opens the heart to God and causes it to yield to the Spirit of God. Therefore obedience allows God's perfect will and perfect character to touch every part of His creation. Obedience spreads love across the universe. It eradicates legalism because it promotes a form of duty that is so self-sacrificial that law is replaced by mercy. Thus universal bonding through humility and innocence breaks the chains of strife and dissolves all vanity.

Ultimately, obedience in the context of love and faith replaces the image of the demon with the perfect image of God. Obedience through love and faith realigns man with God and reestablishes the innocent perfection of the Garden of Eden where love was so universal that law had no real place; where love was so all-pervasive that God was manifest in every part of His creation. Faith in that context was epitomized by the abundant evidence of God's presence. Through obedience based on love and faith, rebellion and discord completely disappear.

Let nothing be done through strife or vainglory; but in lowliness of mind let each esteem other better than themselves. ... Let this mind be in you, which was also in Christ Jesus: who, being in the form of God, thought it not robbery to be equal with God: but made Himself of no reputation, and took upon Him the form of a servant, and was made in the likeness of men: and being found in fashion as a man, He humbled Himself, and became obedient unto death, even the death of the cross. Wherefore God also hath highly exalted Him, and given Him a name which is above every name (Philippians 2:3,5-9).

Jesus did the opposite of Adam and Eve. Because of satan, Eve wanted to be lifted up to the level of God, but instead was brought low. Jesus, however, thought equality with God was not something to be grasped, although He was the very nature of God! Instead, He humbled Himself before the Father and was exalted!

Obedience in love allows the mind of God and the perfection of God to pervade the universe! It benefits the child of God and the family of God while it heals the whole of humanity. It perfects the hearts and minds of man and the angels! It blesses even animals and plants, and the soil and air!

If we follow the example of Jesus, obedience through faith and love humbles us before man and God, so that we participate in the character of God and are exalted by God from the level of the natural to the level of the supernatural. We are given the image of God that was prepared for us before creation, that was given in Adam and Eve, and that is our inheritance through the Holy Spirit.

This is the holistic healing that comes from love, faith, and obedience. This combination of attributes fulfills the model prayer of Jesus Christ that says, "Thy kingdom come. Thy will be done in earth, as it is in heaven" (Mt. 6:10). It perfects the Body of Christ for the healing of humanity. It exalts the name of Jesus as God promised in Philippians. It confirms the truth and mercy of God by the power of His original plan. It settles the eternal conflict for the angels and man.

Therefore, obedience contains a supernatural power that comes from its ability to align earth with Heaven. The natural benefits that are inherent in the plan and government of God are released by adherence to God's Word and surrender to His Spirit!

Chapter 12

Obedience Preserves Life

God has promised to preserve the life of the righteous in the Genesis story of the fall of man, and in the Psalms, the prophets, and throughout His Word. Solomon declares:

For whoso findeth me [wisdom] *findeth life, and shall obtain favour of the Lord. But...all they that hate me* [wisdom] *love death* (Proverbs 8:35-36).

The labour of the righteous tendeth to life: the fruit of the wicked to sin. ... The fear of the Lord prolongeth days: but the years of the wicked shall be shortened (Proverbs 10:16,27).

As righteousness tendeth to life: so he that pursueth evil pursueth it to his own death. ... The fruit of the righteous is a tree of life; and he that winneth souls is wise (Proverbs 11:19,30).

The wicked are overthrown, and are not: but the house of the righteous shall stand. ... In the way of righteousness is life; and in the pathway thereof there is no death (Proverbs 12:7,28).

God has ordained a legacy of obedience that gives His obedient servants strength in their flesh and power to their bones:

He giveth power to the faint; and to them that have no might He increaseth strength. Even the youths shall faint and be weary, and the young men shall utterly fall: but they that wait upon the Lord shall renew their strength; they shall mount up with wings as eagles; they shall run, and not be weary; and they shall walk, and not faint (Isaiah 40:29-31).

Again in Isaiah 41:10, God admonishes His people: "Fear thou not; for I am with thee: be not dismayed; for I am thy God: I will strengthen thee; yea, I will help thee; yea, I will uphold thee with the right hand of My righteousness."

The deadly effects of sin stand in stark contrast to the life-giving consequences of righteousness. Solomon wrote:

The integrity of the upright shall guide them: but the perverseness of transgressors shall destroy them. ...righteousness delivereth from death. ...but the wicked shall fall by his own wickedness. The righteousness of the upright shall deliver them: but transgressors shall be taken in their own naughtiness. ... The righteous is delivered out of trouble, and the wicked cometh in his stead (Proverbs 11:3-8).

...the righteous shall flourish as a branch (Proverbs 11:28b).

Job speaks of his accumulated evidence for the eventual secret judgment of the wicked:

Drought and heat consume the snow waters: so doth the grave those which have sinned. The womb shall forget him; the worm shall feed sweetly on him; he shall be no more remembered; and wickedness shall be broken as a tree. He evil entreateth the barren that beareth not: and doeth not good to the widow. He draweth also the mighty with His power: He riseth up, and no man is sure of life. Though it be given him to be in safety, whereon he resteth; yet His eyes are upon their ways. They are exalted for a little while, but are gone and brought low; they are taken out of the way as all other, and cut off as the tops of the ears of corn (Job 24:19-24).

More than any other man, Job knew the judgment awaiting the wicked, and that is why he clung to righteousness with all his might.

My righteousness I hold fast, and will not let it go: my heart shall not reproach me so long as I live. ... For what is the hope of the hypocrite, though he hath gained, when God taketh away his soul? Will God hear his cry when trouble cometh upon him? (Job 27:6,8-9)

Job's answer to his own question is a thunderous "No!" He concludes his discussion by saying:

This is the portion of a wicked man with God, and the heritage of oppressors, which they shall receive of the Almighty. If his children be multiplied, it is for the sword: and his offspring shall not be satisfied with bread. Those that remain of him shall be buried in death: and his widows shall not weep (Job 27:13-15).

Throughout the Old Testament, the Lord called His chosen people to obedience and righteousness, but they remained obstinate and rebellious. God spoke through Moses to the children of Israel again and again in the Book of Deuteronomy:

Now therefore hearken, O Israel, unto the statutes and unto the judgments, which I teach you, for to do them, that ye may live... (Deuteronomy 4:1).

All the commandments which I command thee this day shall ye observe to do, that ye may live... (Deuteronomy 8:1).

That which is altogether just shalt thou follow, that thou mayest live... (Deuteronomy 16:20).

See, I have set before thee this day life and good, and death and evil; in that I command thee this day to love the Lord thy God, to walk in His ways, and to keep His commandments and His statutes and His judgments, that thou mayest live and multiply: and the Lord thy God shall bless thee in the land whither thou goest to possess it. But if thine heart turn away, so that thou wilt not hear, but shalt be drawn away, and worship other gods, and serve them; I denounce unto you this day, that ye shall surely perish, and that ye shall not prolong your days upon the land, whither thou passest over Jordan to go to possess it. I call heaven and earth to record this day against you, that I have set before you life and death, blessing and cursing: therefore choose life, that both thou and thy seed may live: that thou mayest love the Lord thy God, and that thou mayest obey His voice, and that thou mayest cleave unto Him: for He is thy life, and the length of thy days... (Deuteronomy 30:15-20).

Amos cried, "Seek good, and not evil, that ye may live..." (Amos 5:14). Isaiah said, "Incline your ear, and come unto Me: hear, and your soul shall live..." (Is. 55:3). David said, "What man is he that desireth life, and loveth many days[?] ... Depart from evil, and do good" (Ps. 34:12,14a).

The prophet Ezekiel received one of the most far-reaching visions in the Old Testament when he was commanded to prophesy to dry bones.

...O ye dry bones, hear the word of the Lord. Thus saith the Lord God unto these bones; Behold, I will cause breath to enter into you, and ye shall live: and I will lay sinews upon you, and will bring up flesh upon you, and cover you with skin, and put breath in you, and ye shall live; and ye shall know that I am the Lord (Ezekiel 37:4-6).

When Ezekiel prophesied to the bones, they came together, and sinew and flesh covered them. But there was no breath in them. Then the prophet was commanded to prophesy to the wind: "...thus saith the Lord God; Come from the four winds, O breath, and breathe upon these slain, that they may live" (Ezek. 37:9). When the prophet prophesied to the wind, breath came into the flesh and bones, "...and they lived, and stood up upon their feet, an exceeding great army" (Ezek. 37:10).

The vision of Ezekiel embodies God's eternal promise of restoration for His people. It reaches far beyond Israel's captivity in Babylon to embrace the spiritual revival of the Jews, their return to their homeland, and the final reign of Christ (see Ezek. 37:6,21,25). The prophecy is a foretaste of the outpouring of the Holy Ghost at Pentecost and an Old Testament rendition of the resurrection of the dead at Christ's second coming.

In Ezekiel 36, the prophet foretold of a spiritual renaissance:

A new heart also will I give you, and a new spirit will I put within you: and I will take away the stony heart out of your flesh, and I will give you an heart of flesh.

And I will put My spirit within you, and cause you to walk in My statutes, and ye shall keep My judgments, and do them (Ezekiel 36:26-27).

This reveals a new twist in God's promise of life for obedience. Here He promises to empower His people with the Spirit so they may become an *obedient force*. The overall vision is Messianic, and it describes the undeserved mercy of God that provides the physical and spiritual life necessary for God's chosen people to obey. In Ezekiel 37:23, the Lord says, "...I will save them out of all their dwellingplaces, wherein they have sinned, and will cleanse them: so shall they be My people, and I will be their God."

Let us hear the conclusion of the whole matter: Fear God, and keep His commandments: for this is the whole duty of man. For God shall bring every work into judgment, with every secret thing, whether it be good, or whether it be evil (Ecclesiastes 12:13-14).

We, like Israel, are called to life to glorify God! Obedience lifts up and ornaments our God. We were born and given breath for no other reason than to magnify His name. The sin in our flesh makes *restoration* essential if we want to become a part of God's obedient force. Our first state is hopelessness. When we enter life solely in the flesh, we have entered into death. When we are reborn, we are called from hopelessness to life and are imparted the Spirit of God and a new heart!

Obedience and a Diet

The Lord knew the life and the spirit of His creation. He personally imparted His breath (spirit) into man (see Gen. 2:7), but He also declared, "For the life of the flesh is in the blood..." (Lev. 17:11). Knowing this, the Lord denied man the food that gave death and the spirit of death. Adam and Eve tasted the fruit of death anyway, and their descendants developed a taste for death and even grew to crave it. The all-merciful God was unwilling to force their hand, so He permitted them to taste of the tree. He took no pleasure in the sight of souls dying after their fall, but He would not give eternal life to creatures carrying death or the spirit of death in their bodies. Death would ultimately be "swallowed up" in the victory of Christ (see Is. 25:8). There the cup of God's wrath would be filled to the brim and death would be thoroughly destroyed.

Diets From Heaven

The Bible's guidelines for nutrition are generally set aside as "old covenant" standards, but God's limits on nutrition cannot be violated without consequence. Apart from the miraculous powers of faith noted in the Great Commission (see Mk. 16:18), there are certain plants and animals that remain poisonous to the flesh even under the New Testament law of grace. God draws a line between what leads to life and what leads to death in every other area of human behavior. In His absolute sovereignty, God gave us a diet that transcends the line between the Book of Malachi and the Gospel of Matthew.

The Lord God is the Giver and Keeper of life. We recognize God's life-sustaining power every time we drink and eat. Christ is symbolized as bread and water, in acknowledgment of God our Provider. The necessity of eating forces us to seek God's provision every day. Without hunger and thirst, we might believe our lives are self-sustaining.

Food cultivation and food gathering send us back to God for the continuation of life. We must rely on His physical laws in the earth for the miracle of life and growth. We must rely on the law of seedtime and harvest in other forms of life where something living comes out of something else—the fruit that comes out of the seed; the spring bud that comes out of the winter earth. We rely on the life of the created realm to sustain life. It all goes back and relies upon the One who is self-existent, for nothing created comes out of nothing. Simply stated: Eating—with all of its ramifications—leads man back to God.

On the third day God said, "...Let the earth bring forth grass, the herb yielding seed, and the fruit tree yielding fruit after his kind, whose seed is in itself, upon the earth: and it was so" (Gen. 1:11).

And God said [to man and woman], *Behold, I have given you every herb bearing seed, which is upon the face of all the earth, and every tree, in the which is the fruit of a tree yielding seed; to you it shall be for meat. And to every beast of the earth, and to every fowl of the air, and to every thing that creepeth upon the earth, wherein there is life, I have given every green herb for meat: and it was so* (Genesis 1:29-30).

From the beginning, plant life provided food for humans and animals alike. It appears that all of the fruit-bearing trees and seed-bearing herbs were created to be the sole diet for humans. People were not to eat flesh, grass, or herbs that did not bear seed.

The only exception to this diet concerned one tree in the Garden of Eden, the tree of the knowledge of good and evil. No other tree in the garden contained death *except the tree of the knowledge of good and evil* (see Gen. 2:16-17). All fruit would sustain life except the fruit from the tree of the knowledge of good and evil. Its companion, the tree of life, evidently bore physical fruit that, by God's design, literally contained the power of eternal life.

Without considering the spiritual attributes of these two trees in the middle of the Garden of Eden, we can conclude that from the very beginning God made diet and obedience the critical issues of life. Diet and obedience together posed the life and death conditions for Adam and Eve's existence. God's divine interest in diet and obedience is given a high profile in man's relationship to God.

God chose not to make physical strength, or words, or titles, or the use of land and water the critical issues of life in the beginning. He could have denied or limited man's relationship to others or appointed rituals of devotion that could not be broken. Instead, He restricted their diet and made original sin a "violation of appetite." In broad terms, then, obedience was originally tied to diet.

The Eden story is well known to Christians and Jews around the world. Man disobeyed God and ate the deadly fruit of the tree of the knowledge of good and evil, changing life from that day on. Death entered the bloodstream of Adam and Eve, and the moment the two of them came to know good and evil, the human race was contaminated with a terminal "virus" called death. The Bible says God drove Adam and his wife out of Eden, "…lest he put forth his hand, and take also of the tree of life, and eat, and live for ever" (Gen. 3:22).

The ground was cursed because of Adam's sin, and thorns and thistles sprang up everywhere. Most of the trees evidently stopped producing fruit, while most of the plants became inedible. Many of them were now poisonous, and others tore Adam's flesh. Weeds and bramble covered the earth, and man's painful work of survival after the curse began.

Man now had to fight against the thorny elements of nature just to squeeze a meager livelihood from the earth. A brisk and carefree walk through the forest became a dangerous lurch into risky terrain because man was now at war with both animals and plants. Nature had turned against its keeper, and man was now forced to *dominate* rather than merely care for nature. Worst of all, the virus had forever turned man against man! The curse also changed the human diet. Now the first couple could not eat the wide variety of plant life available before their fall. So they turned to *cultivated* plant life for food (see Gen. 3:18).

Just before God drove Adam and Eve out of Eden, He sacrificed an innocent animal to make "coats of skins" for them (see Gen. 3:21). This sacrifice of an innocent animal to cover their nakedness demonstrated His covering protection and care for the humans and pointed to the sacrifice of Christ Himself. It was a graphic illustration of the wages of sin—death. It was also a sign of the altered relationship between humans and animals; the animals were transformed into another source of food and clothing for the couple's survival.

Within five verses, the Bible describes Abel as "a keeper of sheep," and Cain as "a tiller of the ground" (see Gen. 4:2). Abel "brought of the firstlings of his flock and of the fat thereof" (Gen. 4:4). The fat represented the flesh offering from the sacrificed lamb. This makes it clear that Abel produced flesh food and presented it to God, while Cain produced vegetable and plant foods. The flesh of other animals besides sheep was also consumed, according to Genesis 4:20: "And Adah bare Jabal: he was the father of such as dwell in tents, and of such as have cattle."

We can only speculate about why flesh was eaten. Perhaps it was eaten because of the curse over the fruit of the ground described in Genesis 3:17. Plant foods may have been in relative scarcity, since humans were unaccustomed to working for or cultivating their food. Flesh may have been eaten because people needed the fur and hides of the animals, and did not want to waste the flesh and bones. There was also an enmity created between men and animals that led to man's conquest and domination of the animal kingdom. This ultimately led to the killing of animals for the purposes of sport, fashion, and festivity.

It is not until Genesis chapter 9 that God recognizes flesh foods as a dietary complement in His account of blessings to

Noah and his sons after the flood (see Gen. 9:1-7). The wording in Genesis 9 is a parallel to that of Genesis 1:28-29. Both passages describe blessings to "first families" with promises of superiority over animals, and both provide dietary plans for man.

Noah was, in a sense, a "restored" Adam, a fresh progenitor after the Great Flood. Noah was given even more authority than Adam, and he received a different dietary plan. Adam and Eve were given dominion related to cultivating and organizing the earth's resources, which included training and organizing the animals. Noah's commission appears to be based on antagonism, fear, and dread. The cultivated herb diet of Adam and Eve was replaced by a diet of herbs and flesh foods.

> *And the fear of you and the dread of you shall be upon every beast of the earth, and upon every fowl of the air, upon all that moveth upon the earth, and upon all the fishes of the sea; into your hand are they delivered. Every moving thing that liveth shall be meat for you; even as the green herb have I given you all things. But flesh with the life thereof, which is the blood thereof, shall ye not eat* (Genesis 9:2-4).

Noah could eat any moving thing, except flesh with blood in it (this provision continued into the New Covenant in Acts 15:20,29; 21:25). God withdrew His explicit guidance and left man to find his own limits within broad guidelines. Nonetheless, the Lord did talk to Noah about "clean and unclean beasts" just before the Flood, saying, "Of every clean beast thou shalt take to thee by sevens, the male and his female: and of beasts that are not clean by two, the male and his female" (Gen. 7:2). For this reason, Genesis 9:3, which allows the eating of "every moving thing," appears to be a more permissive restatement of God's more restrictive divisions of "clean" from "unclean" beasts in Genesis 7:2.

It is the character of God not to force His will upon us. He gave Noah the right to choose between what is good and what is not good. He allows men to use what builds them up as well as what tears them down. From this standpoint, the clean and unclean beasts are like the tree of life and the tree of knowledge of good and evil. Noah could eat of every moving thing upon the face of the earth, but he had been taught that some things are unclean.

The formal law and priestly function in the Book of Leviticus restored the designations of beasts as either clean or unclean (see Lev. 11). The Jewish diet today is still more restrictive than the one given in Genesis 9:3. The Lord sets out several rules governing the clean and unclean in the Book of Leviticus:

1. "Whatsoever parteth the hoof, and is clovenfooted, and cheweth the cud, among the beasts, that shall ye eat" (Lev. 11:3). The camel, coney, hare, and swine are unclean, although they meet some of the criteria.

2. "...Whatsoever hath fins and scales in the waters, in the seas, and in the rivers, them shall ye eat" (Lev. 11:9). The shark, the whale, the eel, the seahorse, the catfish, the jellyfish, and all shellfish are unclean.

3. "All fowls that creep, going upon all four, shall be an abomination unto you" (Lev. 11:20), though you may eat the locust, the bald locust, the beetle, and the grasshopper.

4. The Lord named the following fowl unclean: "...the eagle, and the ossifrage, and the osprey, and the vulture, and the kite after his kind; every raven after his kind; and the owl, and the night hawk, and the cuckoo, and the hawk after his kind, and the little owl, and the cormorant, and the great owl, and the swan, and the pelican, and the gier eagle, and the stork, the

heron after her kind, and the lapwing, and the bat" (Lev. 11:13-19).

5. "And whatsoever goeth upon his paws, among all manner of beasts that go on all four, those are unclean unto you..." (Lev. 11:27a).

6. "These also shall be unclean unto you among the creeping things that creep upon the earth; the weasel, and the mouse, and the tortoise after his kind, and the ferret, and the chameleon, and the lizard, and the snail, and the mole" (Lev. 11:29-30).

7. "And every creeping thing that creepeth upon the earth shall be an abomination; it shall not be eaten" (Lev. 11:41).

8. "Whatsoever goeth upon the belly, and whatsoever goeth upon all four, or whatsoever hath more feet among all creeping things that creep upon the earth, them ye shall not eat; for they are an abomination" (Lev. 11:42).

9. The eating of flesh with the blood in it, and the eating or drinking of blood itself, are prohibited in Genesis 9:4, Leviticus 17:10, Deuteronomy 12:23, and other Scriptures.

Diet and the New Testament

The New Testament presents diet as a matter of individual preference. The Pauline epistles clearly forbid making any diet a matter of command. In a letter to Timothy, Paul said:

Now the Spirit speaketh expressly, that in the latter times some shall depart from the faith, giving heed to seducing spirits, and doctrines of devils; speaking lies in hypocrisy; having their conscience seared with a hot iron; forbidding to marry, and commanding to abstain from meats, which God hath created to be received with thanksgiving of them which believe and know the truth (1 Timothy 4:1-3).

The writer of the Book of Romans declared, "I know, and am persuaded by the Lord Jesus, that there is nothing unclean of itself: but to him that esteemeth any thing to be unclean, to him it is unclean" (Rom. 14:14). Uncleanliness then is a violation of conscience and of the voice of the Spirit. The old written universal standard gives way to the law written on the heart of the particular believer. Apart from any betrayal of personal conviction, however, "...every creature of God is good, and nothing to be refused, if it be received with thanksgiving: for it is sanctified by the word of God and prayer" (1 Tim. 4:4-5).

The Gospel of Matthew discusses food from several perspectives. When a group of Pharisees asked Jesus: "Why do Thy disciples transgress the tradition of the elders? for they wash not their hands when they eat bread" (Mt. 15:2), Jesus responded with perfect insight. He ripped through their thinly veiled hatred and deep-seated resentment for His ministry by asking, "Why do ye also transgress the commandment of God by your tradition?" (Mt. 15:3b) Later He told the multitude:

Not that which goeth into the mouth defileth a man; but that which cometh out of the mouth, this defileth a man. ... Do not ye yet understand, that whatsoever entereth in at the mouth goeth into the belly, and is cast out into the draught? But those things which proceed out of the mouth come forth from the heart; and they defile the man. For out of the heart proceed evil thoughts, murders, adulteries, fornications, thefts, false witness, blasphemies: these are the things which defile a man: but to eat with unwashen hands defileth not a man (Matthew 15:11,17-20).

Jesus reached deep into the controversy between good and evil. The seed of sin planted in the flesh defiles the man. The evil thoughts and murderous plans of the Pharisees defiled them. The Pharisees came to trap and kill our Lord, while appearing to be clean on the outside. Their outer appearance and demeanor deceived the simple and naive and concealed the evil intentions that lurked beneath. Jesus stripped away their pretense and exposed the corruption in their hearts.

Those who subvert the law of God while pretending to be holy because they wash, dress, and eat in socially accepted ways are but wolves in sheep's clothing. Christ warned in His Sermon on the Mount, "Beware of false prophets, which come to you in sheep's clothing, but inwardly they are ravening wolves. Ye shall know them by their fruits. ..." (Mt. 7:15-16). Paul said, "They profess that they know God; but in works they deny Him, being abominable, and disobedient, and unto every good work reprobate" (Titus 1:16).

Eve originally thought, perceived, moved, ate, and spoke according to the dictates of the Spirit of God in the Garden of Eden. Once sin entered in, she was transformed from the inside out. Her thoughts were changed from good to evil. Her eyes could now see the flesh that once was hidden by the glory of the Spirit. Her hands, feet, and mouth had a new nature that was contrary to the Spirit and law of God. Her Creator had carefully given her instructions in cleanliness, but she craved the taste of the unclean and ignored God's instructions, reaping death.

The Father has patiently accommodated the object of His love. Though He had forbidden divorce, He allowed Moses, because of man's obstinacy, to give a bill of divorcement (see Mt. 19:8). Although He ordained a theocracy over Israel, He permitted the making of kings (see 1 Sam. 8:5-7). "But God knoweth your hearts: for that which is highly esteemed among men is abomination in the sight of God" (Lk. 16:15b).

In the New Testament, the work of the Spirit is reversed. Clean diets, clean hands, and clean clothes could not accomplish the reversal of the curse. Only rebirth by water and spirit could do that. Obedience demanded a sacrifice of the old and the creation of a new. Only the indwelling Spirit of God had the power to transform from within, renewing the mind and changing human behavior to conform to the image of God. When the Spirit comes inside and transforms a person from the inside out, even those things that were unclean are sanctified by the prayers of the faithful. Even if a believer in the will of God drinks any deadly thing, it shall not harm him or her (see Mk. 16:18).

In the end times, sin will have had its perfect work. Not only will thorns, thistles, and fruitless vines abound, but air, water, plant foods, and animal foods will yield to the defiling effects of transgression, for God's Spirit will cease to strive with man.

Like the "weeping prophet" Jeremiah, we might lament:

For these things I weep; mine eye, mine eye runneth down with water, because the comforter that should relieve my soul is far from me: my children are desolate, because the enemy prevailed. ...I have rebelled against His commandment: hear, I pray you, all people, and behold my sorrow: my virgins and my young men are gone into captivity. I called for my lovers, but they deceived me: my priests and mine elders gave up the ghost in the city, while they sought their meat to relieve their souls. Behold, O Lord; for I am in distress: my bowels are troubled; mine heart is turned within me; for I have grievously rebelled..." (Lamentations 1:16,18-20).

Chapter 13

Obedience and the Body

In the days of Adam and Eve, there were giants in the land, men of great stature, unusual strength, and remarkable stamina, and women of equal size with enchanting beauty and grace. Their minds were keenly developed and they had a vast capacity for learning. They could remember an enormous volume of minute details for their entire lives. Their sheer mental capacity eliminated the need for written material. All of the earth's knowledge was stored in the memories of these awesome human beings and passed on by oral tradition. Their bodies were impervious to pain and presented a nearly perfect barrier to disease and stress. Their eyes were sharper than those of eagles. Their hearing was more acute than that of the greyhound. They had a massive capacity for joy.

Once sin entered the human race, however, their bodies began to decay. Their muscles ached from work. Their hands and brows showed lines of work and worry. Their skin began to wrinkle and sag, and pain became a daily burden. Misery and fear drained their minds. Their bones hardened and their teeth rotted. Their vision slowly diminished and their hearing became dull. Every passing year brought more loss, more weakness, more sickness, and more signs of aging, until finally death became the solitary remedy for a wound that would not heal—sin.

* * * * *

A quick glance through God's Word reveals the loss of longevity because of sin. According to the genealogy in Genesis chapter 5, Adam lived 930 years; Seth lived 912 years; Enos lived 905 years; Cainan lived 910 years; Mahalaleel lived 895 years; Jared lived 962 years; Enoch lived 365 years; Methuselah lived 969 years; and Lamech lived 777 years!

By the sixth chapter of Genesis, however, the earth was far more populated. The Bible says, "And God saw that the wickedness of man was great in the earth, and that every imagination of the thoughts of his heart was only evil continually" (Gen. 6:5). God set a limit on age in that period: "And the Lord said, My spirit shall not always strive with man, for that he also is flesh: yet his days shall be an hundred and twenty years" (Gen. 6:3). Noah lived to be 950 years old, but his sons and descendants showed a rapid decline in longevity. According to Genesis 11, Shem lived 600 years; Arphaxad lived 438 years; Salah lived 433 years; Eber lived 464 years; Peleg lived 239 years; Reu lived 239 years; Serug lived 230 years; Nahor lived 148 years; and Terah lived 205 years.

The human life span continued to drop after Terah, the father of Abram. Abraham lived 175 years according to Genesis 25:7. Isaac lived 180 years (see Gen. 35:28); Jacob lived 147 years (see Gen. 47:28); and Joseph lived only 110 years (see Gen. 50:26). The promise of prolonged life for the righteous clearly came to pass in specific cases like that of Moses, who lived to be 120 years old (see Deut. 34:7). We must conclude that the overall length is only relative to the average life span for the time.

God included a promise of prolonged life in His response to Solomon's prayer for understanding:

And I have also given thee that which thou hast not asked, both riches, and honour: so that there shall not be any among the kings like unto thee all thy days. And if thou wilt walk in My ways, to keep My statutes and My commandments, as thy father David did walk, then I will lengthen thy days (1 Kings 3:13-14).

David did not live an impressively long time. According to Josephus, the Jewish historian, David died at the age of 70. Historians estimate that Solomon lived to be 60 years old. Clearly, he did not keep God's commandments like his father David (1 Kings 11:6). Thanks to the effects of sin over the centuries, the actual number of years lived may not reflect the blessing God gives those who are obedient. Psalm 90, which is attributed to Moses, says, "The days of our years are threescore years and ten; and if by reason of strength they be fourscore years, yet is their strength labour and sorrow; for it is soon cut off, and we fly away" (Ps. 90:10).

Moses seems to bemoan the brevity of life, noting that the best years are full of work and sadness. Yet Moses lived a long life by his own estimate, and he maintained physical strength to the end! "And Moses was an hundred and twenty years old when he died: his eye was not dim, nor his natural force abated" (Deut. 34:7). Also, Joshua lived to be 110 years old (see Josh. 24:29).

Physical strength and general good health are great blessings from God (see Job 12:12-13,16). He makes the strong to "skip like a calf," and dance even like a unicorn (Ps. 29:6). Proverbs advised us, "...fear the Lord, and depart from evil. It shall be health to thy navel, and marrow to thy bones" (Prov. 3:7-8). The prophet Isaiah declares that if you keep the fast of the Lord, "then shall thy light break forth as the morning, and thine health shall spring forth speedily" (Is. 58:8a). Psalm 105:4a tells us, "Seek the Lord, and His strength." Psalm 84 says, "Blessed is the man whose strength is in Thee... They go from strength to strength..." (Ps. 84:5,7).

I will feed My flock, and I will cause them to lie down...I will...bind up that which was broken, and will strengthen that which was sick: but I will destroy the fat and the strong; I will feed them with judgment (Ezekiel 34:15-16).

A soldier and king [David] once said, "Thine, O Lord, is the greatness, and the power, and the glory, and the victory, and the majesty....in Thine hand is power and might; and in Thine hand it is to make great, and to give strength unto all" (1 Chron. 29:11-12). Attend to the words of the wise: "For they are life unto those that find them, and health to all their flesh" (Prov. 4:22).

Human life expectancy has probably corroded from the earliest times to the present, and though God prolonged the life and strength of a few like Moses and Joshua, and even took some to Heaven without tasting death (like Enoch and Elijah), in general, sin cut short the human life span. Each new generation is more susceptible to disease and ill health than the previous one. At one time, humans lived for hundreds of years; now they barely live to 70 or 80. For all the lofty claims of modern science, there have been no major increases since the time of Moses, judging by Psalm 90:10. In the same way, the strength, endurance, and sheer joy of life appear to have diminished over the years.

Obedience and Physical Healing

Obedience produces physical stamina and physical healing! Moses told the children of Israel in the wilderness:

> *...If thou wilt diligently hearken to the voice of the Lord thy God, and wilt do that which is right in His sight, and wilt give ear to His commandments, and keep all His statutes, I will put none of these diseases upon thee, which I have brought upon the Egyptians: for I am the Lord that healeth thee* (Exodus 15:26).

This promise was essentially repeated in Exodus 23:25, where God says He "will take sickness away from the midst of thee." (See also Deuteronomy 7:15.)

God healed a number of women from infertility, of whom many of their offspring were ultimately in the bloodline of the Messiah. The prayers of Abraham led to the supernatural healing of Abimelech, and the opening of his wives' and maidservants' wombs (see Gen. 20:17). God gave Sarah a son in her old age, though she had been unable to conceive (see Gen. 18:14; 21:2). He caused Rebekah to bear twins though she was barren, because her husband Isaac entreated Him on her behalf (see Gen. 25:21).

The Lord first opened the womb of Leah, Jacob's wife, because of His mercy (see Gen. 29:31). Later He remembered Rachel, Jacob's second wife, who called on His name (see Gen. 30:22). In the days of the judges, Hannah poured out her heart unto the Lord in the "abundance of her complaint and grief" for she was barren (see 1 Sam. 1:5-28). She vowed to give her child to the Lord if He would give her a man-child, and the Lord answered her prayer. She conceived and bore Samuel, a prophet called of God as a child. The Book of Judges also records the story of Manoah, a Danite whose wife was barren.

An angel visited her and foretold the miraculous birth of their son, Samson, destined to be a judge over Israel (see Judg. 13:2-24).

The Book of Second Kings speaks of a childless Shunammite woman in her later years. The prophet Elisha responded to her hospitality toward him by interceding to God on her behalf, and she miraculously gave birth to a son (see 2 Kings 4:12-17). Elisabeth, the mother of John the Baptist, was barren until the Lord appeared to her husband in the Holy of Holies. Nine months later she gave birth in her old age to the great prophet who would herald the coming of the Messiah (see Lk. 1:7,13-17,57)!

God is not slow to hear the petitions of the righteous, and His strength is not weakened by the multitude of our infirmities. He told the children of Israel that obedience would heal the barren among them!

> *Wherefore it shall come to pass, if ye hearken to these judgments, and keep, and do them, that the Lord thy God shall keep unto thee the covenant and the mercy which He sware unto thy fathers: and He will love thee, and bless thee, and multiply thee: he will also bless the fruit of thy womb.... Thou shalt be blessed above all people: there shall not be male or female barren among you, or among your cattle* (Deuteronomy 7:12-14).

The Psalmist says of God, "He maketh the barren woman to keep house, and to be a joyful mother of children..." (Ps. 113:9). The power of healing comes from God and God alone. *Jehovah-Ropheka*, Jehovah the healer, declares, "See now that I, even I, am He, and there is no god with Me: I kill, and I make alive; I wound, and I heal: neither is there any that can deliver out of My hand. ...I live for ever" (Deut. 32:39-40).

When the children of Israel presumptuously said they loathed the manna God had miraculously provided for them in the middle of a desert, He sent fiery serpents among them that bit and killed many. In fear and reconciliation, the people repented of their sin and begged Moses to ask God to take away the serpents. God commanded Moses to mount a brass serpent on a pole so that those who were bitten could look at the serpent and live (see Num. 21:8-9). This was a dramatic type and shadow of the role of Christ as the Healer of all mankind. Though He was sinless, Jesus carried our sins to the cross and "became sin" for us. Because of His sacrifice as He was lifted up on the tree, whoever looks to Him in faith and obedience today receives eternal life.

> *Bless the Lord, O my soul: and all that is within me, bless His holy name. Bless the Lord, O my soul, and forget not all His benefits: who forgiveth all thine iniquities; who healeth all thy diseases; who redeemeth thy life from destruction; who crowneth thee with lovingkindness and tender mercies; who satisfieth thy mouth with good things; so that thy youth is renewed like the eagle's. ...bless the Lord, O my soul* (Psalm 103:1-5,22).

The Old Testament has many proofs showing that obedience leads to physical restoration. Naaman the leper dipped his body seven times in the muddy waters of the Jordan River, and "his flesh came again like unto the flesh of a little child, and he was clean" (2 Kings 5:14). Isaiah the prophet told Judah's King Hezekiah that he was about to die, but the king asked for a cure for his terminal illness and prayed, "I beseech Thee, O Lord, remember now how I have walked before Thee in truth and with a perfect heart, and have done that which is good in Thy sight..." (2 Kings 20:3). Even before Isaiah could leave the palace and go into the city, God added 15 years to the life of Hezekiah (see 2 Kings 20:5-6).

When the son miraculously born to the Shunammite woman suffered a sunstroke and died, the Lord raised him back to life in perhaps the most extraordinary cure of the Old Testament! Elisha the prophet "...prayed unto the Lord. And he went up, and lay upon the child, and put his mouth upon his mouth, and his eyes upon his eyes, and his hands upon his hands: and he stretched himself upon the child; and the flesh of the child waxed warm" (2 Kings 4:33-34).

Years earlier, in an almost identical display of His healing power, God restored the life of the son of a widow at Zarephath through the intervention of the prophet Elijah. The widow had provided shelter for Elijah, and later in her life her son died of a grave illness. The widow asked Elijah if the death was because of her sins. Elijah merely took the child from her bosom and carried him up into a loft where he stayed. He laid the child on a bed and cried out to the Lord. He stretched himself out on the child three times and petitioned God, saying, "...let this child's soul come into him again. And the Lord heard the voice of Elijah; and the soul of the child came into him again, and he revived" (1 Kings 17:21-22). When Elijah returned the child to the widow, she said, "...Now by this I know that thou art a man of God, and that the word of the Lord in thy mouth is truth" (1 Kings 17:24).

When King David's disobedient decision to take a census of his people brought a plague on the nation, David quickly repented and offered burnt offerings and peace offerings to the Lord. He had placed his trust in the numbers of his subjects instead of in the Almighty. When God sent a three-day plague that killed 70,000 people, David obeyed the instructions of the prophet Gad and made offerings to God and "...entreated for the land, [so that] the plague was stayed from Israel" (2 Sam. 24:25). It was in this context that David cried to the Lord, "O Lord my God, I cried unto Thee, and Thou hast healed me" (Ps. 30:2).

I will say of the Lord, He is my refuge and my fortress: my God; in Him will I trust. Surely He shall deliver thee from the snare of the fowler, and from the noisome pestilence. He shall cover thee with His feathers, and under His wings shalt thou trust: His truth shall be thy shield and buckler. Thou shalt not be afraid for the terror by night; nor for the arrow that flieth by day; nor for the pestilence that walketh in darkness; nor for the destruction that wasteth at noonday. A thousand shall fall at thy side, and ten thousand at thy right hand; but it shall not come nigh thee. ... Because thou hast made the Lord, which is my refuge, even the most High, thy habitation; there shall no evil befall thee, neither shall any plague come nigh thy dwelling. ... Because he hath set his love upon Me, therefore will I deliver him: I will set him on high, because he hath known My name. He shall call upon Me, and I will answer him: I will be with him in trouble; I will deliver him, and honour him. With long life will I satisfy him, and shew him My salvation (Psalm 91:2-7,9-10,14-16).

Obedience to God does not mean that troubling times will not come. Life on this earth will always involve pain until Jesus comes. Sin guarantees this, if nothing else. Jesus Christ was sinless, and though He never experienced sickness, He nevertheless suffered because of the sins and weaknesses of others. Even the "holiest" among us will probably be confronted by physical illness and death. Healing is, therefore, an important part of God's loving care extended to us. God longs to give us spiritual and physical wholeness.

Job was a *righteous man* who suffered great losses and physical affliction at the hand of satan. The adversary "...smote Job with sore boils from the sole of his foot unto his crown. And he took him a potsherd to scrape himself withal;

and he sat down among the ashes" (Job 2:7-8). Job's wife literally encouraged him to curse God and die, but Job said, "...Thou speakest as one of the foolish women speaketh. What? shall we receive good at the hand of God, and shall we not receive evil?..." (Job 2:10). Satan had caused this affliction believing that Job would curse God to His face, but the Scriptures say, "...In all this did not Job sin with his lips" (Job 2:10).

Job's story is one of abiding faith and obedience. He said, "If a man die, shall he live again? all the days of my appointed time will I wait, till my change come" (Job 14:14). Job was healed and restored to his former station in life. The Lord accepted Job and "...turned the captivity of Job...also the Lord gave Job twice as much as he had before" (Job 42:10).

New Testament Healing

The prolific ministry of Jesus Christ made miraculous healings more common in the New Testament than in the Old. Of the 35 separate miracles of Jesus, 26 are acts of healing! What did our Lord do?

1. He made the lame to walk (Lk. 13:10-17; Jn. 5:1-9).
2. He healed the paralytic (Mt. 8:5-13; 9:2-8; Mk. 2:3-12; Lk. 5:18-26; 7:1-10).
3. He restored a shriveled hand (Mt. 12:9-13; Mk. 3:1-5; Lk. 6:6-10).
4. He cooled a fevered brow (Mt. 8:14-15; Mk. 1:29-31; Lk. 4:38-39).
5. He cleansed lepers (Mt. 8:2-4; Mk. 1:40-45; Lk. 5:12-14; 17:11-19).
6. He gave sight to the blind (Mt. 9:27-31; 12:22; 20:29-34; Mk. 8:22-26; 10:46-52; Lk. 18:35-43; Jn. 9:1-7).
7. He healed the mute (Mt. 9:32-33; 12:22; Mk. 7:31-37; Lk. 11:14).

8. He cast out demons (Mt. 8:28-34; 9:32-33; 12:22; 17:14-18; Mk. 1:23-28; 5:1-20; 9:16-27; Lk. 4:33-36; 8:26-39; 9:38-42; 11:14).

9. He healed a woman with an issue of blood (Mt. 9:20-22; Mk. 5:25-34; Lk. 8:43-48).

10. He healed a man with dropsy (Lk. 14:1-6).

11. He replaced an ear (Lk. 22:49-51).

12. He raised the dead (Mt. 9:18-19,23-26; Mk. 5:22-24, 35-43; Lk. 7:11-15; 8:41-42,49-56; Jn. 11:14-44).

Jesus Christ healed many others whose accounts are not detailed in the Gospels (see Mt. 8:16; Mk. 1:32; Lk. 4:40). The Lord's ministry was one of healing as much as anything else! Salvation is the *ultimate form of healing*. After the Day of Pentecost, God worked many signs and wonders through the apostles, including a number of miraculous healings.

The apostle Peter commanded a lame beggar seeking alms at the gate "Beautiful" of the temple of Herod, "In the name of Jesus Christ of Nazareth rise up and walk." When Peter took him by the right hand and lifted him to his feet, his feet and ankle bones immediately received strength and he walked and leaped and praised God (see Acts 3:1-8). Peter prayed for the resurrection of a benevolent disciple named Tabitha or Dorcas. When he commanded the body of the deceased woman to arise, she opened her eyes and sat up (see Acts 9:36-40)! Peter told Aeneas, who for eight years had been bedridden with the palsy, "Jesus Christ maketh thee whole: arise, and make thy bed." The Bible says Aeneas immediately arose (see Acts 9:33-34).

The apostle Peter moved in such supernatural power that multitudes of people came out of the cities around Jerusalem, bringing the sick, the bedridden, and the possessed, hoping Peter's shadow would pass over them because it brought the healing of God! The Bible tells us that every one who came to be healed was cured! (See Acts 5:15-16.)

The apostle Paul regained his sight after Ananias, a disciple at Damascus, laid hands on him in obedience to the instructions of God (see Acts 9:17). Paul was used by God to cure a cripple at Lystra on his first missionary journey (see Acts 14:8-10). By the power of God, the Scriptures say he worked "special miracles...so that from his body were brought unto the sick handkerchiefs or aprons, and the diseases departed from them, and the evil spirits went out of them" (Acts 19:11-12).

Paul was used by God on the isle of Melita to heal the father of Publius, a chieftain among the islanders, who had fever and a "bloody flux" (see Acts 28:8). The Scriptures say others who had diseases on the island were also healed (see Acts 28:9). Paul himself also suffered no ill effects from the venomous snake bite of a viper at Melita because of God's intercession for his life (see Acts 28:3-6).

Sin leads to sickness and death, and obedience through faith leads to healing and wholeness. Sin's "perfect work" is to thoroughly defile God's creation, but the "perfect work" of obedience through faith is to heal God's creation! John the apostle describes the new Jerusalem of his heavenly vision:

And God shall wipe away all tears from their eyes; and there shall be no more death, neither sorrow, nor crying, neither shall there be any more pain: for the former things are passed away. ... And there shall in no wise enter into it any thing that defileth... (Revelation 21:4,27).

The Blind Man

Once a blind man heard the Master,
On the road to Bethany.
And he hoped that Christ would touch him,

Or His robe might even brush him,
So he might be made to see.

Though a mob was gathered 'round Him,
The blind man yelled with all his might,
So that when the Lord passed near,
He heard a voice that was sincere.
Then He restored the old man's sight.

Although the old man followed Jesus,
He soon got lost and left behind
And though it would have been his pleasure
To thank Him for this priceless treasure
The Lord was much too hard to find.

After a year had come and gone
Since the great feat had been performed,
The old man came to wonder if,
Occasion might present itself
With the Savior's soon return.

But it seemed that Christ would never
Come again to Jericho,
Though the news of all His dealings
And His mighty works of healings,
All the world would come to know.

So one day the old man reasoned,
Perhaps Jerusalem is where,
During the feast of holy days
When the Jewish nation prays,
He might find the Master there.

But the city lay in darkness.
Someone said the Lord had died.
But the old man didn't believe them;
Still he hoped somehow to please Him—
'Til he found Him crucified.

Then his heart sank deep within him
As he realized at last,
That his purpose and his vision
That had fueled this great decision
Were a thing of the past.

As he sat along the roadside,
He recalled what Christ had said,
That if he would just believe Him,
And his heart would just receive Him,
He would live, though he be dead.

So he closed his eyes, and clasped his hands, and
Said a little prayer,
"Oh Lord God, forgive me; I have looked most
everywhere.
And my newfound eyes are red and weary
From a search that brought me here.
If this Christ is sent from Heaven, as I'm led to be
aware,
Let His fingers touch my eyelids, and His hands ca-
ress my hair."

In a moment, while the little prayer
Still floated in the morning air,
This gentle Man with loving hand
Reached out and touched his eyes and hair.

But more than this,
The Savior lifted him off his knee
He showed the wounds that He'd received
From when He'd hung upon the tree.
And vanishing, left this decree:
"You were once blind, but now you see."

Chapter 14

Obedience and Emotional Strength

Our physical state is closely tied to our emotional state, and vice versa. That is why our Creator so often deals directly with our emotions with the statement, "Fear not, for God is with you," especially when His angelic messengers or He Himself confronts us face to face. (See Genesis 15:1 with Abram; Genesis 26:24 with Isaac; Matthew 1:20 with Joseph; and Matthew 28:5 with the angels at the tomb of Jesus.)

Emotions exist, whether we want to admit it or not. God gave them to us, and the godly way to deal with emotions is through obedience to God! The Scriptures attest to the fact that obedience to God overcomes negative emotional states like shame, sorrow, doubt, strife, contempt, and anger. Obedience also promotes the positive emotional states of boldness, hope, joy, and peace. Obedience (or the lack of it) has a direct effect on our emotional state.

Fear

Perhaps our greatest source of failure is fear, or the dread of harm or loss. Fear produces a crippling paralysis that can totally inhibit productive action. In a crisis situation, fear can freeze us at a time when *any response* would be better than none at all! Fear is often called "the killer of dreams and hope." (Hebrews 2:15 speaks of our fear of death.)

Fear stems from uncertainty, and it is a natural emotional expression when we confront the unknown or face a known danger. Fear turns our muscles to jelly and shuts off the brain. It makes our voices quiver and dulls our senses, blocking the flow of vital information from our surroundings. Fear exaggerates every threat and makes mountains out of molehills. When fear sets in, faith is altogether lost because fear and faith are incompatible. Perfect love casts out fear (see 1 Jn. 4:18), and obedience by faith shuts it down. Love, faith, and obedience help control the paralyzing, demoralizing effects of fear in our lives by removing their source.

> *For ye have not received the spirit of bondage again to fear; but ye have received the Spirit of adoption, whereby we cry, Abba, Father* (Romans 8:15).

> *For God hath not given us the spirit of fear; but of power, and of love, and of a sound mind* (2 Timothy 1:7).

Fear is not of God; it is a failure of faith. It may seem to be a natural response to crisis, but is actually the consequence of *momentary reliance upon the flesh* and the enemy. It is often the result of a long-standing pattern of disregard for the sovereignty and protection of God! Fear is from satan, and it is a result of sin.

Adam and Eve knew no fear as long as they were obedient to the Lord. It was only after they submitted to the temptation of the serpent that we find them cowering behind bushes to avoid the presence of the Lord God (see Gen. 3:8). When God called out, "Where art thou?" Adam admitted that he had heard God's voice in the garden, but he said he was *afraid*! He said he hid himself because he was naked (see Gen. 3:9-10). *It is no accident that one of Adam's first emotional responses in his fallen sin nature was fear.* The tree of sin bears the fruit of fear.

Fear is a common emotion among the wicked, the faithless, and the distracted. The Scriptures say, "The wicked flee when no man pursueth: but the righteous are bold as a lion" (Prov. 28:1). Psalm 91 has much to say about fear and our godly response to its threats:

He that dwelleth in the secret place of the most High... [shalt] *not be afraid for the terror by night; nor for the arrow that flieth by day; nor for the pestilence that walketh in darkness; nor for the destruction that wasteth at noonday* (Psalm 91:1,5-6).

Solomon the wise made the exhortation that we be obedient to godly wisdom with a calming description of its reward:

Then shalt thou walk in thy way safely, and thy foot shall not stumble. When thou liest down, thou shalt not be afraid: yea, thou shalt lie down, and thy sleep shall be sweet. Be not afraid of sudden fear, neither of the desolation of the wicked, when it cometh. For the Lord shall be thy confidence, and shall keep thy foot from being taken (Proverbs 3:23-26).

Obedience will overcome fear, if for no other reason than because it lifts the *dread of retaliation* and punishment from your mind! Fear is also lifted when we have an assurance of God's covering and protection. Israel possessed the land of Canaan with this promise: "If ye walk in My statutes, and keep

My commandments, and do them, ... I will give peace in the land, and ye shall lie down, and none shall make you afraid" (Lev. 26:3,6a). One of the most important truths in life is found in the Book of Proverbs: "The fear of man bringeth a snare: but whoso putteth his trust in the Lord shall be safe" (Prov. 29:25).

God Almighty has continually encouraged His servants, "Fear not!" and "Be not afraid!" in His Word, reassuring them that He Himself would fight their battles! These divine words of comfort found their way into the lives and destinies of:

1. Abram (Gen. 15:1) with "I am thy shield"

2. Hagar (Gen. 21:17)

3. Isaac at Beersheba (Gen. 26:24)

4. Jacob (Gen. 46:3)

5. the children of Israel in the exodus (Ex. 14:13; 20:20)

6. Moses (Num. 21:34)

7. Joshua and Caleb (Num. 14:9)

8. Joshua alone (Deut. 31:6,8; Josh. 1:9; 8:1; 10:8; 11:6)

9. the judges of Israel (Deut. 1:17,29)

10. the Levites (Deut. 18:22)

11. Gideon (Judg. 6:23)

12. the widow of Zarephath through Elijah (1 Kings 17:13)

13. Solomon through David (1 Chron. 28:20)

14. Jehoshaphat (2 Chron. 20:17)

15. Isaiah for King Ahaz (Is. 7:4)

16. Israel as a nation (Deut. 20:1; Is. 41:10,13-14; 43:1,5; 44:2,8; 51:7; 54:4,14; Jer. 23:4; 46:27-28)

17. Judah as a nation (Joel 2:21; Zeph. 3:16; Hag. 2:5)

18. Hezekiah by Isaiah (2 Kings 19:6; Is. 37:6)

19. Judah as a nation by Hezekiah (2 Chron. 32:7)

20. Israel and Judah together (Is. 8:12; 10:24; Jer. 10:5; 30:10; 42:11; 46:27; Lam. 3:57; Ezek. 34:28; Zech. 8:13,15)

21. Jeremiah (Jer. 1:8)

22. Ezekiel (Ezek. 2:6)

23. Daniel (Dan. 10:12,19)

24. Zecharias (Lk. 1:13)

25. Mary the mother of Jesus (Lk. 1:30)

26. the shepherds who were told of Jesus' birth (Lk. 2:10)

27. the disciples of Christ (Mt. 10:26,28,31; 14:27; 17:7; 28:10; Mk. 6:50; Lk. 12:4,7,32; Jn. 6:20; 14:27)

28. Jairus (Lk. 8:50)

29. the women at Jesus' tomb (Mt. 28:5)

30. John the Revelator (Rev. 1:17)

31. the church at Smyrna (Rev. 2:10)

Now I am repeating it right here for you: *Fear not, for the Lord God Omnipotent reigns!*

The righteous have no cause to fear rulers (see Rom. 13:3-4), the reproach of men (see Is. 51:7), false gods or superstitions (see Deut. 18:22; Jer. 10:5), or the armies of the wicked (see Deut. 20:1; Ps. 3:6). The righteous should not fear anything that threatens life or limb (see Lk. 12:4; Heb. 13:6). Obedience itself is a cover of sure protection. Indeed, "the moth shall eat them up [the wicked enemy] like a garment, and the worm shall eat them like wool: but My righteousness shall be for ever..." (Is. 51:8). Only the ungodly have reason to fear; and only the hypocrite must shiver (see Is. 33:13-16). God is a shield, a rock, and a fortress (see Ps. 3:3, 18:2; 31:3). He is our guiding light and our sure defense (see Ps. 27:1; 7:10).

They That Be With Us...

In the Book of Second Kings, God protected Israel by revealing to Elisha the prophet every scheme and plot the King of Syria devised, even the secret things he whispered behind closed doors! When the Syrian army encamped in one spot, God told Elisha where they were, and he warned the Israelites in time to escape the Syrian attack. After several incidents like this, the Syrian king called in his closest companions and chief officers to find out who was acting as a traitor. To the king's apparent surprise, someone reported that Elisha, the Jewish prophet, was telling the king of Israel *every word he spoke in his bedchamber*! The Syrian king angrily dispatched a great army and surrounded the city of Dothan during the night (see 2 Kings 6:9-14).

Elisha was asleep when the Syrians arrived, and it was the prophet's servant who first saw the huge Syrian army circling the city. Shaken with panic, he frantically asked the prophet what they should do. Elisha calmly answered, "...Fear not: for they that be with us are more than they that be with them" (2 Kings 6:16). Then Elisha asked God to open his servant's eyes to see the invincible armies of God. "...And the Lord opened the eyes of the young man; and he saw: and, behold, the mountain was full of horses and chariots of fire round about Elisha" (2 Kings 6:17).

Elisha stood firm in faith and was unmoved when a whole army of Syrian soldiers encircled a city to capture him! He already knew God would protect him. His strong faith let him see with spiritual eyes that he was surrounded by the invisible and fiery armies of God! Once a man sees the power of God, how can he fear the puny forces of mere men?

Like Elisha, we can take hold of God's promises of protection and believe that His love is our dwelling place of safety.

"...God is love; and he that dwelleth in love dwelleth in God, and God in him. ... There is no fear in love..." (1 Jn. 4:16,18). "Ye are of God, little children, and have overcome them: because greater is He that is in you, than he that is in the world" (1 Jn. 4:4). Open our eyes, Lord, that we might see the endless armies of horses and chariots of fire that are sent to protect us. Please, Lord, open our eyes.

Shame

I believe that the moment fear made its dreadful appearance in the human mind, it was accompanied by the painful emotion of *shame*. When the eyes of Adam and Eve were opened by sin, "...they knew that they were naked; and they sewed fig leaves together, and made themselves aprons" (Gen. 3:7). Before they sinned, "...they were both naked...and were not ashamed" (Gen. 2:25). Disobedience led to knowledge, but that knowledge gave birth to shame for the first time in their existence!

Shame is "disgrace in the eyes of another." It describes dishonor, embarrassment, disappointment, and self-condemnation. Adam and Eve had shame because they had failed to live up to God's command. Their fallen spiritual condition preceded their depressed emotional condition.

The ever-changing western morality has a problem attaching "nakedness" with shame. But, we as believers cannot be confused in this area because the Bible clearly makes a connection between shame and nakedness through the aprons sewn by Adam and Eve, and through Adam's response to God's question, "Where art thou?" Adam answered, "...I was afraid, because I was naked; and I hid myself" (Gen. 3:10).

Satan had led them to believe that after eating the fruit they would become gods and see God on His level. Instead they were brought low, and now saw Him through the eyes of their terminal weakness and need! This was the fruit of the knowledge of good and evil. It included the new feelings of fear and shame. Instead of placing them face-to-face with God, it exchanged their companionship with God for a continuing relationship with satan's lie. Distrust of others would now become a major consequence of their entrapment.

Adam and Eve also discovered their sin had opened their senses to the raging forces of the lust of the flesh. Once they indulged in the forbidden fruit, I believe they felt lustful passion surge through their bodies like poisonous venom. They had experienced supreme pleasure before the fall. Now they tasted lust with the love of God removed. I do not think it was very pleasant. I believe this was the moment when God's love, as described in First Corinthians 13, initially separated and distinguished itself from erotic love, removing the holy influence from the natural desire. The result was diabolical!

Although sin leads to shame, obedience leads to glory. God's Word reveals the contrast. Proverbs 13:5 says, "...a wicked man is loathsome, and cometh to shame." But Romans 10:11 says, "...Whosoever believeth on Him [Christ] shall not be ashamed."

Shame comes to those who say there is no God, to those who are confederates against God (see Ps. 53:1-5; 83:2,16-17). It comes to the enemies of God (see Jer. 50:12; Ezek. 32:24-25, 30; Mic. 7:10; Nahum 3:4-5; Lk. 13:17; Tit. 2:7-8). Idolatry leads to shame (see Is. 44:9-11; 45:16; Jer. 48:13; Hos. 9:10; Zech. 13:4). Pride leads to shame, as does laziness, wastefulness, and hastiness (see Prov. 11:2; 10:5; 19:26; 18:13). So does riotous behavior, lack of discipline, avarice, drunkenness, and ungodly counsel (see Prov. 28:7; 29:15; Hab. 2:10,16; Is. 30:5). The enemies of God's servants will be ashamed (see Ps. 132:18; Is. 41:11; 66:5), along with false prophets (see Jer. 23:40; Mic. 3:7). God has decreed a destiny of everlasting shame for every wickedness and abomination (see Ezek. 7:18; Dan. 12:2).

Jeremiah the prophet cried, "O Lord, the hope of Israel, all who forsake You will be put to shame. Those who turn away from You will be written in the dust because they have forsaken the Lord, the spring of living water" (Jer. 17:13 NIV).

And now, little children, abide in Him; that, when He shall appear, we may have confidence, and not be ashamed before Him at His coming (1 John 2:28).

Sorrow

Profound sorrow is the end product of every evil work, and part of each negative emotion. It is in every bad experience. Although it is often related to death and linked to grief, it also closely follows every pain, loss, disappointment, separation, and disaster. Sorrow comes hand in hand with every negative consequence of sin, including fear, shame, sickness, and pain.

After God questioned Adam and Eve about their disobedience, He named their sorrows for them, although their sorrows had already begun. "Unto the woman He said, I will greatly multiply thy sorrow...And unto Adam He said... cursed is the ground for thy sake; in sorrow shalt thou eat of it all the days of thy life; ...unto dust shalt thou return" (Gen. 3:16-17,19).

The aftertaste of sin was a death sorrow, a deep emotional pain of the most piercing and lingering variety. It cannot be overemphasized that sin produced death sorrow and the unnerving fear that springs from death consciousness. This death awareness is so all-consuming that it is the central prevailing issue of our lives. It produces the most powerful motivation for human behavior, whether voluntary or involuntary. Sin in every way leads to sorrow.

Because of rebellion, the unrepentant sinner has no hope in life and only sorrow in his death (see 1 Thess. 4:13). Sin is his inescapable captivity, and sorrow his unwelcome bedfellow. In "the day of the Lord" there will be fear, sorrow, and anguish to the sinner (see Is. 13:8-9). Christ said the sign of the end of the world would literally be the multiplication of sin and of sorrow! (See Matthew 24:5-8.)

In contrast, the Psalmist says, "Blessed is he whose transgression is forgiven, whose sin is covered" (Ps. 32:1). Isaiah prophesied to the redeemed, "Surely He [Jesus] hath borne our griefs, and carried our sorrows" (Is. 53:4a). "The blessing of the Lord, it maketh rich, and He addeth no sorrow with it" (Prov. 10:22). Jeremiah declared a message of hope for the restored Israel:

For the Lord hath redeemed Jacob, and ransomed him from the hand of him that was stronger than he. Therefore they shall come and sing in the height of Zion, and shall flow together to the goodness of the Lord...and their soul shall be as a watered garden; and they shall not sorrow any more at all (Jeremiah 31:11-12).

Doubt and Confusion

Doubt comes before sin just as pride comes before a fall. Satan must cast doubt on God's Word to effectively corrupt His servants. Doubt is satan's vehicle to draw the children of God away from the protection of God's Word. His diabolical lies exist solely to cast doubt upon the promises of God, and thus, to cast doubt upon God Himself.

"...[Satan] said to the woman, 'Did God really say, "You must not eat from any tree in the garden"?' " (Gen. 3:1 NIV) Satan didn't ask this question to get an answer; his true motive was to plant doubt in Eve's mind about the motives and fairness of God with the *implied* suggestion: "Why not eat from every tree in the garden? What is God hiding from you?"

Doubt quickly festers into sin because we lose our bearing once we abandon direction from God. "...Adam and his wife hid themselves from the presence of the Lord God amongst the trees of the garden" (Gen. 3:8). Where could they go from the presence of God? (See Psalm 139:1-12 and Amos 9:1-4.) Where could the first couple hide? Clearly they had lost their bearing because of disobedience.

Once sin had "opened" the eyes of Adam and Eve, their response was an act of pure confusion. The very act of questioning God caused them to lose perspective on the character of God (and thus, of themselves). They trusted satan's lies and expected to see God more clearly because of their sin, but their actions made them see Him less clearly! This carnal knowledge did not lift them up toward God in deeper knowledge of His word and character; it cast them into self-centered introspection and myosis of the soul, causing them to see God more in smaller human terms than in the unlimited realm of the divine. Doubt breeds disobedience, and disobedience breeds more doubt and confusion.

"For God is not the author of confusion, but of peace..." (1 Cor. 14:33), "...and he that believeth on Him shall not be confounded" (1 Pet. 2:6). God hates discord (see Prov. 6:16,19). He will cut off the proud, the flattering, and those who speak with a double heart (see Ps. 12:2-3). Sin causes doubting (see Deut. 28:66), and they who walk in sin walk in blindness and confusion because they have sinned against the voice of God (see Dan. 9:7-11). "The way of the wicked is as darkness: they know not at what they stumble" (Prov. 4:19; see also Jer. 23:12).

Satan is the father of lies (see Jn. 8:44), and every false impression, false counsel, and false god is an invention of satan to cast doubt upon God. "Molten images are wind and confusion," according to Isaiah 41:29. "They shall go to confusion together that are makers of idols" (Is. 45:16b). Idolatry provokes the sinner to his own confusion (see Jer. 7:18-19).

God does not disappoint faith. "...If ye have faith, and doubt not...whatsoever ye shall ask in prayer, believing, ye shall receive" (Mt. 21:21-22). The doubter, the double-minded, and the wavering receive nothing from God (see Jas. 1:6-8) because to doubt is sin: "...for whatsoever is not of faith is sin" (Rom. 14:23). For that reason, the apostle James admonishes us to submit to God, resist satan, and purify our double-minded hearts (see Jas. 4:7-8). He says those who endure temptation and are steadfast will receive the crown of life (see Jas. 1:12). "But the fearful, and unbelieving...and all liars, shall have their part in the lake which burneth with fire and brimstone..." (Rev. 21:8).

Anger, Strife, Hopelessness, Envy, and Contempt

Every negative emotion can be linked to sin. The Book of Job says the wicked have no hope in this life nor in the resurrection to come. Even wealth gives no hope to the wicked, since God will take away his soul (see Job 27:8-23). "For what portion of God is there from above? and what inheritance of the Almighty from on high? Is not destruction to the wicked? and a strange punishment to the workers of iniquity?" (Job 31:2-3) Job links sin to anger, fear, envy, and hopelessness, and says destruction is the sure reward of sin.

The Book of Proverbs says, "He loveth transgression that loveth strife" (Prov. 17:19a). The apostle James says, "For where envying and strife is, there is confusion and every evil work" (Jas. 3:16). Sinners reap all the anguish of those harmful emotions, not the righteous. Daniel prophesied that in the end times sin would cause many to awaken to shame and everlasting contempt (see Dan. 12:2). Paul elaborated on Psalm 62:12 and Proverbs 24:12 in his letter to the Romans:

God "will give to each person according to what he has done." To those who by persistence in doing good seek glory, honor and immortality, He will give eternal life. But for those who are self-seeking and who reject the truth and follow evil, there will be wrath and anger. There will be trouble and distress for every human being who does evil: first for the Jew, then for the Gentile; but glory, honor and peace for everyone who does good: first for the Jew, then for the Gentile (Romans 2:6-10 NIV).

Eve's Song

Today is the day
  to believe Him,
the Strength that we can find
No other way.

The call of all the world
  has grown so cold and
    unappealing; and,
nothing that they say can we believe.

We've taken all the time that
  we can give to them,
    and find, there is no hope inside—
      the way they've made it seem.

Today is the day
  to believe Him,
the Truth we knew was
  right there all along.

There's still enough time today
to reach back where
  we lost our way
  and try to learn the lessons
    that we left so far behind.

Tomorrow will be another bright and shining star.
We only have to put our hope in what we've learned thus
far.
    But now is our tomorrow on the way. Because
Today is the day
  to believe Him,
the Faith that waited while we grew inside.
    We'll place all of our yesterdays in one big bag of
dreams,
    and carry them beside us, though we know just what they
mean.
    Then we'll find all our tomorrows here today.

Boldness and Confidence

The Scriptures are bursting with proof that righteousness leads to positive emotional consequences. If wickedness leads to fear, then righteousness must lead to boldness, confidence, and certainty! "The wicked flee when no man pursueth: but the righteous are bold as a lion" (Prov. 28:1). Isaiah says, "And the work of righteousness shall be peace; and the effect of righteousness quietness and assurance for ever" (Is. 32:17). He eloquently expands his point in the following chapter:

> *The sinners in Zion are afraid; fearfulness hath surprised the hypocrites. Who among us shall dwell with the devouring fire? who among us shall dwell with everlasting burnings? He that walketh righteously, and speaketh uprightly; he that despiseth the gain of oppressions, that shaketh his hands from holding of bribes, that stoppeth his ears from hearing of blood, and shutteth his eyes from seeing evil; he shall dwell on high: his place of defence shall be the munitions of rocks: bread shall be given him; his waters shall be sure (Isaiah 33:14-16).*

The Lord has given words of emotional strength to His obedient servants, but the disobedient must dwell in their own self-imposed isolation from God's counsel. He told Joshua that if Israel would "cleave" to the Lord, then "one man of you shall chase a thousand: for the Lord your God, He it is that fighteth for you. ... [But if you turn away, then your enemies] ...shall be snares and traps unto you, and scourges in your sides, and thorns in your eyes..." (Josh. 23:10,13).

God promised a "sure house" to David, Solomon, and Jeroboam, if they avoided evil and kept His commandments (see 1 Sam. 25:28; 1 Kings 2:4; 11:38). Proverbs says, "The merciful man doeth good to his own soul: but he that is cruel troubleth his own flesh. The wicked worketh a deceitful work: but to him that soweth righteousness shall be a sure reward" (Prov. 11:17-18). Paul told Timothy, "...the foundation of God standeth sure...depart from iniquity" (2 Tim. 2:19). Peter said:

...Make every effort to add to your faith goodness; and to goodness, knowledge; and to knowledge, self-control; and to self-control, perseverance; and to perseverance, godliness; and to godliness, brotherly kindness; and to brotherly kindness, love. ... Therefore, my brothers, be all the more eager to make your calling and election sure. For if you do these things, you will never fall (2 Peter 1:5-7,10 NIV).

Our confidence and hope in God is the anchor of our souls (see Heb. 6:13-19). God is the "confidence of all the ends of the earth" (Ps. 65:5). "...His compassions fail not. They are new every morning: great is Thy faithfulness" (Lam. 3:22-23).

Joy

God is the Father of joy. He founded joy before the earth was made, for when He stretched the line and measure of the

earth and laid its cornerstone, the morning stars sang together and all the sons of God shouted for joy! (See Job 38:4-7.)
The joy of the Lord is eternal, and David declared, "in Thy
presence is fulness of joy" (Ps. 16:11).

Joy is a defining characteristic of the Kingdom of God (see
Rom. 14:17). Through His Son, God gives "...beauty for ashes,
the oil of joy for mourning, the garment of praise for the spirit
of heaviness; that they might be called trees of righteousness,
the planting of the Lord, that He might be glorified" (Is. 61:3).
Unspeakable joy springs forth from our faith in the invisible
God! (See First Peter 1:8.)

> *Seek ye the Lord.... For ye shall go out with joy, and be
> led forth with peace: the mountains and the hills shall
> break forth before you into singing, and all the trees of
> the field shall clap their hands* (Isaiah 55:6,12).

> *Many sorrows shall be to the wicked: but he that
> trusteth in the Lord, mercy shall compass him about.
> Be glad in the Lord, and rejoice, ye righteous: and
> shout for joy, all ye that are upright in heart* (Psalm
> 32:10-11).

Joy is a blessing reserved for God's chosen (see Ps. 65:13;
132:16). "For God giveth to a man that is good in His sight wisdom, and knowledge, and joy: but to the sinner He giveth tra-
vail..." (Eccles. 2:26). Know this to be sure, the first fruit of the
Spirit is love, but the second one is *joy* (see Gal. 5:22).

Gladness and Happiness

God also blesses us with two gifts that are closely related
to joy: gladness and happiness. They may come to the just or
the unjust, but they are *promised* to the just, and are literally
the *endowments* of righteousness. The Psalmist writes:

Ye that love the Lord, hate evil: He preserveth the souls of His saints; He delivereth them out of the hand of the wicked. Light is sown for the righteous, and gladness for the upright in heart (Psalm 97:10-11).

The righteous before God should have happy expectations, for "the hope of the righteous shall be gladness: but the expectation of the wicked shall perish" (Prov. 10:28). The righteous are glad simply because God is on their side! David said, "I have set the Lord always before me: because He is at my right hand, I shall not be moved. Therefore my heart is glad..." (Ps. 16:8-9). God promises happiness to everyone who obeys His Word:

Blessed is every one that feareth the Lord; that walketh in His ways. For thou shalt eat the labour of thine hands: happy shalt thou be, and it shall be well with thee (Psalm 128:1-2).

Happy is that people, whose God is the Lord (Psalm 144:15b).

And whoso trusteth in the Lord, happy is he (Proverbs 16:20b).

Happy is the man that feareth alway (Proverbs 28:14a).

But he that keepeth the law, happy is he (Proverbs 29:18b).

The Promise of Peace

God declared in Isaiah 45:7, "I make peace." His name, *Jehovah Shalom*, means "God is peace" (see Judg. 6:24; Heb. 13:20). Jesus Christ is the "Prince of Peace" (see Is. 9:6). Surely the children of God are children of peace (see Mt. 5:9), and heirs to a legacy of peace (see Rom. 14:17). God's Word says the Lord God gives peace to His people (see Ps. 29:11).

"When a man's ways please the Lord, He maketh even his enemies to be at peace with him" (Prov. 16:7). "Great peace have they which love [God's] law: and nothing shall offend them" (Ps. 119:165). When we remember God's law and keep it, "...length of days, and long life, and peace, shall they add to thee" (Prov. 3:2). If you walk in His statutes, and keep His commandments, God will give peace to your land (see Lev. 26:3,6). "They that trust in the Lord shall be as mount Zion, which cannot be removed.... As the mountains are round about Jerusalem, so the Lord is round about His people..." (Ps. 125:1-2).

The work of righteousness is peace (see Is. 32:17), and all the paths of wisdom lead to peace (see Prov. 3:17; Jas. 3:17). The Bible says righteousness and peace have "kissed" each other (see Ps. 85:10). Just as the unfailing love of God will not be shaken, neither will His covenant of peace be taken away (see Is. 54:10). "[God] wilt keep him in perfect peace, whose mind is stayed on [Him]: because he trusteth in [God]" (Is. 26:3).

But the wicked are like the troubled sea, when it cannot rest... There is no peace.... (Isaiah 57:20-21).

The way of peace they know not; and there is no judgment in their goings: they have made them crooked paths: whosoever goeth therein shall not know peace (Isaiah 59:8)

God takes away the peace of the wicked (see Jer. 16:5; Lam. 3:17). "For to be carnally minded is death; but to be spiritually minded is life and peace" (Rom. 8:6). There is anguish for the evil one, but peace to them that do good (see Rom. 2:9-10).

God has called us to peace (see 1 Cor. 7:15). Our feet are to be shod with the preparation of the gospel of peace (see Eph. 6:15), a peace from God our Father and from the Lord Jesus Christ (see Phil. 1:2). It is the "...peace of God, which passeth all understanding" (Phil. 4:7a).

For yet a little while, and the wicked shall not be: yea, thou shalt diligently consider his place, and it shall not be. But the meek shall inherit the earth; and shall delight themselves in the abundance of peace. The wicked plotteth against the just.... The Lord shall laugh at him: for He seeth that his day is coming. ... Mark the perfect man, and behold the upright: for the end of that man is peace (Psalm 37:10-13,37).

Safety and Security

If ye walk in My statutes, and keep My commandments, and do them; ...ye shall...dwell in your land safely. And I will...rid evil beasts out of the land, neither shall the sword go through your land (Leviticus 26:3,5-6).

Wherefore ye shall do My statutes, and keep My judgments, and do them; and ye shall dwell in the land in safety. And the land shall yield her fruit, and ye shall eat your fill, and dwell therein in safety (Leviticus 25:18-19).

But if ye will not hearken unto Me, and will not do all these commandments; ...ye shall be slain before your enemies.... I will punish you seven times more for your sins. ... I will also send wild beasts among you, which shall rob you of your children, and destroy your cattle, and make you few in number.... And I will bring a sword upon you, that shall avenge the quarrel of My covenant... (Leviticus 26:14,17-18,22,25).

For the turning away of the simple shall slay them, and the prosperity of fools shall destroy them. But whoso hearkeneth unto Me shall dwell safely, and shall be quiet from fear of evil (Proverbs 1:32-33).

The horse is prepared against the day of battle: but safety is of the Lord (Proverbs 21:31).

...whoso putteth his trust in the Lord shall be safe (Proverbs 29:25b).

There is none like unto the God of Jeshurun, who rideth upon the heaven in thy help, and in His excellency on the sky. The eternal God is thy refuge... (Deuteronomy 33:26-27).

The name of the Lord is a strong tower: the righteous runneth into it, and is safe (Proverbs 18:10).

The fear of the Lord tendeth to life: and he that hath it shall abide satisfied; he shall not be visited with evil (Proverbs 19:23).

For the Lord is our defence; and the Holy One of Israel is our king (Psalm 89:18).

Chapter 15

Obedience
and the Family

*T*he triune God exists in a collective unity. God is three in one. Each lives for the other. Each is bound up in the other. Each is fully surrendered to the other by love, faith, and obedience.

Likewise, we are not as separate as we think. We are bound one to another through spiritual and physical attributes. Thus the weight of sin within us is multiplied with time so that every new generation is less able to see and overcome it. The power of God's Spirit must also increase with time to meet the final challenge of the enemy.

God's form is a mirror of the form man must also take. God manifests Himself in the persons of the Father, the Son, and the Holy Ghost. These three manifestations are the perfect

---

"figure" or illustration of the character of God *fit to the purposes of His creation.* They represent a *community that is interconnected by an unbreakable bond of love.* They represent the identity and purpose of God as He relates to the universal family of spiritual entities above and below, and fallen flesh.

God the Son

1. Jesus is the perfect reflection of the Father (Jn. 8:19).
2. He is one with the Father (Jn. 14:10).
3. The Father loves Him with perfect love (Jn. 15:9; 17:23).
4. He and the Father have all things in common (Jn. 16:15; 17:10).
5. They receive from us as one (Jn. 15:23).
6. Jesus came out of the Father (Jn. 16:28).
7. He is fully obedient to the Father (Jn. 8:29; 14:31).
8. The Father always bears witness of His Son (Jn. 8:18).
9. The Father never leaves the Son (Jn. 8:16,29; 16:32).
10. The Father does all things for the Son (Jn. 8:28).

God the Holy Spirit

1. The Holy Spirit, like the Son, came forth from the Father (Jn. 15:26).
2. The Spirit is fully surrendered to the Son who is fully surrendered to the Father (Jn. 8:26; 14:31; 16:13)
3. He will manifest the love of the Son and of the Father (Jn. 14:21).
4. He will be the eternal presence of the Son and of the Father (Jn. 14:16-20).

We are the children of the Father if we receive His Son (see Jn. 1:12). Then we go forth in the power and the presence of the Son (see Jn. 14:13; 15:16). Even as the Father has sent the Son, so the Son has sent us (see Jn. 20:21). He has sent us in the power of the Spirit (see Jn. 20:22-23). So we proceed in the reflection of Christ and by the authority given to His name. Jesus said to Mary at the resurrection, "...I ascend unto My Father, and your Father; and to My God, and your God" (Jn. 20:17).

We are to be one as They are one (see Jn. 17:11,21-22). Yet in our first generation, the righteous line of God was broken, and we were made children of the fallen angel instead of children of God. We inherited the lineage of the rebels! We became murderers of the righteous just like Cain!

Sin Inherited

Wherefore, as by one man sin entered into the world, and death by sin; and so death passed upon all men, for that all have sinned: ... Nevertheless death reigned from Adam to Moses, even over them that had not sinned after the similitude of Adam's transgression, who is the figure of Him that was to come (Romans 5:12,14).

Adam's transgression brought death to all humanity. Since death came before Sinai, we need not concern ourselves with the law at this point. Paul says death even reigned over those who did not sin like Adam. This "inherited sin" is sin that enters into all flesh because of Adam's disobedience. We cannot separate ourselves from our species, and Adam's primal sin affects all of his seed! If Adam merely transmitted to the race the propensity to sin or the weakness for sin, then we are inseparable *to the degree* that he passed this weakness on to others (See Genesis 3:1-7 for the details of the fall of man.)

Some small part of Adam is found in every newborn infant because Adam's sin banished him *and all of his seed* from eternal existence in Paradise and the company of God. This is how the sin nature became the heritage of every human being. His spiritual deprivation was passed along in a physical and spiritual link, giving each of us the defective capacity and inclination to sin along with the banishment from God's perfect presence and an appointment with the grave. We have to face the fact that sin passes from one person to another.

What above Eve? Nowhere does the Bible say that sin passed from Eve to mankind, although Genesis 3:6 clearly says Eve was the first to disobey. Adam sinned without the "benefit" of deception, while Eve was deceived by the serpent (see 1 Tim. 2:14). Eve's deception did not necessarily make her disobedience an act of ignorance. It was her choice to doubt God, and her actions were carried out with full personal knowledge of God's warning and His directions.

Eve's sin must have been imputed to Adam. Adam was the first human created, and since Eve came out of Adam, she could not physically pass any genetic attribute from herself to Adam. The sin nature could not pass from Eve to Adam through biological inheritance because Eve did not give birth to Adam. For the sin nature to come from Adam instead of Eve, God must have attributed Eve's sin to Adam. Adam was Eve's husband and he became her covering before God. Adam, in this sense, *carried Eve's sin for her*, just as Christ our Head carries and covers our sin:

> *Wives, submit yourselves unto your own husbands, as unto the Lord. For the husband is the head of the wife, even as Christ is the head of the church: and He is the saviour of the body. Therefore as the church is subject unto Christ, so let the wives be to their own husbands in every thing* (Ephesians 5:22-24).

Christ is the Savior of the Church because He carried the sins of the Church and paid the price of redemption for her sins. The price of Adam's leadership is similar to the price of Christ's leadership. Christ gave Himself for the Church according to Ephesians 5:25. In the same way, Adam, who was not deceived, gave himself for the woman. Out of love for Eve, Adam gave up his life rather than go on without her. Man placed woman above God by joining in her transgression. As a consequence, the sins of the woman were imputed to the stronger, more primary, and perhaps more culpable of the two. So husband and wife are not separate in the eyes of God and the sins of the wife may be imputed to the husband (see Mt. 19:5-6).

These are not the only circumstances in which the sins of one person were passed to another. At the giving of the Decalogue at Sinai, God commanded that there be no other gods before Him. He prohibited the making and the worship of any graven image with the warning, "...I the Lord thy God am a jealous God, visiting the iniquity of the fathers upon the children unto the third and fourth generation of them that hate Me" (Ex. 20:5). (See also Numbers 14:18 and Ezekiel 18:19.) The implication is that the sinful habits of parents are learned by their children rather than that God punishes children for their father's sins.

Idolatry, in particular, is difficult to resist or destroy once it has been set up, simply because of societal pressures to conform. Bad systems are self-perpetuating and slow to be put aside, so children can rarely "fix" their father's established sin patterns. The Book of Romans essentially says that refusal to acknowledge God the Creator, in favor of worshiping His creation instead, makes fools of those who consider themselves wise. Chapter 1 says in three separate verses that God gives idolaters over to blindness, unnatural lusts, and a reprobate mind (see Rom. 1:24-26,28). This means that systems of sin, especially when they are made a part of a religious worship, deprive idolaters of the ability to distinguish right from wrong. The subversion of God's law creates the possibility of endless error. Ezekiel put it this way: "The fathers have eaten sour grapes, and the children's teeth are set on edge" (Ezek. 18:2b).

Jesus healed one man who was "blind from his birth." Just before He healed him, however, the Lord's disciples asked him a typical religious question: "...Master, who did sin, this man, or his parents, that he was born blind?" (See John 9:1-2.) The question is based on the assumption that sickness is a result of sin, but it also raises the issue of whether "sickness at birth" is the punishment of sins not yet committed, or sins committed beforehand by others.

The Jews of Jesus' time interpreted Exodus 20:5 to mean that God would punish the children for the father's sins. They recognized the biological transmission of physical traits and the possible effects of learning. Nonetheless, Jesus bluntly dismissed both options: "Jesus answered, Neither hath this man sinned, nor his parents: but that the works of God should be made manifest in him" (Jn. 9:3).

It is interesting to me that Jesus immediately followed that answer with this statement: "I must work the works of Him that sent Me, while it is day: the night cometh, when no man can work" (Jn. 9:4). Although Jesus would face death and return to His Father's side, He also promised to abide with His disciples and followers even after death (see Mt. 28:20). Apparently Jesus was speaking of "night" as the increase of sin in the world and a coming state of universal darkness, perhaps referring to the culmination of many generations of sin. The important point here is that the sin capacity, if not the sin itself, is inherited and that sin is cumulative.

Righteousness Imputed

For if by one man's offence death reigned by one; much more they which receive abundance of grace and of the gift of righteousness shall reign in life by one, Jesus Christ. Therefore as by the offence of one judgment came upon all men to condemnation; even so by the righteousness of one the free gift came upon all men unto justification of life. For as by one man's disobedience many were made sinners, so by the obedience of one shall many be made righteous (Romans 5:17-19).

The sacrificial act of *one* man, Jesus Christ, extended *divine grace* to *all* men. Sin created enmity between God and man, and we desperately needed to be reconciled to God and have our lives restructured. Jesus came to earth both to die for our sins and to demonstrate the righteous life that pleases God. John says, "And He is the propitiation for our sins: and not for ours only, but also for the sins of the whole world. And hereby we do know that we know Him, if we keep His commandments" (1 Jn. 2:2-3). Unlike Adam's sin, we do not inherit the righteous tendency from Christ. Righteousness is not consistent with human nature; it is unnatural to our flesh. The righteousness of Christ is *imputed* to all who accept Christ as their Savior and follow His example.

As a more perfect remedy for inherited sin, along with His body Jesus Christ also gives His Spirit to every born-again believer to help them live a life of righteousness. In one of His departing messages to the disciples, Jesus promised to send them the Spirit of truth.

First He told them, "...no man cometh unto the Father, but by Me" (Jn. 14:6). He made it clear that personal behavior and religious systems apart from His righteousness are incapable of reconciling men to God. Only the *imputed righteousness of Christ* through His death and resurrection can bring us back to God. Then He said:

And I will pray the Father, and He shall give you another Comforter, that He may abide with you for ever; even the Spirit of truth; whom the world cannot receive,

*because it seeth Him not, neither knoweth Him: but ye
know Him; for He dwelleth with you, and shall be in
you. I will not leave you comfortless: I will come to you.
Yet a little while, and the world seeth Me no more; but
ye see Me: because I live, ye shall live also. At that day
ye shall know that I am in My Father, and ye in Me,
and I in you. He that hath My commandments, and
keepeth them, he it is that loveth Me: and he that loveth
Me shall be loved of My Father, and I will love him,
and will manifest Myself to him. ... But the Comforter,
which is the Holy Ghost, whom the Father will send in
My name, He shall teach you all things, and bring all
things to your remembrance, whatsoever I have said
unto you* (John 14:16-21,26).

Righteousness is imputed from Christ to us, and we are inseparable from Christ to the extent that we accept and follow Him. Those who accept Christ inherit His Spirit, receiving Him into their tabernacles (bodies) to teach them truth and lead them into righteousness. Paul said:

*I am crucified with Christ: nevertheless I live; yet not I,
but Christ liveth in me: and the life which I now live in
the flesh I live by the faith of the Son of God, who loved
me, and gave Himself for me* (Galatians 2:20).

By His Spirit, Christ lives inside us and acts to reconcile us unto God. Is righteousness ever imputed from one person to another apart from Christ? That is a big question with a delicate answer. The Scriptures imply that the righteousness of one person can certainly lead to blessings for others (the word "imputed" may be a strong description of that process).

From the Genesis story of the patriarchs, we find several examples of persons being blessed because of the righteousness of another. Isaac and his offspring were blessed because of the obedience of Abraham.

And the Lord appeared unto him, and said…I will be with thee, and will bless thee…in thy seed shall all the nations of the earth be blessed; because that Abraham obeyed My voice, and kept My charge, My commandments, My statues, and My laws (Genesis 26:2-5).

The broad range of blessings included in the "blessing of Abraham" anticipates the coming of Jesus Christ, who blessed "all the nations of the earth." Those blessings cannot be separated from the righteousness of Christ, though they span many generations. In a very real sense, a son and his family are blessed because of the obedience of the father.

Isaac's son, Jacob, brought blessings to Laban, his father-in-law, who said, "…I pray thee, if I have found favour in thine eyes, tarry: for I have learned by experience that the Lord hath blessed me for thy sake" (Gen. 30:27). Laban was blessed because of Jacob. God often blesses a relative by marriage because of the righteousness of His servant. The Lord also blessed the house of Potiphar, the Egyptian captain of the guard under Pharaoh, because of the presence of Joseph, the son of Jacob:

And it came to pass from the time that he [Potiphar] *had made him* [Joseph] *overseer in his house, and over all that he had, that the Lord blessed the Egyptian's house for Joseph's sake; and the blessing of the Lord was upon all that he had in the house, and in the field* (Genesis 39:5).

The blessings of God may even extend beyond the family and pass to employers or those in authority over believers. A common thread connects each of these divine blessings, however. Long before any one of these events took place, God had already promised Abraham that his seed would be blessed (see

Gen. 13:14-17), and that all the families of the earth would be blessed through him (see Gen. 12:3).

Each one of these examples involves a single family line and a common line of obedience and righteousness. Each looks forward to the obedience of Christ as a universal ransom for sin, fulfilling the promises to Abraham. Under the new and better covenant, all who believe on and obey Christ *are children of Abraham by faith* (see Gal. 3:7; Heb. 8:6). All righteousness is found in Christ—there is no other source. All spiritual blessings flow from the obedience of Christ and the faithfulness of God to fulfill His plan through Christ (see Is. 64:6; Rom. 3:21-25).

The work of redemption is a single work that spans across the law and the prophets to culminate in the death of Christ Jesus on the tree and His resurrection three days later. The giving of the Decalogue at Sinai foreshadowed the work done in the upper room at Pentecost. The same Spirit that descended upon Mount Sinai also filled the room occupied by the 120 disciples at Jerusalem! He communed with Moses between the Cherubim of the Ark and was promised by Christ at the Last Supper. That Spirit was the Spirit of Christ. Though He be in the Father (see Jn. 14:20), and all things of the Father are His (see Jn. 16:15), the earthly work of the Father was given to Him. All power in Heaven and earth was given to Him (see Mt. 28:18), and He is the power and the wisdom of God to us (see 1 Cor. 1:24).

Christ openly claimed to be the "I Am" Yahweh of the Old Testament several times before many witnesses, both friendly and hostile, which ignited a fire of religious indignation among the Pharisees and teachers of the law (see Jn. 6:35; 8:12; 10:7-9,11,14; 11:25; 14:6; 15:1,5). Consider the following statements made by Jesus (I have omitted the unstated pronouns added to the translation to conform to the English language):

> *God is a Spirit: and they that worship Him must worship Him in spirit and in truth. ...I that speak unto thee **am** (Jn. 4:24,26).*

> *I said therefore unto you, that ye shall die in your sins: for if ye believe not that **I am**, ye shall die in your sins (Jn. 8:24).*

> *...When ye have lifted up the Son of man, then shall ye know that **I am**... (Jn. 8:28).*

> *...Before Abraham was, **I am** (Jn. 8:58).*

> *Now I tell you before it come, that, when it is come to pass, ye may believe that **I am** (Jn. 13:19).*

I believe the Spirit of Christ descended at Sinai, and I believe the Spirit of Christ filled the upper room at Pentecost. Christ appeared to Moses in the form of a burning bush (see Ex. 3:2), and wrestled with Jacob near the river Jabbok (see Gen. 32:24-28; Hos. 12:4). Christ was the ransom for our sins at Calvary, and He was the *shekinah* glory of God revealed above the mercy seat of the Ark.

All righteousness is of God (see Is. 54:17), and that righteousness is imputed to you and me because of Christ alone. He laid the foundation of our faith at Sinai in the giving of the law and finished the work at Calvary and on the Day of Pentecost! "For by one offering He hath perfected for ever them that are sanctified" (Heb. 10:14). Because of Christ, righteousness is imputed from the obedient father to his son, from the obedient employee to the employer, and from one believer to another. He covers our homes, our marriages, and our children with His righteousness and blessings when we obey His commands and serve Him as our Lord.

Lifelines

In time, the line is broken
Like so many words in canyons spoken
But in bits and pits and crevices
Are dripping down like golden tokens
Into ponds, into ponds, into ponds

In time, the frame is marriage
So our blood be not disparaged
'til they swear with air, dust, foliage
And the life of love is carriage
To our graves, to our graves, to our graves

Outside of time the chain is tightly woven into strains
Of fine and fanciful renames of still some other whole
Design outside of time

Eternal light in streams of bright and dandy
Colored seamless rounds of life in beams
Unscattered by our sounds

In time the line is broken
Like so many words in canyons spoken
But in bits and pits and crevices
Are dripping down like golden tokens
Into ponds, into ponds, into ponds

Jesus is the unbroken line from the Father. He is completely in the Father, and the Father is completely in Him.

The seed of the upright shall be blessed. David says, "I have been young, and now am old; yet have I not seen the righteous forsaken, nor his seed begging bread. He is ever merciful, and lendeth; and his seed is blessed" (Ps. 37:25-26). Psalm 37:27-31 may be taken as a paraphrase of God's promise to Abraham, which culminated in Christ. "Depart from evil, and do good; and dwell for evermore. For the Lord loveth judgment, and forsaketh not His saints; they are preserved for ever: but the seed of the wicked shall be cut off" (Ps. 37:27-28).

God seeks a godly seed. For this reason, the offspring and spouse of the believer are blessed by the believer's presence. Paul counsels the unbelieving spouse with these words: "For the unbelieving husband is sanctified by the [believing] wife, and the unbelieving wife is sanctified by the [righteous] husband: else were your children unclean; but now are they holy" (1 Cor. 7:14). God delights to bless the righteous and even their children's children!

> *Praise ye the Lord. Blessed is the man that feareth the Lord, that delighteth greatly in His commandments. His seed shall be mighty upon earth: the generation of the upright shall be blessed. Wealth and riches shall be in his house: and his righteousness endureth for ever* (Psalm 112:1-3).

Here is the promise of wealth. The blessing of prosperity is given to the obedient family. Riches and wealth are the rewards of those who obey the Word of God (see Ps. 1:1-3). It is God who gives the power to get riches in this life (see Deut. 8:18). The promise of earthly gain is the endowment and legacy of the righteous family (see Prov. 13:22)!

Chapter 16

The Extrinsic Rewards of Obedience

It is easy to see that truthfulness builds confidence, and that marital fidelity may avert disease. It takes deep faith, however, to appreciate and exercise total surrender to God, and it is only this level of profound commitment to God that allows us to see the hand of the Creator in every detail of our lives. Total surrender puts the upright believer in line to receive such an abundance of God's blessings that they will seem to flow like rivers of water! Jesus told the Samaritan woman:

> *...Whosoever drinketh of this* [natural] *water shall thirst again: but whosoever drinketh of the water that I shall give him shall never thirst; but the water that I shall give him shall be in him a well of water springing up into everlasting life* (John 4:13-14).

Wells were few in the dry terrain of that area, so water was a precious commodity. A well that never failed was a source of continual satisfaction and a vital resource that drew people to its refreshing waters again and again. When Jesus offered this woman an *endless stream of water to quench every thirst* in life, He immediately had her attention! Once she learned that the water from the Lord's inexhaustible well sustained life eternally, it must have staggered her imagination! The same thing happens to every believer who seriously studies the great promises of God made to the faithful:

> *Blessed is the man that walketh not in the counsel of the ungodly, nor standeth in the way of sinners, nor sitteth in the seat of the scornful. But his delight is in the law of the Lord; and in His law doth he meditate day and night. And he shall be like a tree planted by the rivers of water, that bringeth forth his fruit in his season; his leaf also shall not wither; and whatsoever he doeth shall prosper* (Psalm 1:1-3).

> *...Eye hath not seen, nor ear heard, neither have entered into the heart of man, the things which God hath prepared for them that love Him* (1 Corinthians 2:9; see also Isaiah 64:4).

> *...No good thing will He withhold from them that walk uprightly* (Psalm 84:11).

It is God's good pleasure to richly reward the righteous! "He that spared not His own Son, but delivered Him up for us all, how shall He not with Him also freely give us all things?" (Rom. 8:32) Christ said He came that we "...might have life, and that [we] might have it more abundantly" (Jn. 10:10). Jesus promised us, "If ye abide in Me, and My words abide in you, ye shall ask what ye will, and it shall be done unto you" (Jn. 15:7). He also said, "For every one that asketh receiveth;

and he that seeketh findeth; and to him that knocketh it shall be opened" (Lk. 11:10).

This may sound strange or unbelievable, but the blessings of God are *His to give*, not ours to demand. God's blessings don't come by *merit*. We may wish we could "earn" them or acquire them by our own efforts, wealth, talent, intellect, or position—but it cannot be done. The riches of God are His own to give in His own time and way.

Jacob probably knew about God's incredible promise to his grandfather, Abraham. He may have believed as a boy that he was the one destined to carry the seed of the promised nation. It is even likely that Jacob knew in his spirit that God had chosen him to be the father of Israel. Rebekah was aware of his election even before his birth because the Lord had told her that "the elder shall serve the younger" (Gen. 25:23).

One day Jacob took advantage of his elder brother's fatigue and traded some red pottage for his brother's birthright (see Gen. 25:29-34). He also deceived his father, Isaac, into giving him the blessing that should have gone by custom and right to Esau, the firstborn (see Gen. 27:6-29). Despite the deception, God promised to bless all the earth through the seed of Jacob! (See Genesis 28:14-15.)

Even though he had the promise of divine blessing, Jacob's deceptive ways estranged him from his family, and for the next 14 years his uncertainty about his relationship with God drove his constant attempts to make amends for his misdeeds. He had deceived his father; now he suffered from the deception of his brother-in-law, Laban. He worked for 14 years instead of 7 years for the woman he wanted to marry. Though Jacob became rich, he still had not made peace with God or his fellow man in those years.

Jacob finally decided to return home to Canaan to reunite with his family. That meant he had to confront Esau, the brother he'd wronged. Although God had instructed him to return and had promised to be with him (see Gen. 31:3), Jacob was afraid Esau would kill him (see Gen. 32:7). Thinking everything he had built was about to crumble, Jacob prepared for the worst. He took account of all he had gained in life and divided his goods and family into two companies. He thought one might escape if Esau attacked the other. He sent ahead of him several droves of camels, colts, cattle, asses, and foals as gifts to Esau, hoping to soften his brother's heart. He sent away his wives and 11 sons and waited for Esau alone.

That night must have been the lowest point in Jacob's life, yet it was at this low point that God visited Jacob and changed human history. An "angel" wrestled with Jacob all through the night and into the morning light (see Gen. 32:24-30; Hos. 12:3-4). Somehow, perhaps through desperation, Jacob would not let go of his adversary until he had blessed him. The angel said, "...Thy name shall be called no more Jacob, but Israel [prince of God]: for as a prince hast thou power with God and with men, and hast prevailed" (Gen. 32:28).

Would Jacob have stood in line with the ancestors of our Lord had he not received the blessing of his father? Since God had already chosen Jacob from his mother's womb, he was destined to fulfill God's purposes. Jacob's own deceptive efforts to win a birthright were feeble and misguided and caused more problems than good. Jacob needed God's blessing to fulfill the promises set upon him, but his own efforts could not secure those promises. Only God can fulfill the promises He has made to us!

Jacob "the supplanter" desperately needed the blessing of God to overcome the stain of sin left by his deceptive acquisition of a birthright. He literally needed a new identity. His "new identity" is a type and shadow of the new birth in Christ. With God's blessing and his new identity, Jacob escaped the pursuit of Laban whom he had robbed (see Gen. 31:21-29); he avoided the vengeance of Esau (see Gen. 33:1-15); and he overcame the angry reprisal of the Canaanites after the murders of Shechem and the men of his city (Gen. 34:25–35:5). Every time we follow Jacob's footsteps by failing to trust God and trying to win God's blessings our own way, we are sure to fall into error, sorrow, and pain. We need to remember that our heavenly Father already knows what we need (see Mt. 6:8).

The promise of God also found its way around human weakness in the life of Moses. This great prophet and man of God seemed to have circumvented his destiny by presumptuously killing an Egyptian to protect a Hebrew slave and win the approval of the Hebrew people. Moses must have known that he was to be the great deliverer of his people. He knew the miraculous circumstances of his birth: how he had been saved from Pharaoh's massacre of Jewish males (see Ex. 2:1-6). He probably knew he had been nursed by his own mother (Ex. 2:7-10).

All of these point to a special purpose for his life. Moses must have felt well prepared for leadership, too, because of his unique position in Pharaoh's house with the privileges of formal learning. Moses might have viewed himself as someone strategically placed in the Egyptian political structure to bring civil reform. His impulsive murder of an Egyptian, instead, estranged him from the very people he was born to lead! We will go God's way, or no way! God's timing and God's plans are just as important as God's call! Moses left Egypt in fear and disgrace to be further molded by the hands of the Creator in the wilderness.

In the desolate land of the Midianites, he joined the household of an Arabian shepherd and priest named Jethro. As the years went by, Moses reflected upon the truths of God as he tended sheep. God's word seemed to contrast sharply with the false concepts of Egypt. He communed with God and nature and was humbled by the Creator's awesome proportions.

Forty years in Midian erased every identity and "qualification" Moses had known. For 40 long years, he kept the flock of Jethro, now his father-in-law. Jethro's daughter, Zipporah, had become his wife and had borne him two sons, Gershom and Eliezer. Moses become a different man during those 40 years. The Lord invaded his new life on the mount of God, called Horeb, and called Moses to be the deliverer of His people! The once-proud Moses answered God with the question, "Who am I?" (see Ex. 3:11) This self-appointed judge, trained statesman, soldier, and prince raised in Pharaoh's royal household, had waited for 40 long years to be formally recognized by God. Not one day was wasted by God—every detail of Moses' life was charted by God's appointment. Every title he had earned and all the knowledge he had acquired would be needed to accomplish the supernatural task God would set before him.

Moses become smaller in his own eyes when he humbled himself to ask, "Who am I?" But His God had become larger when he asked the Lord, "Who are You?" (See Exodus 3:13.) Like Jacob, Moses had to wait for *Jehovah Raah*, the "Lord my Shepherd" (see Ps. 23:1), to give him a new identity in God's plan and to make him prince and judge. Nothing Moses might have done could have forced the hand of El Shaddai, the Almighty God (see Gen. 17:1). Nothing and no one but God could have placed him in the stream of events that led to his eventual position and power as the Deliverer of Israel!

Only *El Olam*, the "Everlasting God" (see Is. 40:28), could direct the hands of time. Only *Jehovah Nakeh*, the "Lord who smites" (see Ezek. 7:9), could raise or cast down kings, pharaohs, and leaders of men! Only *Jehovah Jireh*, "God my Provider" (see Gen. 22:13-14), could plan and never fail. Human wealth, human talent, and human intellect or power could never accomplish what *Jehovah Shammah*, the "Omnipresent God" (see Ezek. 48:35), had planned. The blessings of *Jehovah M'kaddesh*, our "Holy God" (see Ex. 31:13), and the appointments of *El Elyon*, the "Most High God" (see Is. 14:13-14), are only His to give—in His own perfect time and in His own perfect way. Our own "goodness" or "merit" cannot force the hand of God. *Jehovah Tsidkenu* is "God our righteousness" (see Jer. 23:6). *Jehovah Nissi* is "God our banner" (see Ex. 17:15). *Jehovah El G'mulah* is "God our recompense" (see Jer. 51:56).

Jacob and Moses were called of God for a special purpose. They tried to find God's purpose for their lives in every way possible, just as you and I have! They wanted to do God's will, but they tried it under their own power. Even the patriarchs tried to do things in their own strength in an earnest effort to please God. When the folly of our ways is exposed, all of us have to turn more completely to God and to His way, growing in our faith and obedience to His will. This is the path that leads to maturity. Others want what God can give rather than to do God's will. They hope to fulfill *their own purposes* through *God's power*. They seek the blessings, but without the sacrifice and without obedience.

Simon Magus, who was a sorcerer in Samaria, had bewitched the people of that region, making himself out to be someone powerful (see Acts 8:9-24). He had convinced nearly everyone there that he possessed the power of God, but he was actually a demon-possessed soothsayer and charlatan at enmity with God. Simon was excited by the miracles worked through Philip the evangelist. Simon believed the teachings of Philip and was baptized. He followed Philip around constantly as the evangelist spread the gospel in the area of Sychar.

When Peter and the apostles visited Samaria to authenticate the believers there, Simon saw the laying on of hands and the receipt of the Holy Ghost. Moved by greed and power, Simon offered money to learn or receive the power to "give the Holy Ghost" to others by the laying on of hands (see Acts 8:19). Simon probably intended to use this power to enhance his trade in the art of divination. Peter rebuked Simon for his presumption and said, "...Thy money perish with thee, because thou hast thought that the gift of God may be purchased with money" (Acts 8:20).

Simon's mistake is common: He thought he could receive the blessings and power of God *without allegiance to God*. Eve desired the power of God without obeying the command of God, too! Church tradition has it that Simon was so convinced of himself that he asked to be buried alive to prove that he would rise from the dead on the third day!

The rich young ruler esteemed God's blessing of less value than material possessions (see Mt. 19:16-22; Mk. 10:17-22; Lk. 18:18-23). He had position, fortune, and character and felt the need of a blessing from the Lord. The young man was a member of the Jewish religious council who kept the law and saw himself as devout. He had been so deeply moved by the words of the Savior that he ran to Jesus and kneeled at His feet, asking, "...Good Master, what shall I do to inherit eternal life?" (Lk. 18:18) When Jesus asked him to give up his money (his first love), he hung his head. The esteem of men and the pride of human accomplishment kept that young ruler from appreciating the value of the heavenly treasure Christ had set before him!

The Savior's call to us is reasonable: "Take up your cross and follow Me" (see Mt. 10:38; 16:24; Mk. 8:34; Lk. 9:23; 14:27). People who love the world more than Christ are in the same predicament as the rich young ruler! They want the gift of God without allegiance to God. They want the gift without the Giver! They put their life before His life and their concerns before His concerns. They put their families before His family, along with their jobs, houses, cars, and friends! They have not stopped to count the price He paid at Calvary. "For what shall it profit a man, if he shall gain the whole world, and lose his own soul?" (Mk. 8:36)

Chapter 17

The Qualifications

There are at least two absolute qualifications every believer must meet to obtain the blessings and power of God. First, we must choose God's way. The only way to God's treasures is the "Way" God gives us. It is ridiculous to believe there can be any other way or any shortcuts between "here and there." Any other way leads to deception by satan with the fruits of destruction and eternal damnation. Jesus was blunt and to the point: "...*I am the way*...no man cometh unto the Father, but by Me" (Jn. 14:6).

Secondly, we must remember that only God can fulfill His promises and bestow His blessings on us. He does this when He wants and how He wants for He is sovereign. God knows the end and the beginning, and He weighs and balances the deeds of the flesh with those of faith. There is no blessing in any other way. There is no hope, no light, no strength. The end of every other path is destruction.

Verily, verily, I say unto you, He that entereth not by the door into the sheepfold, but climbeth up some other way, the same is a thief and a robber. ...I am the door of the sheep. All that ever came before Me are thieves and robbers: but the sheep did not hear them. ... The thief cometh not, but for to steal, and to kill, and to destroy: I am come that they might have life, and that they might have it more abundantly. I am the good shepherd: the good shepherd giveth His life for the sheep (John 10:1,7-8,10-11).

The Guarantee

God's blessings, power, and gifts are completely guaranteed. Through Christ and in God our ultimate victory over every obstacle is absolutely guaranteed. Obedience by faith guarantees the victory. It guarantees the power and presence of God for every problem in this life, and it guarantees the life to come. Victory and power are available now, and they are guaranteed!

Jesus in the Wilderness

After Jesus submitted to the baptism of John and the Spirit of God had come upon Him, the Spirit led Him into a wilderness to be tempted by satan (see Mt. 4:1; Mk. 1:12-13; Lk 4:1). Jesus prepared Himself for spiritual warfare by fasting and praying for 40 days and 40 nights (see Mt. 4:2; 17:21). He knew the adversary would attack His purpose and identity, so He covered Himself with the full armor of God (see Eph. 6:14-17). Jesus knew the Word of God was a sure defense and an invincible spiritual weapon for attacking and subduing the enemy.

When satan appeared to Christ, I believe he came in the form of a gentle, wise, helpful, and godly "angel of light" (see 2 Cor. 11:13-14), hoping to disguise his true character and murderous intent. He wanted to disarm the Lord and destroy His mission of mercy. Perhaps the devil's confidence was boosted by seeing the Son of God clothed in the familiar flesh of Adam's children.

Satan hoped he could lead Jesus into sin as he'd done with one-third of Heaven's angelic hosts and with Adam and Eve! If he could bring the Christ to the slightest point of doubt, he could forever steal the hope of reconciliation with God from the souls of fallen men! Had Jesus fallen, we would have all been doomed to eternal separation from the Father, for Christ Himself would have fallen into the hands of satan to do his bidding!

Jesus went into the contest "with both hands tied behind His back" because He refused to defeat satan *by use of His divine power*! Jesus could have exercised His divinity and squashed the evil angelic rebel like a roach, but He was on a mission. He had to pave the way for every human being who would face attack by satan. He was determined to respond only with those weapons available to human beings, becoming a living example for every human facing the Valley of Temptation.

The tempter began by *questioning Christ's identity* as the Son of God. (He does the same to us today!) He hoped to arouse fleshly pride in Jesus. Perhaps he could prod the Christ to indulge in a hasty, self-motivated display of His divinity! (After all, that's what he would do in Christ's place!) He wanted the same response he'd seen in the Garden of Eden. (Adam and Eve also wielded the power of God, but they doubted His Word and presence.) If he could shake the faith of Jesus Christ, he could control His mind, and hence, His behavior.

Should Jesus ever question His identity, He would subvert the promise and election of God and call all faith into question! That stage was set as satan slyly suggested: "...*If* Thou be the Son of God, command that these stones be made bread" (Mt. 4:3; see also Lk. 4:3). Satan first assaulted Christ's identity at the level of base physical appetite because he knew Jesus had not eaten for 40 days and nights.

The tempter knew most men and women would quickly abandon faith at the first whimper of their fleshly appetites. Whether it was baited with food, sex, wealth, or other material possessions, the temptation of the flesh was satan's most successful weapon against the faith of men who knew God!

The tactic he used on Jesus had been absolutely successful with Adam and Eve and thousands of humans after them. He hoped that the lust of the flesh would somehow blur the Lord's identification with God the Father. If not, maybe Jesus would compromise His knowledge of His sonship just long enough to "satisfy His hunger." He hoped Jesus would reason, "What could be wrong with making something to eat?" He hoped to replay the scene with Eve when he persuaded her to consider God's ordinance about the tree to be "sheer pettiness."

Jesus didn't take the bait. He boldly answered, "...It is written, Man shall not live by bread alone, but by every word that proceedeth out of the mouth of God" (Mt. 4:4; see also Lk. 4:4). Jesus devastated the tempter's assault by placing the Word of God in its rightful place: *above every requirement of the flesh!* The children of God can only have power over the enemy when they bring their passions and appetites into submission to God's Word by His Spirit.

"Then the devil taketh Him up into the holy city, and setteth Him on a pinnacle of the temple" (Mt. 4:5). Still stinging from the inescapable blow of God's Word, the devil took Jesus to a high spot above the city of Jerusalem. Jesus stood over the temple, the chosen people, and the nations of the earth. He was in the position of high priest and mediator between God and His people. At that point, satan turns to Scripture himself and says, "...If Thou be the Son of God, cast Thyself down: *for it is written*, He shall give His angels charge concerning Thee:

and in their hands they shall bear Thee up, lest at any time Thou dash Thy foot against a stone" (Mt. 4:6).

All the power of God's celestial armies were at the disposal of Christ, the Captain of the heavenly host! Satan, in his desperation, had almost conceded the spiritual unity of Christ with God! He had to bring Him to a point above the temple, and he had actually referred to the hated and feared passage in Psalm 91 that predicted the coming of the Messiah! The tempter only went to these painful efforts because *he hoped to appeal to presumption and pride* (which he assumed were in everyone!). Would Christ satisfy satan's "innocent" request to see a sign—without meeting the great spiritual needs of the Jewish people?

This particular satanic appeal, which he uses on us as well, probes for arrogance of faith that has lost its grounding in a higher source. His subtle suggestion encourages insecure spiritual leaders to affirm themselves and enhance their reputations *through the power of God.* His hope is to divert God's power toward selfish purposes instead of bringing glory to God and divine deliverance and forgiveness to others. If Jesus had accepted the challenge, He would have been, in essence, requiring God the Father to prove Himself as God, as though the Son did not already know Him.

Satan subtly quoted from the Scriptures, assuming the "learned character" of a master, hoping to inflate Christ's sense of self-worth. Satan still had the appearance of an angel of light and probably felt he was meeting the Lord on His own ground by using the quoted Word. He ended up falling into his own trap! Satan unwisely chose a passage reminiscent of Genesis 3:15, where the Lord God told the serpent in the garden, "...thou shalt *bruise His heel.*" He had hoped to twist the Word, but he just couldn't shake the foreboding declaration of God: "...it [the seed of the woman] shall bruise thy head..."

(Gen. 3:15). Christ Jesus again destroyed satan's hopes by replying with authority, "...It is written again, Thou shalt not tempt the Lord thy God" (Mt. 4:7).

As a last resort, satan took Christ to an even higher elevation at the top of a very high mountain. There satan showed Him "all the kingdoms of the world," and said, "...All these things will I give Thee, if Thou wilt fall down and worship me" (Mt. 4:9; Lk. 4:5-7). All pretense was gone. Every disguise was stripped aside. Satan was revealed in all of his diabolical hunger for godhood and worship. He no longer bothered to couch his temptation in sly phrases. He openly conceded that Christ was the Messiah and Savior. Throwing aside all pretense, the fallen angel made a final, desperate appeal to the lust of the eye! He told Jesus, in essence, "These kingdoms of the world are *mine to rule*, but I will give them all to You if You will worship me just once!"

Perhaps satan knew the sacrifice awaiting the Lamb of God, and he was hoping Jesus would take his offer to avoid the anguish of crucifixion. After all, Jesus could still "achieve His goal" of reclaiming the dominion of the earth. The truth was—and is—that the earth's kingdoms already belonged to Christ. The Psalmist declared, "The earth is the Lord's, and the fulness thereof; the world, and they that dwell therein" (Ps. 24:1). It is true that the tempter was called the "prince of the power of the air" (Eph. 2:2), but he only dominates the wicked world system. Satan cannot claim the cosmos; it belongs to Jesus Christ who made it. The Gospel of John says, "All things were made by Him; and without Him was not any thing made that was made" (Jn. 1:3). If satan was only promising to give Jesus the world system, then he could have rested assured that Christ did not want it.

The "father of lies" was promising something that was not his to give in order to gain what he could not otherwise take!

His temptation was nothing more than one lie based upon another. He had no intention of giving up anything, even if it were his to give. He came only to steal and destroy (see Jn. 10:10). At the same time, Christ was fully aware of His Kingdom and His power (see Jn. 18:36; Rev. 19:16), and He already knew He would reign forever (see Dan. 7:27b).

Christ's victory over satan was essential to His kingship. Satan himself would be forced to worship Christ because of His victory over sin (see Is. 45:23; Rom. 14:11). Jesus prophetically proclaimed to satan, "...Thou shalt worship the Lord thy God, and Him only shalt thou serve" (Mt. 4:10; Lk. 4:8), and ordered him to be gone, thereby establishing His authority even over the devil's movements. With these words, He crushed the head [or rule] of the serpent that had successfully tempted Adam. He took the first great step to regain the keys to the kingdom and reestablish God's order in the world system.

Jesus showed us what we can do if we only trust the Word of God and obey it to the letter. Satan would return to tempt and hinder Jesus, but Christ-come-in-the-flesh had already established His dominion over the angel of darkness. Although satan returned many times, he merely presented the same old challenges in new forms, and Christ always repeated the same victory.

The Father sent angels from Heaven to feed our Lord and minister to Him after the temptation in the wilderness. Unlike the bread suggested by satan, this food was a blessing of obedience (see Mt. 6:31-33). Jesus had continued His pattern of total submission to His Father and walked in the blessing given by God at His baptism in the Jordan, "...This is My beloved Son, in whom I am well pleased" (Mt. 3:17), words that satan himself had heard with envy.

We must do as Jesus did. "Submit yourselves therefore to God. Resist the devil, and he will flee from you. Draw nigh to God, and He will draw nigh to you..." (Jas. 4:7-8).

Israel's Trials in the Wilderness

Jesus spent one day in the wilderness for every day the spies of Israel spent in the Promised Land, and for every year of judgment Israel spent in the wilderness for their sin before God. Israel spent 40 years wandering in the desert, but unlike the Savior, the Israelites were ultimately unable to achieve victory over satan because they often doubted the promises and presence of God. The Lord was always faithful and true to His Word. When they were obedient, He delivered them. When they were disobedient or doubtful, He had compassion on them. When they fell into patterns of sin, however, He sometimes allowed sin's deadly consequences to follow. Obedience guarantees victory, and disobedience ultimately guarantees defeat.

The Scriptures reveal how the Lord carved out a nation for Himself, revealed His power and governing principles, and established a way for man to tap into the power He had demonstrated in the Books of Exodus, Leviticus, Numbers, and Deuteronomy. God revealed Himself to Moses as *Yahweh*, or "I Am That I Am" (see Ex. 3:14), after Moses asked, "What shall I tell them when they ask, 'What is God's name?' " (See Exodus 3:13.) God also demonstrated His power over kings, nature, demons, false gods, and life and death through the ten plagues He brought upon Egypt (see Ex. 7:14–12:36).

Despite God's victory over Egypt and His awesome displays of power, the Hebrew children doubted His presence and loving care in the wilderness. Failing to take arms against satan by prayer and fasting, they fell to the wiles of the tempter at the level of their lusty appetites. At a town called Marah, they complained of bitter water (see Ex. 15:22-24). In the

Desert of Sin, they complained of lack of food (see Ex. 16:1-3). At Rephidim, they complained about lack of water (see Ex. 17:2-3), and tempted the Lord, saying, "Is the Lord among us, or not?" (Ex. 17:7) Finally, at Sinai they made and worshiped a golden calf. In short order, the Hebrew people failed every test that Jesus would later face and overcome. Even when they confronted the occupants of the Promised Land, they refused to attack them (see Num. 13:31-33). At one point they actually conspired to stone the prophet Moses (Ex. 17:4)!

Without faith, you surely cannot please God; but even more basically, without faith you cannot see Him or recognize His power. Real success in the face of insurmountable odds requires believers to rest in God's power and ride on His might. "...He that cometh to God must believe that He is, and that He is a rewarder of them that diligently seek Him" (Heb. 11:6). It is too simple and inviting for us to focus on our weaknesses instead of God's strength. When we do, we can easily become convinced that God will not or cannot fight our battles and win! Victorious faith must rise beyond speculation and hesitation. It must stir the spirit to "undaunted, blind, crazy obedience" before it can take on the impossible.

Two of the 12 Israelite spies were faithful in their report about the Promised Land. One was Moses' assistant, Joshua, an Ephraimite and the son of Nun (see Num. 13:8); the other was Caleb, the son of Jephunneh, of the tribe of Judah (see Num. 13:6). When the Hebrew people foolishly talked of "choosing a leader for themselves" to lead them back to Egypt, Joshua and Caleb "tore their clothes," and told the people:

> ..."The land we passed through and explored is exceedingly good. If the Lord is pleased with us, He will lead us into that land, a land flowing with milk and honey, and will give it to us. Only do not rebel against the Lord. And do not be afraid of the people of the land, because we will swallow them up. Their protection is

gone, but the Lord is with us. Do not be afraid of them" (Numbers 14:7-9 NIV).

Joshua and Caleb were permitted to enter the Promised Land because of their faith and obedience (see Num. 14:30; Josh. 14:6-14). They had endured the trials of satan with the rest, and they had stood among the many who fell into the traps satan placed before them. They saw many of their comrades die the death of infidels, but in the end, they stood on God's Word and reaped the rewards of obedience.

We stand on this side of Calvary enjoying a more perfect covenant than that of Sinai (see Heb. 8:6-13) because Christ was victorious over satan. He stands at the pinnacle of the Church as mediator between God and man. By Him, we are saved to the utmost, and He makes intercession to the Father on our behalf (see Heb. 7:25). His victory is our permanent guarantee of eternal life (see Heb. 7:22-28) and entrance into the Promised Land.

These are the things Jesus Christ guarantees to those who *choose His way* and *trust Him to fulfill His promises*:

*But my God shall **supply all your need** according to His riches in glory by Christ Jesus* (Philippians 4:19).

But seek ye first the kingdom of God, and His righteousness; and all these things [food, clothes, etc.] ***shall be added** unto you* (Matthew 6:33).

*...**What things soever ye desire,** when ye pray, believe that ye receive them, and ye shall have them* (Mark 11:24).

***And whatsoever ye shall ask in My name, that will I do,** that the Father may be glorified in the Son* (John 14:13).

*If any man serve Me...**him will My Father honour*** (John 12:26).

*He that hath My commandments, and keepeth them, he it is that loveth Me: and he that loveth Me shall be **loved of My Father**, and **I will love him**, and will **manifest Myself to him*** (John 14:21).

*Hitherto have ye asked nothing in My name: **ask, and ye shall receive**, that **your joy may be full*** (John 16:24).

*Verily, verily, I say unto you, **He that believeth on Me hath everlasting life*** (John 6:47).

*I am the living bread which came down from heaven: if any man eat of this bread, he shall **live for ever**...* (John 6:51).

*I am the good shepherd, and know My sheep, and am known of Mine. ... My sheep hear My voice, and I know them, and they follow Me: and **I give unto them eternal life**; and they shall never perish, neither shall any man pluck them out of My hand* (John 10:14,27-28).

If we believe God's Word, we shall receive all of His blessings. If we obey God's Word, we will be endowed with His power. Guaranteed. We will receive the intrinsic blessings of obedience, along with the extraordinary blessings that overflow unto eternal life. These include unlimited access to God and to His love, honor, joy, and abundant supply of our needs and desires. We inherit both the promises of Sinai and the promises of Jesus Christ to become priests and kings of God.

But ye are a chosen generation, a royal priesthood, an holy nation, a peculiar people; that ye should shew forth the praises of Him who hath called you out of darkness into His marvellous light (1 Peter 2:9).

"[We] can do all things through Christ which strengtheneth [us]" (Phil. 4:13), we have power over all the power of the enemy (see Lk. 10:19). "And whatsoever we ask, we receive of Him, because we keep His commandments, and do those things that are pleasing in His sight" (1 Jn. 3:22). All things are possible because we believe (see Mk. 9:23).

The Living Way

And when the Lord commanded Noah
To build that fateful ark,
He could only see the borders of
God's plan before his start.

But then he labored, though uncertain
Of when the flooding rain would come,
And put his faith in God's own promise to
Deliver him unharmed.

There's a ship that we call Jesus
That sails through storms of doubt and sin
With a cargo load of mercy
If we believe and follow Him.

We can see past the dark clouds blinding us
With fear and disbelief
And behold a rainbow of God's love
With joy and hope and peace.

Come, all aboard that ark!
With faith, you can embark.
Give up your misery;
Sail for eternity!

Come, all aboard that ark!
Render your soul and heart.

Leave all the storm outside.
Leave out your lust, your pride.

$*$ $*$ $*$ $*$ $*$

Before the courts of mighty Pharaoh,
God said, "Let My people go!"
He had promised them a new land
Where the milk and honey flow.

First He grouped in bands of thousands
For the caravans to go,
But before they'd see that new land,
God would have their faith to grow.

So He guided them through desert
With their caravans in flight,
Led by clouds ahead in daylight
And a ball of fire at night.

Now the Guide, of course, is Jesus,
And the desert is our doubt.
'Til by faith in Christ He frees us,
We cannot find our way out.

And the devil's right behind us
To make sure we don't get free,
But the Lord will open every door
Make a pathway through the sea.

Come all join hand in hand
In God's great caravan.
Give up your vanity.
Let Jesus set you free.

Come all and join that band,
That holy caravan.
Put hand in Jesus' hand,
March to the Promised Land.

$*$ $*$ $*$ $*$ $*$

Upon a sacred spot called Bethel,
The Lord appeared to lowly man.
And a ladder went from Heaven's gate
To the ground on which we stand.

There were angels on that ladder,
Coming down and going up,
And the Lord stood up above them all
With a gift for all of us.

Now we know Jesus is that ladder,
That each of us must climb,
From our sinful state, humanity,
To the heights above, divine.

And the angels will assist us
If we repent and turn from sin.
They will carry us to Heaven's gate,
And the Lord will let us in!

Come all and make that climb.
Renew your hearts and minds.
The angels here will say,
"Come, children, come today."

How can we dare neglect
So great salvation? Yet
Our Savior paid the debt.
Our course to God is set.

Part V

The Power
of the Word

The Word of God is the basic unit of power. It is the most elemental component of creation. As such, it is often used synonymously with God. Flesh is the antithesis. It is the opposing matter. The Word is spirit, but flesh is mammon. The Word is life everlasting, but flesh is sure death. The Word is power, but flesh is weakness. The Word is for God, by God, and through God. The flesh is against God. The Word has the power to heal, to deliver, and to invoke divine strength. The flesh will sicken, weaken, and repel the divine. The Word will last forever, but the flesh will pass away. The flesh is doomed to destruction.

Chapter 18

The Word Is a Contract for Power

Regardless of how we interpret it, divide it, or dissect it, the Word of God is a contract. It is an agreement between fallen man and the Supreme Being. It is a covenant, a compact, an understanding, a testament, a pact, a bond, a collective bargain, a treaty, a set of promises, and an arrangement between God and man. As offensive as this may sound to modern ears, take it or leave it. *The Word of God is a contract!*

All higher creatures, whether human or angelic, operate in contractual relationship with their Creator. Lucifer the archangel violated the terms of his contract in Heaven and was thrown out (see Is. 14:12-15). Adam and Cain each violated contracts, although the precise terms and scope of their arrangements are unknown to modern writers.

"Then the Lord said to Cain, '...*If you do what is right*, will you not be accepted? But *if you do not do what is right*, sin is crouching at your door; it desires to have you, but you must master it'" (Gen. 4:6-7 NIV). Cain apparently knew the "terms" necessary to win "acceptance" for his offerings to God, but he chose to violate them. God simply reminded Cain of the terms of the contract he chose to ignore.

Modern readers think of contracts as legal documents for arranging mutually-beneficial relationships between parties. Since we separate law from religion in our minds, the idea of a "divine contract" seems to be a contradiction of terms. The contradiction is in our thinking. The concept that law is separate from religion is a recent and unproven notion.

Church and state are only beginning to separate for much of the world's population. Throughout human history (and in many countries today) religion was the "legal" arm of the state. Courts were often composed of clergy; laws were ecclesiastical and rooted in the mores of the Church; and community legal records were kept by churches until recent times. Have you ever wondered why so many births and deaths were recorded in Bibles?

All of our laws come from God, though many have gone off course. Every modern western code of law and its rational formulation are traceable to the laws Moses received from God! God is the creator of legal contracts in the first place. Most legal contracts ultimately contemplate the divine order of things, whether they are written or implied, explicit or implicit. They simply restate God's intended relationships for man to man and man to God. World history may be described as the record of man's deviation from perfect law and perfect compliance with divine order.

Most Bible students point to the laws given to Moses at Sinai as the major legal contract in the Word of God. These laws covered the following subjects:

1. Moral conduct (Ex. 20)

2. Treatment of servants (Ex. 21:1-11)

3. Injuries (Ex. 21:12-36)

4. Theft (Ex. 22:1-4)

5. Property damage (Ex. 22:5-6)

6. Dishonesty (Ex. 22:7-15)

7. Immorality (Ex. 22:16-17)

8. Civil and religious obligations (Ex. 22:18–23:9)

9. Sabbaths and feasts (Ex. 23:10-19)

10. Conquests (Ex. 23:20-33)

11. The tabernacle (Ex. 25:1–31:18; 35:1–40:38)

12. Sacrifices (Lev. 1–10)

13. Sanctification (Lev. 11–27; Num. 5:1–10:10)

We call them "laws," but to Moses they comprised a contract in the form of a treaty between a powerful Ruler and His subjects! The Mosaic laws contain a preamble (see Ex. 19:3), a historical introduction emphasizing the benevolence of God (see Ex. 19:4), the specific obligations of the subjects, the witnesses to the treaty, and a list of blessings or consequences for keeping or breaking the terms of the treaty (from the footnote to Exodus 19:3, The Holy Bible, New International Version, 1986, The Moody Bible Institute).

"Reciprocal terms" are a major aspect of the Mosaic Code, unlike civil and criminal "laws" that simply state the nature of the offenses and the penalties for breaking them. God's contract with Israel includes *a promise of great rewards* for obedience! God made this proposal to the children of Israel through Moses:

Now therefore, if ye will obey My voice indeed, and keep My covenant, then ye shall be a peculiar treasure unto

*Me above all people: for all the earth is Mine: and ye
shall be unto Me a kingdom of priests, and an holy nation...* (Exodus 19:5-6).

Obedience to God's Word always provides access to God
by virtue of a special relationship. In this sense, the Word of
God is *a contract for power*. Obedience to it creates a special
identity. It gave the Hebrew people power through their ability to call on God. The Hebrew people could call on God for
help if they were obedient because they had an "agreement"
with God!

God outlined all the benefits earned by those who kept
the terms of His contract, and He ratified the contract in
glowing terms. He promised plentiful harvests, *food* (see Lev.
26:4-5,10; Deut. 28:8,12), *peace* (see Lev. 26:6), astonishing
military *might* (see Lev. 26:7-8; Deut. 28:7), *fertility* for offspring (see Lev. 26:9), and *guidance* provided through His
continual presence (see Lev. 26:11-12). He also promised
worldwide *recognition* (see Deut. 28:10), unusual *prosperity*
(see Deut. 28:11), and a *supernatural competitive edge* (see
Deut. 28:13). He even promised the same blessings and benefits for their children (see Deut. 28:4), regardless of season, oc-
cupation, or life changes (see Deut. 28:6,8,12)!

This is an offer you cannot refuse! It is a contract you dare
not break. It covers every detail of life, and it promises health,
wealth, and happiness for choosing the only true God as sovereign and king.

God had already proven to the Israelites that He could
keep His end of the bargain through many splendid displays of
His awesome power (see Ex. 19:4). He had destroyed the
greatest earthly kingdom at the time, along with all of its false
gods. He demonstrated the power to take life and to give it,
towering over all of nature. He made a dry road in the middle
of a sea and called forth water from a rock. He rained down

food from the heavens and sent quail in the middle of a desert. He descended in fire to a mountaintop and He spoke with the voice of a trumpet. What god before or after ever came so close to man? What god has called man "holy" and offered the most precious opportunity of all of earth's long story? Only the Almighty God, Yahweh, came to visit man and held out His great hand in covenant.

There could be no neutral ground with God's contract; everyone must either choose or refuse Him. God must have authority over all things. Nothing and no one could stand outside His power. Nothing could be so small that it would avoid His mindful attention. Nothing could be too big for Him to do. God's contract, of necessity, left nothing to mere chance. God was prepared to prove Himself in every circumstance. He would never turn His back upon the earth and His creation. He would never turn His back upon His Word.

Nonetheless, the children of Israel broke their contract with God through unbelief after publicly ratifying the law and promising that "all the words which the Lord [had] said [they would] do" (Ex. 24:3). They rejected God as sovereign, and sacrificed to a dumb idol cast in the shape of a calf (see Ex. 32:1-10).

The very first commandment received on Mount Sinai prohibited worship of gods other than Jehovah. God had warned Israel, "I am the Lord thy God, which have brought thee out of the land of Egypt, out of the house of bondage. Thou shalt have no other gods before Me. Thou shalt not make unto thee any graven image...thou shalt not bow down thyself to them, nor serve them..." (Ex. 20:2-5).

Moses had been gone for 40 days receiving God's law in tablets of stone on Mount Sinai (see Ex. 24:18) when the people grew impatient. They were tired of waiting for Moses, so they gathered the gold they had received from their Egyptian neighbors and made an idol in the form of a calf (see Ex. 32:4).

They worshiped the image of a lower animal, framing their rebellion in words that contradicted God's Word, His revelation, His deliverance, and the living Spirit. Their rebellion denied that God had ever spoken, led them out of captivity, been with them, or ever saw them. The idol of a lower animal symbolized the elevation of their lower instincts or animal urges and drives above the Most High God! It was only natural that their worship consisted of drunkenness, nakedness, and sexual excess (see Ex. 32:6,25; 1 Cor. 10:7-8).

They broke God's law in a way that clearly rejected everything that was powerful, holy, and true. They rejected deliverance from evil, and even worse, they rejected the presence and Spirit of God!

Moses interceded for Israel, offering his own life in exchange for the lives of the children of Israel (see Ex. 32:31-32); but the consequences of sin could not be avoided by the perpetrators. God did not destroy them altogether, but "the Lord plagued the people, because they made the calf, which Aaron made" (Ex. 32:35). When the people repented, the covenant was renewed (see Ex. 34).

The rebellion at Mount Sinai, however, became a prototype of continual rebellion, unbelief, and disobedience (see Ps. 78:56-64). Moses recounts the trail of rebellion with compassion and encouragement:

> *Remember, and forget not, how thou provokedst the Lord thy God to wrath in the wilderness: from the day that thou didst depart out of the land of Egypt, until ye came unto this place, ye have been rebellious against the Lord. Also in Horeb ye provoked the Lord to wrath, so that the Lord was angry with you to have destroyed you. ... And at Taberah, and at Massah, and at Kibrothhattaavah, ye provoked the Lord to wrath. Likewise when the Lord sent you from Kadeshbarnea,*

*saying, Go up and possess the land which I have given
you; then ye rebelled against the commandment of the
Lord your God, and ye believed Him not, nor heark-
ened to His voice* (Deuteronomy 9:7-8,22-23).

Despite it all, Moses adds: "Thy fathers went down into
Egypt with threescore and ten persons; and now the Lord thy
God hath made thee as the stars of heaven for multitude.
Therefore thou shalt love the Lord thy God, and keep His
charge, and His statutes, and His judgments, and His com-
mandments, alway" (Deut. 10:22–11:1).

Unfortunately, the Israelites lost sight of God again and
again until they made of themselves a dispossessed people.
Their rebellion was so persistent that the covenant of God was
passed from the Hebrews to non-Hebrew peoples of the world,
to people who were not endowed with the oracles of God or the
physical seed of the Messiah.

The will of God will be done in all the earth (see Mt. 6:10),
and the salvation of Christ will be preached to all the nations,
according to a plan set forth before the worlds were ever made!
The Hebrew people were to spread the knowledge of God to all
the Gentile world and they were to become "a light to lighten
the Gentiles" (Lk. 2:32a; see Is. 42:6; 49:6; 60:1-3; Mt. 4:16;
Acts 13:47; 28:28). So, despite their childish unruliness, insur-
rection, and idolatry, they would still reap the fruits of the
covenant and still bring forth the Messiah. Unfortunately,
some of the fruits would be bitter.

God has always known about the weaknesses of men and
women (see 1 Sam. 16:7; 1 Chron. 28:9; Jn. 2:24-25; 6:64; Acts
1:24). He knew that the covenant would be broken before He
ever made it, but He has used every human weakness and
misdirection to show us even more of His love and His mercy.
By the power of His Word, He came closer to His creation. By
the presence and character of Christ, God walked with and experienced the embodied life of His creation. By the Spirit of

Christ in the earth, God gave life to His laws, His expectations, and His contract. In His sojourn among men, He fashioned a *new contract* with His people from the pattern and fabric of the old. Through it all, God never abandoned His people.

> *Behold, the days come, saith the Lord, that I will make a new covenant with the house of Israel, and with the house of Judah: not according to the covenant that I made with their fathers in the day that I took them by the hand to bring them out of the land of Egypt; which My covenant they brake, although I was an husband unto them, saith the Lord: but this shall be the covenant that I will make with the house of Israel; after those days, saith the Lord, I will put My law in their inward parts, and write it in their hearts; and will be their God, and they shall be My people* (Jeremiah 31:31-33).

Jesus ratified the new contract by the shedding of His own blood (see Mt. 26:26-28). The rules governing sacrifices were renewed and accomplished once and for all in the sacrifice of Jesus Christ. The Messiah who was promised by the prophets of old satisfied the penalty for sin by giving up His life. Now He would make eternal intercession for the wrongs of mankind. Jesus Christ, the Righteous Branch, assumed the throne of David to rule forevermore. He is the eternal High Priest for the remission of sins (see Heb. 7:17-28). He is the ultimate and eternal fulfillment of the law for all who trust Him and obey His commandments (see Mt. 5:17).

> *In those days, and at that time, will I cause the Branch of righteousness to grow up unto David; and He shall execute judgment and righteousness in the land. ... For thus saith the Lord; David shall never want a man to sit upon the throne of the house of Israel; neither shall the priests the Levites want a man before Me to offer*

burnt offerings, and to kindle meat offerings, and to do sacrifice continually. ... As the host of heaven cannot be numbered, neither the sand of the sea measured: so will I multiply the seed of David My servant, and the Levites that minister unto Me (Jeremiah 33:15,17-18,22).

Jeremiah spoke clearly of Jesus Christ in prophecy. Even before the Lord Jesus came in the flesh, an angel of the Lord had identified Him as the eternal King and Son of the Highest:

And the angel said unto her, Fear not, Mary: for thou hast found favour with God. And, behold, thou shalt conceive in thy womb, and bring forth a son, and shalt call His name JESUS. He shall be great, and shall be called the Son of the Highest: and the Lord God shall give unto Him the throne of His father David: and He shall reign over the house of Jacob for ever; and of His kingdom there shall be no end (Luke 1:30-33).

God's contract was not destroyed in the wilderness around Sinai with the worship of the calf. It did not end after Israel disobeyed. Instead, God came to earth in the form of a man, Jesus Christ, to restore His creation to its perfect beginning. He came to demonstrate His absolute and unconditional love for mankind. He came to give power to those who believe, and to renew the promises made at Sinai. He came to satisfy and extend the terms of the old contract with more perfect benefits and the assurance of eternal life.

Jesus Christ, therefore, is God. "For in Him dwelleth all the fulness of the Godhead [God the Father, God the Son, and God the Holy Ghost] bodily" (Col. 2:9). Jesus asked His disciple, Philip, "...Have I been so long time with you, and yet hast thou not known Me, Philip? he that hath seen Me hath seen the Father... Believe Me that I am in the Father, and the

Father in Me..." (Jn. 14:9,11). Another time, Jesus said, "I and My Father are one" (Jn. 10:30).

Nearly 800 years before the angel appeared to Mary, Isaiah the prophet foretold the coming of the eternal king:

> *For unto us a child is born, unto us a son is given: and the government shall be upon His shoulder: and His name shall be called Wonderful, Counsellor, The mighty God, The everlasting Father, The Prince of Peace. Of the increase of His government and peace there shall be no end, upon the throne of David, and upon His kingdom, to order it, and to establish it with judgment and with justice from henceforth even for ever. The zeal of the Lord of hosts will perform this* (Isaiah 9:6-7).

Since Jesus was prophetically declared to be the "everlasting Father" and "The mighty God" who will govern forever, surely His contract with man cannot differ from the contract given at Sinai. The laws established in the old covenant must be the laws of the new covenant. The promises and rewards of the old contract must be the promises and rewards of the new contract.

It is clear that Jesus came to *complete* the work of God, with the crowning distinction that the new contract would be *based on faith* in Jesus Christ and would extend to Gentiles and Jews alike. So the promises of old have now come to all who believe and obey the words of Jesus Christ.

Knowing that man would not comprehend His character from the heavens, God entered His own created world to draw mankind back to Himself with a personal appeal and a tangible demonstration of His love. While the Jews in the wilderness wanted a God whom they could see (see Ex. 17:7; 32:1), they never dreamed that Jehovah would come in the flesh and tabernacle among His people! They didn't realize that He would touch their lives so intimately that He would feel their sorrows, share their struggles, and experience their pain! Little did they know that He would even die for them.

Calvary demonstrated the depth of God's utter hatred for sin and disobedience. It revealed the price of discipleship and the reality of God's unconditional love for mankind. Calvary paid the price for disobedience, won victory over sin and death through the resurrection, and made available to all mankind the promises and riches of God's contract. Because of Calvary, Christ dispatched the Holy Spirit to reconcile creation unto its Creator God.

Righteousness is based on faith. Even Abraham was considered righteous because it was *imputed to him* because of his faith (see Rom. 4:16–5:1). Even faith requires a sacrifice and discipline. God accepts us the way we are, but once He cleanses our hearts He requires us to *discipline the flesh*. In theory, if a believer could keep the law to the letter, he would be able to receive all the blessings of God and receive *unlimited power* because God could reach into his life without the obstructions of sin and satan. The sacrificial work of Christ calls us to reach for a higher state of holiness than the letter of the law requires. This comes only through faith in Jesus Christ and obedience to His Word. Those who accept His challenge will become children of God. He places His Spirit in our hearts and, ultimately, He will bring us into perfect unity with the Father.

The reward of obedience is the inheritance of Christ. God transforms those who abide by His contract into His children, and He gives them access to His wealth and His power (see Ex. 19:5-6).

The law is only for the beginners. It is merely a "basic protocol" for walking in line with God's plan. Paul urges us to go beyond the basics to a profound commitment that requires radical change and the deepest type of faith. Christ made that ultimate transformation a reality. Even in the Sermon on the Mount, He extended the written commandments to cover even the sins of thought! Adultery and murder could then "be committed" simply by *thinking* lustfully or with malicious anger. He required sacrificial love and separation from worldly pursuits. This new emphasis went to the core of our character and tapped the deepest reserves of faith.

The radical changes demanded by these new requirements set by Jesus can only be accomplished by the presence of His Spirit in our hearts! *We must receive the Holy Ghost to walk in righteousness.* Christ came to finish the work begun at Sinai, and the new contract is the logical extension of the old contract. Now we are led into obedience by the indwelling Spirit, and by that same Spirit we become children of God—we become Christlike.

What kind of God has all power bound up in Himself, and yet lavishes such sacrificial love and grace upon such insignificant creatures, giving us gifts so magnificent that imagination can't comprehend them! He gives us life without end and power to accomplish every positive thing we can conceive. He plants within us the Spirit that makes it happen. This sovereign King of the universe asks only that we recognize Him for who He is and that we remain within His protective plan. He took the form of a servant to illustrate His willingness to give everything in His benevolent hands to lift us up to our greatest potential and fulfill our greatest sufficiency! The omnipotent God of the universe even suffered the agony of death on a cross to demonstrate the passion of His commitment to our maximum empowerment.

Everything He said and did, from Genesis to Revelation, was geared to accomplish this purpose. God's intent was to rescue His creation from the throes of self-destruction. He put everything in place to remind us of His love. He pressed the earth with such delights of nature that only the blind of heart and mind could doubt there is a God. He preserved the record of His actions from the first moment He made us, and recorded His great love as a parent would for His child. He laid out a plan before us, mapping every obstacle. He sent us one reminder after the next, urging us to follow the path He made. He gave us every chance to see the glory set before us. Even now He urges us, "Just choose Me. Choose Me. Choose Me. And you'll win."

If we do not grasp anything else from the law, the prophets, and the Gospels, let us realize that they are a record of our *contractual obligation* to the One and Almighty God. They document the only way to win. The conclusion of the matter is this: "...Till heaven and earth pass, one jot or one tittle shall in no wise pass from the law, till all be fulfilled" (Mt. 5:18); "And it is easier for heaven and earth to pass, than one tittle of the law to fail" (Lk. 16:17).

The contract is valid forever; it will always be enforceable. The contract made in the law of Moses will never be put aside. Never! The agreement is infallible, and the rewards and judgments are sure. In the vast stretches of eternity, God's plan will still hold true.

"The Lord is not slack concerning His promise, as some men count slackness; but is longsuffering to us-ward, not willing that any should perish, but that all should come to repentance" (2 Pet. 3:9). Just because the promises were made a long time ago, and just because Jesus has not returned yet, does not mean He is not going to come. All of the law and the prophets depend on this single occurrence! Jesus said He would come, and He is coming!

John declares, "But as many as received Him, to them gave He power to become the sons of God, even to them that believe on His name" (Jn. 1:12). Those who receive Jesus also receive the promises made at Sinai! They receive all the privileges, rights, blessings, and power of a child of the one and only omnipotent God! "For I am not ashamed of the gospel of Christ: for it is the *power* of God unto salvation to every one that believeth; to the Jew first, and also to the Greek" (Rom. 1:16). *The Word is a contract for power.*

Common Sense

Nothing could be more unfair
Than a God who stayed up in the air,
Then made us guess from all we knew,
What He expected us to do.

You know the devil was not curt.
He got right down here in the dirt,
And the mess he made from carrying on
Got folk not knowing right from wrong.

And, by the way, there's something more
I have to ask to just be sure.
I'm not the kind with words to mince,
But, what became of common sense?

The children, they all run amok.
If parents try, they lock them up.
The state is giving out the drugs,
And laws are made to help the thugs.

Oh, Lord, we need Your Word real bad.
It is the only guide we've had.
Any other way, I can surely tell
Is straight up from the pits of hell.

Boy! Am I glad You wrote things down,
And sent some folk to spread it 'round.

'Cause if I know just what to do,
You can believe I'll pay my due.

And one more thing I need to say
To folk who want the easy way.
That as for me, I've come to see,
If it's worthwhile, it sure ain't free!

Chapter 19

The Word Is an Empowering Creed

The Word of God comes from God Himself. It is not a clever invention of human intellect or a man-made scheme to control mass behavior. God's Word exceeds the boundaries of man's knowledge and power. It bears the mark of the Author's infinite wisdom, supreme benevolence, and ultimate power. It is the imprimatur of God upon the nature, character, and history of man. As such, it is to be revered, received, and consumed as an exquisite delicacy. It is to be the object of daily devotion and continual meditation and study. It is to be believed, committed to memory, and taken to heart. It will mold and transform our doubtful character into the perfect image of God. The apostle Paul says:

All scripture is given by inspiration of God, and is profitable for doctrine, for reproof, for correction, for instruction in righteousness: that the man of God may be perfect, throughly furnished unto all good works (2 Timothy 3:16-17).

The apostle Peter adds:

...No prophecy of the scripture is of any private interpretation. For the prophecy came not in old time by the will of man: but holy men of God spake as they were moved by the Holy Ghost (2 Peter 1:20-21).

No Scripture is the product of any person's individual interpretation of events. The Bible is not some "collective unconscious motivation of several men" or their joint sociological considerations about God. It is not a collection of "cunningly devised fables" (2 Pet. 1:16), nor is it a library of well-preserved political expediencies or powerful sectarian dogmas. The Scripture is nothing less than the mind of God revealed to mankind. Men of God wrote these awesome words as they were led by the Holy Spirit. Therefore, Scripture contains direction from God, protection by God, and instructions from God—for hope, for strength, for righteousness, and for judgment.

The authorship of God distinguishes the Word from every other written document in human history! The Word comes from God Himself; thus it is in a category wholly different and apart from other literature. It is elevated above the merely allegorical, metaphorical, anecdotal, or scientific record. God's authority elevates it to the level of the divine. The Bible is an object of belief; it is a creed—not to be simply read and understood, but to be pondered, penetrated, and pursued with all the determination of a convicted heart and hungry mind!

God's living Word is to be lived, loved, and died for. It is a creed because it is the essence of faith, since "faith cometh by hearing, and hearing by the word of God" (Rom. 10:17).

When was the last time you read a novel with the objective of *living out the life of the protagonist* or fulfilling the expectations of the author? Only the misguided would finish a story and then go out to repeat the actions of the characters. No one would be expected to study *Alice in Wonderland* or *Huckleberry Finn*, for example, and then try to become Alice or Huckleberry to satisfy the expectations of Lewis Carroll or Mark Twain!

The Word of God is unique. God is the author and the main character. The Author clearly invites every reader to do as He does and to become what He is: "...If any man will come after Me, let him deny himself, and take up his cross, and follow Me" (Mt. 16:24). Allegiance unto death is the demand of the disciples of Jesus Christ.

To believe the Word is to do it. The apostle James declared, "Even so faith, if it hath not works, is dead, being alone" (Jas. 2:17). He encourages us:

> *But be ye doers of the word, and not hearers only, deceiving your own selves. For if any be a hearer of the word, and not a doer, he is like unto a man beholding his natural face in a glass: for he beholdeth himself, and goeth his way, and straightway forgetteth what manner of man he was. But whoso looketh into the perfect law of liberty, and continueth therein, he being not a forgetful hearer, but a doer of the work, this man shall be blessed in his deed* (James 1:22-25).

The power of inspired faith has no limits (see Mt. 17:20), but it hinges on recognizing God in His Word. Those who change the Word wash away their faith and weaken their power. Those who doubt can have nothing (see Jas. 1:6-8) because "without faith it is impossible to please Him: for he that cometh to God must believe that He is, and that He is a rewarder of them that diligently seek Him" (Heb. 11:6). The Word of God is a creed that empowers the "diligently seeking" believer. It is "the power of God unto salvation" (Rom. 1:16), and the "righteousness of God revealed" (Rom. 1:17). It is our hope (see Ps. 130:5), our strength (see Ps. 119:28), and our judgment (see Is. 28:13). At its very core, it is the presence of God acknowledged and exalted.

The Psalmist declared that the Word of his Counselor helped him avoid evil: "...by the word of Thy lips I have kept me from the paths of the destroyer" (Ps. 17:4). He said, "Thy word have I hid in mine heart, that I might not sin against Thee" (Ps. 119:11), and "Thy testimonies also are my delight and my counsellors" (Ps. 119:24). He prayed, "Open Thou mine eyes, that I may behold wondrous things out of Thy law" (Ps. 119:18). The Word of God unravels the mysteries of life and reveals them to us.

In Psalm 119, King David repeatedly declared the blessings and benefits of living by God's Word. He declared, "Blessed are the undefiled in the way, who walk in the law of the Lord" (Ps. 119:1), and "Blessed are they that keep His testimonies, and that seek Him with the whole heart" (Ps. 119:2). David asked one of the most common and important questions a person can ask: "Wherewithal shall a young man cleanse his way?" Then he answered his own question: "By taking heed thereto according to Thy word" (Ps. 119:9).

Psalm 119 is the longest chapter in the Bible, and it is totally dedicated to describing the divine value and worth of God's Word: "And I will walk at liberty: for I seek Thy precepts" (Ps. 119:45). "This is my comfort in my affliction: for Thy word hath quickened me" (Ps. 119:50). "The law of Thy mouth is better unto me than thousands of gold and silver" (Ps. 119:72). "Unless Thy law had been my delights, I should then have perished in mine affliction" (Ps. 119:92). "Thou through Thy commandments hast made me wiser than mine enemies: for they are ever with me" (Ps. 119:98). "I have more understanding than all my teachers: for thy testimonies are my meditation." (Ps. 119:99). "I rejoice at Thy word, as one that findeth great spoil" (Ps. 119:162).

In this one chapter, the Psalmist declared that joy, peace, wisdom, long life, and even salvation and righteousness may be found in the Word of God! He said the Word of God was established to be everlasting and is settled in Heaven. He confessed that he clings to the Word in affliction and persecution to find comfort from his pain. It protected him against shame and he never turned away from it. He said God is to be found in His Word (see Ps. 119:57-64).

God Himself is the source of power in His Word! The Word of God contains His Spirit as much as it contains His wisdom, affection, and direction. The Word of God is to us what the Nazarite vow was to Samson—the key or the place where the power of God may be found and applied to our situation. Without His Word, we are lost and undone as other men and women. The Word of God has the power to open our spiritual eyes to see more deeply into the things of this world and the next. If we fail to acquire this faith and power, we will waste our lives and possibly injure the breadth of creation. If we overlook God's Word, we will sever the line and the branch of a soul intended to reach God.

"Whoso despiseth the word shall be destroyed: but he that feareth the commandment shall be rewarded" (Prov. 13:13). "Therefore as the fire devoureth the stubble, and the flame consumeth the chaff, so their root shall be as rottenness, and their blossom shall go up as dust: *because they have cast away the law of the Lord of hosts, and despised the word of the Holy One of Israel*" (Is. 5:24).

Hear the Word of the Lord (Jer. 22:29)

...If ye continue in My word, then are ye My disciples indeed; and ye shall know the truth, and the truth shall make you free (John 8:31-32).

...Behold, their ear is uncircumcised, and they cannot hearken: behold, the word of the Lord is unto them a reproach; they have no delight in it (Jeremiah 6:10).

Whosoever therefore shall be ashamed of Me and of My words in this adulterous and sinful generation; of him also shall the Son of man be ashamed, when He cometh in the glory of His Father with the holy angels (Mark 8:38).

...If a man love Me, he will keep My words: and My Father will love him, and We will come unto him, and make Our abode with him (John 14:23).

It is "not as though the word of God hath taken none effect" (Rom. 9:6a). If we walk away from God's Word, we might as well take the sun from the sky or watch the stars die one by one! God withholds the latter rain to those who deny His Word. Our stretch of land (our life) will turn to barren heaps of dust and cracking clay with crusty clods above and nothing down below. It is the Word of God and His promises that make us children of God. The seed of Abraham did not of itself blossom into trees of righteousness. It did not make Isaac's children sons of God. Only the divine Word of promise made them the children of God (see Rom. 9:7-14). Without the Word of God and His promises, every green thing would die on its vine and hope in the Father would be a certain vanity. Praise God our Redeemer lives, and our faith is built upon a sure hope (see Heb. 6:19):

He that is of God heareth God's words (John 8:47a).

If ye abide in Me, and My words abide in you, ye shall ask what ye will, and it shall be done unto you (John 15:7).

Verily, verily, I say unto you, If a man keep My saying, he shall never see death (John 8:51).

...He that heareth My word, and believeth on Him that sent Me, hath everlasting life, and shall not come into condemnation; but is passed from death unto life (John 5:24).

O earth, earth, earth, hear the word of the Lord (Jeremiah 22:29).

Chapter 20

The Word Is a Power Tool

God's Word has carved out the whole world. It has turned the soil. It has planted meadows. It has raised the mountaintops.

God puts His Word into our hearts. He validates the word of all His children. He substantiates the words that fall down from their lips.

* * * * *

Creation itself and the call of life and death are bound up in the breath of God, and in the power of His Word. Our life is sustained by the Word of God, for we cannot live by bread alone, but by every word that proceeds out of His mouth (see Deut. 8:3; Mt. 4:4; Lk. 4:4).

"By the word of the Lord were the heavens made; and all the host of them by the breath of His mouth. ... For He spake, and it was done; He commanded, and it stood fast" (Ps. 33:6,9). "…The worlds were framed by the word of God, so that things which are seen were not made of things which do appear" (Heb. 11:3). "But the heavens and the earth, which are now, by the same word are kept in store, reserved unto fire against the day of judgment and perdition of ungodly men" (2 Pet. 3:7).

God's Word is spirit and life (see Jn. 6:63). It breaks the ice of ages past and quickens the day of salvation:

He sendeth forth His commandment upon earth: His word runneth very swiftly. He giveth snow like wool: He scattereth the hoarfrost like ashes. He casteth forth His ice like morsels…. He sendeth out His word, and melteth them… (Psalm 147:15-18).

All of nature bows its knee to the powerful Word of God:

Praise ye Him, sun and moon: praise Him, all ye stars of light. Praise Him, ye heavens of heavens, and ye waters that be above the heavens. Let them praise the name of the Lord: for He commanded, and they were created. He hath also stablished them for ever and ever: He hath made a decree which shall not pass (Psalm 148:3-6).

God's Word will never fail:

For as the rain cometh down, and the snow from heaven, and returneth not thither, but watereth the earth, and maketh it bring forth and bud, that it may give seed to the sower, and bread to the eater: so shall My word be that goeth forth out of My mouth: it shall not return unto Me void, but it shall accomplish that which I please, and it shall prosper in the thing whereto I sent it (Isaiah 55:10-11).

"For I will hasten My word to perform it." (Jer. 1:12b). "Is not [God's] word like a fire?...like a hammer that breaketh the rock in pieces?" (Jer. 23:29) It is a blazing plow to till the soil for seed, a fervent torch to melt the crystal glazier, a hot and crackling spark to set the world in motion!

"Great is our Lord, and of great power: His understanding is infinite" (Ps. 147:5). It is this wonderful, powerful Word that the Lord freely lends to His children! For Christ delivered the Word, and God has granted power to the Word received in His name: "Behold, I give unto you power..." (Lk. 10:19). "He that heareth you heareth Me; and he that despiseth you despiseth Me; and he that despiseth Me despiseth Him that sent Me" (Lk. 10:16).

*I have manifested Thy name unto the men which Thou gavest Me out of the world: Thine they were, and Thou gavest them Me; and they have kept **Thy word**. Now they have known that all things whatsoever Thou hast given Me are of Thee. For I have given unto them the **words** which Thou gavest Me; and they have received them, and have known surely that I came out from Thee, and they have believed that Thou didst send Me. ... I have given them Thy **word**; and the world hath hated them, because they are not of the world, even as I am not of the world. I pray not that Thou shouldest take them out of the world, but that Thou shouldest keep them from the evil. They are not of the world, even as I am not of the world. Sanctify them through Thy truth: Thy **word** is truth. As Thou hast sent Me into the world, even so have I also sent them into the world* (John 17:6-8; 14-18).

The Lord has given us the words of the Father that sanctify us through faith and bring us into perfect oneness with

Christ. He ratifies His Word upon our lips so all the world may know that He has sent us.

> *Verily I say unto you, Whatsoever ye shall bind on earth shall be bound in heaven: and whatsoever ye shall loose on earth shall be loosed in heaven. Again I say unto you, That if two of you shall agree on earth as touching any thing that they shall ask, it shall be done for them of My Father which is in heaven* (Matthew 18:18-19).

When we come into unity with Jesus Christ, the power of the spoken Word of God illuminates the channels of our faith by the presence of the Holy Ghost inside of us and is validated by God Himself. This proves the righteousness of our Lord, propels the work of healing mankind, and reveals the love and allegiance of Jesus Christ in His ongoing redemption of the world.

God will not let His Word in us fall down to the ground. We have become a showpiece of God's power. He sets us up on His banqueting table like a grand bouquet of flowers from His garden (see Mt. 5:14-16).

Our God has often changed the earth to demonstrate His awesome power. He has stopped the sun and moon (see Josh. 10:12-14); He has "dried" the dark rain clouds (see 1 Kings 17:1). Also, He can move mountains (see Mt. 21:21) and stand seas upright like the old Great Wall of China. He would remake the earth all over again before He would let His words fail to follow their intended course (see Lk. 21:33).

He has sent armies of hornets, locusts, and flies against those who defy Him (see Ex. 8:20-24; 10:12-15; 23:28), and He has darkened the brightest sky (see Ex. 10:21-26). He has showered down storms of ice and fire to show His strong commitment to His people (see Ex. 9:22-26; 1 Kings 18:37-38). God will even raise satan to his greatest strength to demonstrate the power of His Word! (See Revelation 13.)

Return to your first love, dear child of God. The Father is waiting for you. He said, "...Israel is My son, even My first-born" (Ex. 4:22). This is the symbol that Jesus wore to Calvary, the emblem of God's beloved Church. We are His sons and daughters; not just *any* son or daughter, we are the first and favored objects of His love whom He has made oracles of His Word. Fulfill your destiny and speak with the power of God behind each and every word! *Pray* in God's great shower of His strength. *Cast out demons* from the earth with confidence! *Speak in tongues* into universal understanding for the angels and for men. God gives the comprehension from outside and from within. *Prophesy* and place things in time. God will verify your words as His very thoughts come from your mind! Be bold to *declare God's healing* to mend bodies, minds, and souls! *Speak* with the *power* of Him who owns the universe. Speak with all the *creativity* of Him who made the earth.

This is unleashed power, a nuclear explosion of our faith. God rests, rules, and rides upon the power of the Word within us. Speak power over the earth, for you carry the Word and promise of God!

But first, you must return to God. First, take the step of *love* with all of your heart, mind, soul, and strength. The first step calls for total involvement. Look to Calvary for the test of how much love it takes to yield full empowerment. It is absolute and undiluted love.

Secondly, exercise your *faith* to step outside of self and into God. Let your faith translate you away from the mundane things of the earth. Yield to the full work of faith to totally transform your mind. Faith's goal is the full transfiguration of everything we think so we might stand with holy men of yesteryear without doubt, without question, and without fear.

Faith goes to God with proof of our unremitted loyalty (see Jn. 20:17). Have the faith that bears each circumstance without giving sin a chance. Stand in faith and call out what is not as though it is!

Third, you must be *obedient* beyond what you think or see. Like trusting children, we must humbly walk for the Lord into death and hell for the cause of eternity—being obedient to the letter, obedient to the Spirit—poised to prove the righteousness of God. Our lives must say to our Father the words He has said to us (carefully read what I'm saying now):

Ask me, Lord, and it shall be given You; seek me, Lord, and Ye shall find me; knock, and I will open up my heart and soul and mind! (See Matthew 7:7.)

Up to now, dear Lord, You have asked nothing of me to do. Ask me, Lord, that I may prove I am loyal, faithful, and true (see John 16:24).

* * * * *

Within His Majesty

I love the Lord; He rescued me.
He gave me joy. He taught me liberty.
And now my soul is kept within the depth
Of His blessed sanctity.
And when the times get hard,
I find my Lord where I know that He will be—
Within His victory,
That's where He comforts me.
Within His majesty,
I love the Lord.

I love the Lord, and He loves me.
He showed me how to live life peaceably.
So now the thing we've got is such a lot,

More than the world can see.
But when my heart grows weak,
I know to seek Him where He'll always be—
Within His royalty,
That's where He strengthens me,
Within His majesty,
I love the Lord.

I love the Lord; He set me free.
When I was lost, His mercy lifted me.
And now my hope will rest on nothing less
Than what He's promised me.
So when the world is cold,
I've learned to hold on to the truth He made me see.
Within His sovereignty,
That's where He pardons me,
Within His majesty,
I love the Lord.

I love the Lord; He died for me.
He took the blame and all the penalty.
And there's a star above, unselfish love,
That all the world may see.
Before the end is here,
Let's all come near and give Him loyalty.
The Lamb that is worthy,
The One who died for me,
Within His majesty,
I love the Lord!

Oh beloved,

Be born again by the Word of God (1 Pet. 1:23).

Be sanctified by the Word of God (Jn. 17:17).

Be fed by the Word of God (Lk. 4:4; 1 Pet. 2:2).

Be filled by the Word of God (Col. 3:16).

Be protected by the Word of God (Heb. 4:12).

Be guided by the Word of God (Ps. 119:105).

Be strengthened by the Word of God (Ps. 119:28).

Oh, Lord, order our steps in Your Word.

Chapter 21

The Word Is God

Jesus Christ is the revelation and complete expression of the Father. He is the manifestation of God's holiness in the highest character of man. He is the extraction of God's essence, the undefiled carriage of His person, and our earthly reference and personal depiction of His nature. Jesus Christ is God. "In the beginning was the Word...and the Word was God" (Jn. 1:1).

When time first awakened, Jesus Christ was there. He made the first ray of light and brought to earth the first stream of air. Of Jesus Christ there is no beginning and no end. His feet have trod the corridors of eternity. He has come from everlasting to everlasting. His day is infinite!

When God made the heavens and appointed to each star a certain orbit, He was there. He was in the Father when the compass of the earth was rolled between His palms and when the ancient clay was spun into its form. He made the fine division between the darkest dawn and daybreak. He closed the evening shadows with the falling lids of night. It was He who breathed life into the hollow soul of man.

Your father Abraham rejoiced to see My day: and he saw it, and was glad. Then said the Jews unto Him, Thou art not yet fifty years old, and hast Thou seen Abraham? Jesus said unto them, Verily, verily, I say unto you, Before Abraham was, I am (John 8:56-58).

Lord, Thou hast been our dwelling place in all generations. Before the mountains were brought forth, or ever Thou hadst formed the earth and the world, even from everlasting to everlasting, Thou art God (Psalm 90:1-2).

In Heaven, Jesus said, "...Sacrifice and offering Thou wouldest not, but a body hast Thou prepared Me: ...Lo, I come...to do Thy will, O God" (Heb. 10:5,7). When the fullness of time had come, Jesus prepared Himself to become the sacrificed Lamb of God. He was the supreme revelation of God's love and mercy. Out of God He came, so that out of Him, God would come.

He told Moses, "And let them make Me a sanctuary; that I may dwell among them" (Ex. 25:8). They didn't realize then that the New Covenant sanctuary of God would be the body of Jesus Christ, and those who believe on Him.

Oh! The Lord God Himself went high and low
To Heaven's peak
And down to hell's floor
To save His dear creation,
To bring to earth salvation.
His Spirit and His flesh
He would bestow.
His deepest love, the Lord God
Longed to show.

The prophet Isaiah foretold the coming of the Lord when he proclaimed, "Behold, a virgin shall be with child, and shall bring forth a son, and they shall call His name Emmanuel, which being interpreted is, God with us" (Mt. 1:23). Jesus came to declare the Word of God.

God, who at sundry times and in divers manners spake in time past unto the fathers by the prophets, hath in these last days spoken unto us by His Son, whom He hath appointed heir of all things, by whom also He made the worlds; who being the brightness of His glory, and the express image of His person, and upholding all things by the word of His power, when He had by Himself purged our sins, sat down on the right hand of the Majesty on high (Hebrews 1:1-3).

The Word of God is Jesus Christ. He is in the Father, and the Father is in Him (see Jn. 14:11). Out of Him are the issues of life, and out of Him proceeds the power of new birth from on high. Through Him we may reach the Father (see Jn. 14:6). Apart from Him, no man can know God or see Him. Now we know the Father and have seen Him, for Jesus has declared Him (see Jn. 17:26). This knowledge of God is life eternal (see Jn. 17:3).

For there are three that bear record in heaven, the Father, the Word, and the Holy Ghost: and these three are one. ... If we receive the witness of men, the witness of God is greater: for this is the witness of God which He hath testified of His Son. He that believeth on the Son of God hath the witness in himself: he that believeth not God hath made Him a liar; because he believeth not the record that God gave of His Son. And this is the record, that God hath given to us eternal life, and this life is in His Son. He that hath the Son hath life; and he that hath not the Son of God hath not life. These things have I written unto you that believe on the name of the Son of God; that ye may know that ye have eternal life, and that ye may believe on the name of the Son of God. And this is the confidence that we have in Him, that, if we ask any thing according to His will, He heareth us: and if we know that He hear us, whatsoever we ask, we know that we have the petitions that we desired of Him (1 John 5:7,9-15).

Out of God, He came, so that out of Him, God would come.

Part VI

The Gift of Love

Chapter 22

Merger

*A*nd the Lord God commanded the man, *saying, Of every tree of the garden thou mayest freely eat: but of the tree of the knowledge of good and evil, thou shalt not eat of it: for in the day that thou eatest thereof thou shalt surely die* (Genesis 2:16-17).

For the wages of sin is death; but the gift of God is eternal life through Jesus Christ our Lord (Romans 6:23).

Yet Adam sinned.

Adam's sin separated man from God, the source of life. It created a deep and seemingly impenetrable gorge between the spirit of man and the quickening Spirit of God. Sin set at odds the will of man with the will of his Creator. It tore apart the spiritual connection between the Almighty God and His earthly creation and drained mankind of divine life. Sin loosed the flow of death into the veins of its sad and uncertain victims.

In that very instant, the search for the Messiah began.

Adam had lost his first home. Now, the Spirit who had moved upon the face of the waters, and was light and life to the created son of God, had left the mind, flesh, and spirit of its host. Naked and empty, he was fearful in his new and strange condition. He was weak, wanting, and fallen into shame. The aging clock began at the same time as the search for God. The prayers, pleas, and sacrifices began as mankind searched for the Messiah.

Year after year, the first couple waited. Every new birth kindled afresh their hope: "Is this the one who was promised? Will he crush the serpent's head?" Some hoped that it would be Enoch, but then he "was taken" (see Gen. 5:24). Soon the question was no longer asked and hope faded to the dimmest flicker of light. Darkness covered the earth as "every imagination of the thoughts of [man's] heart was only evil continually" (Gen. 6:5).

The Lord said, "...My spirit shall not always strive with man" (Gen. 6:3a) as His creation was given over to a reprobate mind to do the most abominable things with their hearts filled with all unrighteousness, fornication, wickedness, covetousness, and maliciousness (see Rom. 1:28-29). God looked down upon the earth, and said, "And behold, I, even I, do bring a flood of waters upon the earth, to destroy all flesh, wherein is the breath of life, from under heaven; and every thing that is in the earth shall die" (Gen. 6:17).

The first death was with water, and the second death will be with fire. The first rebirth is with water, and the second rebirth is with fire.

In the years from Noah to Jesus, many prophets came and went, keeping the hope for a "Kinsman Redeemer" alive in the hearts of men. God longed to transform all who believed and obeyed Him into children of God. The dying earth groaned in its longing to give birth to the great Messiah. The prayers of the righteous were caught up in the promise of His coming. All of creation waited with bated breath in anticipation of the coming Lord and King.

His Spirit would fill the earth with new life (see Joel 2:28). He would establish the eternal Kingdom of God described to Adam (see Gen. 3:15), Abram (see Gen. 12:3), Jacob (see Gen. 49:10), Moses (see Deut. 18:15,19), David (see Ps. 16:10), Isaiah (see Is. 52:13–53:12), Jeremiah (see Jer. 23:5; 31:31-33; 33:15), and Daniel (see Dan. 9:24-26). Every nation would submit to His rule (see Mic. 4:1-4). He would reclaim and conquer the domain lost by Adam, and reunite the Spirit of God with the earthly creation. He would win victory over death and the grave (see Is. 25:8).

In a dark hour of national servitude, after 400 years of silence devoid of a true prophetic witness, the authoritative voice of the prophet, John the Baptist, exploded from the barren wilderness with the startling declaration, "The kingdom of heaven is at hand" (Mt. 3:2). The religious rulers asked him who he was, and John shook his head, "And he confessed, and denied not; but confessed, I am not the Christ. ...I am the voice of one crying in the wilderness, Make straight the way of the Lord, as said the prophet Esaias" (Jn. 1:20,23).

John baptized multitudes of people for the remission of sins in the waters of the Jordan River. Just as the Great Flood had symbolized the washing away of sin, as did the passages of Israel through the Red Sea and through the Jordan River, John's baptism was another sign marking the cleansing from sin. Death of the wicked always preceeded the symbolic baptism. In the Great Flood it was the wicked world; at the Red Sea, it was the Egyptian army; and at the Jordan River it was all adults over 20 years old who refused to go up against the Canaanites. In each case the waters symbolically washed away the stain of sin. But John himself spoke of a second baptism that could only be done by the Messiah. He said, "I indeed baptize you with water; but He shall baptize you with the Holy Ghost and with fire" (see Mt. 3:11; Mk. 1:8; Lk. 3:16; Jn. 1:26-33).

The water baptism of John and the promise of the Holy Ghost baptism with fire signaled the beginning of a new era and a new relationship with God. Although the symbols of water and fire were etched in the minds of the Jews from the ancient stories of the journey to Sinai when Israel was led by the cloud of mist by day and the pillar of fire by night, these two baptisms brought all the promises of God to a new height of expectation. But what did John mean by the baptism of the Holy Ghost and fire?

The prophets had already spoken of a new law for the heart. Jeremiah foretold a new covenant that required a new spirit:

Behold, the days come, saith the Lord, that I will make a new covenant with the house of Israel, and with the house of Judah: ...I will put My law in their inward parts, and write it in their hearts; and will be their God, and they shall be My people (Jeremiah 31:31,33).

Ezekiel also prophesied of a new heart and a new spirit:

...Thus saith the Lord God.... And I will give them one heart, and I will put a new spirit within you; and I will take the stony heart out of their flesh, and will give them an heart of flesh (Ezekiel 11:17,19).

Ezekiel also said of God:

A new heart also will I give you, and a new spirit will I put within you: and I will take away the stony heart out of your flesh, and I will give you an heart of flesh. And I will put My spirit within you, and cause you to walk in My statutes, and ye shall keep My judgments, and do them (Ezekiel 36:26-27).

Could it be that the Messiah would make the commandments a part of the character of each individual believer? Would He somehow elevate the human disposition so the believer might live more obediently to God? Would He actually give him the Spirit of God?

John immediately recognized Jesus as the Messiah at the Jordan. He declared, "...Behold the Lamb of God, which taketh away the sin of the world" (Jn. 1:29). John reluctantly baptized Jesus in the Jordan River, and gave this report:

> ...I saw the Spirit descending from heaven like a dove, and it abode upon Him. And I knew Him not: but He that sent me to baptize with water, the same said unto me, Upon whom thou shalt see the Spirit descending, and remaining on Him, the same is He which baptizeth with the Holy Ghost. And I saw, and bare record that this is the Son of God (John 1:32-34).

This was perhaps the first time anyone had been baptized by the Spirit of God. Jesus received the baptisms of water and Spirit at once. The Spirit of God had finally returned to the temple that God had intended as its dwelling place, the body of His creation. At last, the Holy Ghost had entered human flesh to give eternal power and significance to life.

"What? know ye not that your body is the temple of the Holy Ghost which is in you, which ye have of God, and ye are not your own?" (1 Cor. 6:19) "...Ye are the temple of the living God; as God hath said, I will dwell in them, and walk in them; and I will be their God, and they shall be My people" (2 Cor. 6:16; see also Jn. 2:19-21).

The Scriptures say that Jesus never baptized with water (see Jn. 4:2), but He often spoke about the coming Holy Ghost. He once told a Pharisee named Nicodemus, "...Except a man be born of water and of the Spirit, he cannot enter into the kingdom of God" (Jn. 3:5).

At the Jewish Feast of Tabernacles, Jesus said, "He that believeth on Me, as the scripture hath said, out of his belly shall flow rivers of living water" (Jn. 7:38). John, the apostle, noted after this passage, "But this spake He of the Spirit, which they that believe on Him should receive: for the Holy Ghost was not yet given; because that Jesus was not yet glorified" (Jn. 7:39).

Although there is some debate about the meaning of Jesus' words referring to the Spirit, the Gospel is clear that it would only be given after Christ was glorified. Within a few verses, the apostle John traced the time line from the first mention of Jesus' glorification up to the giving of the Holy Ghost. In John 12:16, he says that the disciples understood the triumphant reentry into Jerusalem in the context of Zechariah's prophecy only after He was glorified.

Jesus prepared His disciples for His death by saying, "...The hour is come, that the Son of man should be glorified. Verily, verily, I say unto you, Except a corn of wheat fall into the ground and die, it abideth alone: but if it die, it bringeth forth much fruit" (Jn. 12:23-24). Jesus reminded His disciples that His death is required, and encouraged Judas Iscariot to complete his work of betrayal quickly. Then He comforted His disciples with these words: "...Now is the Son of man glorified, and God is glorified in Him" (Jn. 13:31).

Jesus' comment to the disciples seems to imply that He would be glorified by the crucifixion, yet after His resurrection from the grave, Jesus told Mary, "...Touch Me not; for I am not yet ascended to My Father: but go to My brethren, and say unto them, I ascend unto My Father, and your Father; and to My God, and your God" (Jn. 20:17). This implies that Jesus had to present Himself to the Father before He could give the Holy Ghost. He explicitly acknowledged the new relationship of the disciples to God as both children and subjects. Finally, in John 20:22, Jesus breathed on His disciples and said, "Receive ye the Holy Ghost."

If the chronology in the Gospel of John is accurate, this was the giving of the Holy Ghost predicted by the Old Testament prophets and John the Baptist. It is the first official act of Jesus Christ among His assembled disciples after His resurrection. No doubt, it means that His glorification had occurred the exact same day.

The baptism of Christ foretold by John the Baptist must refer to the gift of the Holy Ghost imparted by Christ after His crucifixion, resurrection, and brief visit to the Father. This baptism is not optional for the believer; Christ told Nicodemus that "except a man be born of water and of the Spirit, he cannot enter into the Kingdom of God (Jn. 3:5)!

To enter into eternal life, one must surrender to God through Jesus Christ, repudiating satan and sin (this is new birth by water), and must take in the Spirit of God (this is new birth by the Spirit).

All the work of Jesus is important for our lives. We need to understand all of His deeds and practice them in some sense. Yet, of all of these, the culminating work of our Savior—the work that makes Him Messiah and not merely prophet—is the work of giving the Holy Ghost after His resurrection. The work of salvation is incomplete without the baptism of the Spirit. According to John the Baptist, Jesus came for the explicit purpose of baptizing with the Holy Ghost and with fire. Yet, this could only be done after His sacrifice and resurrection from the grave (see Jn. 16:7).

According to the prophets of old, the Spirit would be planted into the flesh of the believer, allowing them to embody the eternal covenant of God! That means that God's Word, principles, statutes, ordinances, and ways would literally be carried in the hearts and flesh of the believer!

Remember that God's power derives from His promises and relationship to us (see Ex. 19). The "giving of the Spirit" would therefore be the "giving of power" to the extent that it represented the embodiment of the covenant promises and our identification with the family of God. We have some evidence for this since on the Day of Pentecost, the disciples received the *power* of the Holy Ghost. This was the same calendar day as the "giving of the covenant" at Sinai (see Ex. 12 and 19).

As for the "baptism of fire," it may be synonymous with the baptism of the Spirit, especially since the experience on the Day of Pentecost involved "cloven tongues like as of fire" (see Acts 2:1-4). I believe it also refers to Jesus' final judgment of the world and the destruction of the wicked (see Mal. 3:1-5; 4:1-4).

When Adam lost the fight with satan (see Rom. 5:12a), our whole race become subject to the dominion of the archenemy of our souls. We became slaves to sin, assumed the nature of the evil one, and took on the spirit of rebellion, becoming enemies of God. Death reigned supreme in us from Adam until Christ (see 1 Cor. 15:22) under the rule of satan (see Rom. 5:14a,17a). Because of one man's disobedience, many were lost in sin and separated from their Creator (see Rom. 5:19), and flesh governed the wills of men, who were subject to the domination of lust and pride (see Rom. 3:23; 6:16).

Now Christ is risen from the dead (see 1 Cor. 15:20), and life has swallowed up death in victory (see Is. 25:8). Life conquered death because Christ defeated satan and crushed the head of that old serpent (see Gen. 3:15). By His righteousness, Christ overcame the spirit of the enemy and defied death and sin. Now He reigns as Lord over all the earth, justifying many who were once condemned (see Rom. 5:18).

Christ said, "...how can one enter into a strong man's house, and spoil his goods, except he first bind the strong man? and then he will spoil his house" (Mt. 12:29). He demonstrated this when He bound satan and spoiled his earthly home. We can be sure that He will bind the demon again and destroy him forevermore (see Rev. 20:1-3,7-10).

This Is the Kingdom of God on Earth

Many people were drawn to Jesus because of His miracles and healing, and He was very conscious of the possibility that the fervor of the people for signs and wonders would cause them to overlook His primary role as Messiah, the Giver of the Spirit and the new covenant. He often commanded the people whom He had healed to keep His identity secret, primarily to avoid this possibility (see Mt. 8:4; 9:30; 12:16). He even told His closest disciples to keep the vision of the transfiguration to themselves until He had risen from the dead (see Mt. 17:9). Perhaps He did this to highlight the fact that He was not merely a prophet, but the King who would reign forevermore (see Dan. 2:44).

Jesus answered the antagonistic demand by the scribes and Pharisees that He provide a "sign" with a scathing rebuke:

...An evil and adulterous generation seeketh after a sign; and there shall no sign be given to it, but the sign of the prophet Jonas: for as Jonas was three days and three nights in the whale's belly; so shall the Son of man be three days and three nights in the heart of the earth. The men of Nineveh shall rise in judgment with this generation, and shall condemn it: because they repented at the preaching of Jonas; and, behold, a greater than Jonas is here. The queen of the south shall rise up in the judgment with this generation, and shall condemn it: for she came from the uttermost parts of the earth to hear the wisdom of Solomon; and, behold, a greater than Solomon is here. When the unclean spirit is gone out of a man, he walketh through dry places, seeking rest, and findeth none. Then he saith, I will return into my house from whence I came out; and

when he is come, he findeth it empty, swept, and garnished. Then goeth he, and taketh with himself seven other spirits more wicked than himself, and they enter in and dwell there: and the last state of that man is worse than the first. Even so shall it be also unto this wicked generation (Matthew 12:39-45).

What good is healing, when a man is not changed? What good is the casting out of demons, if the Spirit of God does not come in? What good is a sign to the unbelieving? Peter says, "For if after they have escaped the pollutions of the world through the knowledge of the Lord and Saviour Jesus Christ, they are again entangled therein, and overcome, the latter end is worse with them than the beginning" (2 Pet. 2:20).

To know the truth and then reject it is worse than never to have known truth at all (see Mt. 26:24)! To see the miracles of Jesus and then walk away is worse than never seeing them at all (see Jn. 15:24)! Christ Himself said that to turn our backs on the Holy Ghost is a sin incapable of pardon (see Mt. 12:31). It is the Holy Ghost who changes the inner man, so when we reject His life-changing power, we turn away from the light and condemn ourselves to darkness. When we reject all of the Spirit's urgings to repentance and walk away from God, we have "slammed the door" on grace itself, and rejected the gift of love.

Christ knew the religious leaders' request for a sign was a snare from satan himself. The devil had tried once before to question His divinity by asking for a sign (see Mt. 4:5-7; Lk. 4:9-12). Jesus knew the scribes and Pharisees were in the grip of satan, since their plan was to murder Him (see Mt. 12:14). That is why He pointed them away from the usual signs and toward the resurrection. He gave them a greater sign than they could have hoped for when He pointed them to His victory over the grave and the conquest of sin and satan! It was to be the greatest healing stroke of all time. He also told them about the necessity of receiving the Spirit, so old things would pass away, and all things would become new.

Present-day believers who read the gospel and discover Christ as Healer, Teacher, Feeder, and Helper but fail to discover the Giver of the Spirit, are incomplete. The power of God is not in mere benevolence; nor is it in social and political change. The power of God is found in the giving of the Holy Ghost. Christ did not come simply to rescue the poor or to set the world's affairs in order. He declared, "My kingdom is not of this world" (Jn. 18:36).

Christ did not come merely to heal the physically ill or to cast out demons from the many who were possessed. This is the same mistake the Jews made 2,000 years ago! It is a grave error to see the Kingdom of God as temporal instead of spiritual. It is to think of Christ as a historical hero of social reform but not as Messiah and King.

If we receive power from the indwelling Christ, it will be *for the same purpose*. Our first priority is to look for Heaven, and not for earth; our first goal is spiritual, not temporal (see Mt. 6:19-34). Healing, miracles, and blessings from God are for the Kingdom of God (see Lk. 10:17-20), not simply to establish a kingdom in this world. The Spirit of God, first and foremost, is out to make us citizens of Heaven and children of the Kingdom to come.

Christ came to establish a spiritual Kingdom by planting a spiritual seed that would grow up into life eternal in the bodies of believers. He came to put God on the inside of man and to fashion a Kingdom from within. This indwelling Spirit is the treasure of God's grace and the revelation of Christ in the life of His creation. The Spirit is the outpouring of the Word into flesh, the manifestation of a new and glorious age—the Kingdom of God on earth.

* * * * *

One Holy, Royal Nation

Some of you are solitary figures.
Some of you are building wings, some bridges,
others fixtures.
Some of you are columns, some foundations—
The sum of you, one holy, royal nation.

Some of you have deep, discerning visions.
Some of you will join the foreign missions.
Some of you have tongues, some tongue
interpretation—
The sum of you, one holy, royal nation.

Some of you are rich, and some are poor.
Some of you came straight away, some took a long de-
tour.
Some of you will taste of death, some will see the
revelation—
The sum of you, one holy, royal nation.

The sum of all the parts is not the whole,
Though each of us is some of all.
And all is some of each, but still there is
another pasture and yet another fold.

'Cause some of you are Gentiles, some are Jews.
Some of you know mockery, and some have been
abused.
But none of you will come to condemnation,
Because the sum of you, one holy, royal nation!

Chapter 23

This Is the Seed,
the Spirit of Life

*E*xcept a corn of wheat fall into the ground and die, it abideth alone: but if it die, it bringeth forth much fruit. He that loveth his life shall lose it; and he that hateth his life in this world shall keep it unto life eternal (John 12:24-25).

In the middle of the Garden of Eden, there were two trees— one was the tree of life, and the other was the tree of the knowledge of good and evil (see Gen. 2:9). One tree contained the spirit of life; and the other tree contained the spirit of death. To eat the fruit of the one tree was to live forever (see Gen. 3:22); to eat the fruit of the other tree was to surely die.

* * * * *

The Father above had two sons, one created and the other begotten. The created son was Adam, and the begotten Son was Jesus. Adam carried the spirit of death and separation from God. Jesus carried the Spirit of life, reconciliation, and oneness with God. *One son made us children of satan. One Son made us children of God* (see Jn. 1:12).

The "spirit" of the tree is in the fruit, and the "spirit" of the tree is in the seed. As such, the "spirit" of the fruit is in the "spirit" of the tree, and the "spirit" of the seed is in the "spirit" of the fruit. In the same way, the offspring of the heavenly Father has the Spirit of the Father. The Son is in the Father, and the Father is in the Son. He is not the Son if He does not contain the seed and Spirit of the Father.

Whatever seed a son carries points us to his father. The fruit of a father is in his son, and the fruit of a son is in his father. The seed of every son is from his father, and the fruit of every son contains the spirit and seed of his father.

As believers, we cannot be the children of God unless we have the Spirit of God. If we have the Spirit of God, we should bear the fruit of God (see Mt. 7:20). Jesus came from God, bore the fruit of God, carried the Word of God, and planted the seed of God:

> *...He that believeth on Me, believeth not on Me, but on Him that sent Me. ... For I have not spoken of Myself; but the Father which sent Me, He gave Me a commandment, what I should say, and what I should speak. And I know that His commandment is life everlasting: whatsoever I speak therefore, even as the Father said unto Me, so I speak* (John 12:44,49-50).

> *...My doctrine is not Mine, but His that sent Me* (John 7:16).

...When ye have lifted up the Son of man, then shall ye know that I am He, and that I do nothing of Myself; but as My Father hath taught Me, I speak these things. And He that sent Me is with Me: the Father hath not left Me alone; for I do always those things that please Him (John 8:28-29).

If we are the children of God, we should be able to truthfully say the same things Jesus said of His relationship with the Father! We should be able to say we always do the things that please the Lord, speaking nothing of ourselves. We should truthfully claim to teach only as the Savior has taught us. We are in Christ and Christ is in us. We are never alone, for Christ is always with us. Christ sent us to be His witnesses. He knows us and we know Him, for we have seen Him.

"As the Father knoweth Me, even so know I the Father.... I and My Father are One" (Jn. 10:15,30). "All things are delivered to Me of My Father: and no man knoweth who the Son is, but the Father; and who the Father is, but the Son, and he to whom the Son will reveal Him" (Lk. 10:22). "...Whosoever shall receive Me receiveth Him that sent Me..." (Lk. 9:48). "...No man cometh unto the Father, but by Me" (Jn. 14:6).

The Prodigal Son

And [Jesus] said, A certain man had two sons: and the younger of them said to his father, Father, give me the portion of goods that falleth to me. And he divided unto them his living. And not many days after the younger son gathered all together, and took his journey into a far country, and there wasted his substance with riotous living. And when he had spent all, there arose a mighty famine in that land; and he began to be in want. And he went and joined himself to a citizen of that country; and he sent him into his fields to feed swine. And he would fain have filled his belly with the husks that the swine did eat: and no man gave unto him. And when he came to himself, he said, How many hired servants of my father's have bread enough and to spare, and I perish with hunger! I will arise and go to my father, and will say unto him, Father, I have sinned against heaven, and before thee, and am no more worthy to be called thy son: make me as one of thy hired servants. And he arose, and came to his father. But when he was yet a great way off, his father saw him, and had compassion, and ran, and fell on his neck, and kissed him. And the son said unto him, Father, I have sinned against heaven, and in thy sight, and am no more worthy to be called thy son. But the father said to his servants, Bring forth the best robe, and put it on him; and put a ring on his hand, and shoes on his feet: and bring hither the fatted calf, and kill it; and let us eat, and be merry: for this my son was dead, and is alive again; he was lost, and is found. And they began to be merry. Now his elder son was in the field: and as he came and drew nigh to the house, he heard musick and dancing. And he called one of the servants, and asked what these things meant. And he said unto him, Thy brother is come; and thy father hath killed the fatted calf, because he hath received him safe and sound. And he was angry, and would not go in: therefore came his father out, and intreated him. And he answering said to his father, Lo, these many years do I serve thee, neither transgressed I at any time thy commandment: and yet thou never gavest me a kid, that I might make merry with my friends: but as soon as this thy son was come, which hath devoured thy living with harlots, thou hast killed for him the fatted calf. And he said unto him, Son, thou art ever with me, and all that I have is thine. It was meet that we should make merry, and be glad: for this thy brother was dead, and is alive again; and was lost, and is found (Luke 15:11-32).

All the children of the earth are prodigal children. We have all turned away from the Father and sought our own way. Only the unfallen creatures in the heavenly sphere have remained faithful to the Father. If we repent and return to God, He will take us back as sons and daughters, give each of us a robe of righteousness, a ring of authority through our identity with the Father, and some shoes for our purpose in Him. Will the "elder sons" of God who dwell above find reason to refuse the merriment of the younger prodigal son? Will they murmur against the good man of the house who gives every worker a penny, though some have worked far longer than the others? (See Matthew 20:1-16.)

God is the Father of us all. We, His children, fall and crawl as much as we stand up tall...our numbers include those who were self-righteous, indignant, ungrateful, unrepentant, way-ward, weak, wanton, wild, regretful, and lamented.

Our connection as children with our Father God is spiritual, practical, and volitional. Since we are born in alienation from God, our first move must be to realign ourselves with God *by choice*. We must *choose* God's Kingdom over the kingdom of the world (see Mt. 6:24,33; Jas. 4:4; 1 Jn. 2:15-17). We must *decide* to align ourselves with God's principles and Spirit and cast out satan's spirit and abandon his evil works. We must purify ourselves by obedience to God's Word (see 1 Jn. 3:2-6). John the apostle said:

Little children, let no man deceive you: he that doeth righteousness is righteous, even as He is righteous. He that committeth sin is of the devil; for the devil sinneth from the beginning. For this purpose the Son of God was manifested, that He might destroy the works of the devil. Whosoever is born of God doth not commit sin; for His seed remaineth in him: and he cannot sin, because he is born of God. In this the children of God are manifest, and the children of the devil... (1 John 3:7-10).

John also said, "And he that keepeth His commandments dwelleth in Him, and He in him" (1 Jn. 3:24a). Peter said we are "...born again, not of corruptible seed, but of incorruptible, by the word of God, which liveth and abideth for ever" (1 Pet. 1:23).

If we decide to obey God and abandon sin, then God will manifest Himself and impart His Spirit to us (see Jn. 14:15-17, 21). He will put the Spirit of Christ into our bodies as a guide, teacher, and comforter (see Jn. 14:26; 16:13). When we choose to obey God, our lives are no longer our own. We become the vessels of God, led through the world by the internal presence of God in the same way Israel was led by the pillar of cloud and fire! This is the *merger of God with man*. His Spirit takes up residence in our bodies to lead us into truth and righteousness after we die to self and the world and are born again of the Spirit.

Jesus was the firstborn from the dead (see Col. 1:18), the firstfruits of them that sleep (see 1 Cor. 15:20,23). He gave up His life that we might live. His death imparted spiritual life to all who choose Him, and His resurrection is the hope of each one of His children. In Him, we are quickened unto eternal life. We are like Jesus in that we are called to "die to self" and to the world. If the Spirit is born in us, it will bear fruit in our lives and in the lives of those we touch. The Scripture says, "But the fruit of the Spirit is love, joy, peace, longsuffering, gentleness, goodness, faith, meekness, temperance.... . And they that are Christ's have crucified the flesh with the affections and lusts. If we live in the Spirit, let us also walk in the Spirit" (Gal. 5:22-25).

One of the most basic principles of God is the principle of sowing and reaping. Paul warned us, "Be not deceived; God is not mocked: for whatsoever a man soweth, that shall he also reap. For he that soweth to his flesh shall of the flesh reap corruption; but he that soweth to the Spirit shall of the Spirit reap life everlasting" (Gal. 6:7-8).

Christ confronted the Pharisees about their plot to murder Him and applied this principle with power:

I know that ye are Abraham's seed; but ye seek to kill Me, because My word hath no place in you. I speak that which I have seen with My Father: and ye do that which ye have seen with your father. They answered and said unto Him, Abraham is our father. Jesus saith unto them, If ye were Abraham's children, ye would do the works of Abraham. But now ye seek to kill Me, a man that hath told you the truth, which I have heard of God: this did not Abraham. Ye do the deeds of your father. Then said they to Him, We be not born of fornication; we have one Father, even God. Jesus said unto them, If God were your Father, ye would love Me: for I proceeded forth and came from God.... . Ye are of your father the devil, and the lusts of your father ye will do. He was a murderer from the beginning, and abode not in the truth, because there is no truth in him. When he speaketh a lie, he speaketh of his own: for he is a liar, and the father of it (John 8:37-42,44).

The murderous Pharisees looked only upon the flesh to kill the body; their wicked hearts and blind eyes had failed to see the eternal Spirit in Christ. While they tried to shame Him by pointing to His conception before wedlock, their evil eyes had failed to see that His birth was by the Holy Ghost. Their focus on the flesh and the deeds of the flesh had blinded them to the Spirit and the works of the One whom they called Father and God.

Beloved, we are of God if we have the Spirit of God, if we spread the Word of God and reflect the person of God in Jesus Christ. If we walk outside of God in the flesh, if we teach others to walk outside of God in the flesh, then we have the spirit of satan and are the children of satan and sin. There is no other option in all the universe. The seed of the Father is in the Son, and the fruit of the Father is the fruit of the Son.

There is a certain mystery in the message of Jesus Christ. It is the mystery of the incorruptible seed. It is the message of God's love reflected in the new covenant, and it can be found nowhere else. The message is simple but profound: *The world is going to change from old to new.* The works of the devil will give way to the works of Jesus Christ. The glorious day of His coming will break the barriers of the past, tear open the dawn of a new day, and bridge the chasm of time and space heretofore impassable by mortal flesh.

The key to this new revelation resides within the Spirit-filled believer. It is the *merger of God in Christ with His fallen creation*. One by one, Christ comes inside us to change the whole world through the Spirit.

Many ask why God did not make us perfect in the first place. The answer is that He gave His creation the choice to follow Him or follow evil. Only time can reveal the mystery of how the omnipotent God can give human choice. Nevertheless, those who choose Him receive a gift of infinite love and mercy when they receive the Spirit of God and are changed from corruptible to incorruptible. The coming age of perfection is *here today*, and it is taking place one soul at a time!

Behold, what manner of love the Father hath bestowed upon us, that we should be called the sons of God: therefore the world knoweth us not, because it knew Him not. Beloved, now are we the sons of God, and it doth not yet appear what we shall be: but...we shall be like Him; for we shall see Him as He is (1 John 3:1-2).

The "corn of wheat" in John 12:24 is Jesus Christ. By His death He was able to send the Comforter (see Jn. 16:7) and plant a seed in the life of His disciples. This seed is newness of life on the inside of those who have the indwelling Spirit of God. It is not an emotion, a vague sensation, or a collection of thoughts about holiness. It is a mind-changing, life-altering experience so awesome, so dramatic, and so deep that it forever transforms the life of the recipient. It births an adoration of God so great that it compels change from the smallest details and to our greatest and most secret of sins.

The apostle John was on target! The presence of the Holy Ghost is so profound that it pulls us away from our familiar patterns of sin and demands total attention to its holy internal agenda. It overtakes the surrendered life like a sweeping wave of energy, pressing toward perfection with irresistible urgency. Jesus gave Nicodemus the best description of this process when He said, "The wind blows wherever it pleases. You hear its sound, but you cannot tell where it comes from or where it is going. So it is with everyone born of the Spirit" (Jn. 3:8 NIV).

If you give place to God's presence, the Spirit will take control in a loving way and lead you to new heights of power, faith, and obedience. He produces things in your life that you could never produce on your own. He produces the power of God and renders the gifts of God to establish the Kingdom of God.

The Spirit itself is God. He does not ask for particulars in your life, He asks for your general permission to lead. Once you grant it, you will walk in the power of His presence and experience the deepest love commitment of your whole life! The *Pneuma* (Spirit) of God will breathe in and through your life, blowing like a tropical breeze through the bending palms of your mind and spirit. If you love Him, you will yield to His loving touch and move to His gracious urgings. He softens, sweetens, mends, mellows, and puts together a life in Christ out of nothing of particular value.

O, heavenly treasure in earthen vessels! The resurrected Christ is come on the inside to do a strange work that began with Adam. It passed to Noah, and moved to Abraham, and then to Moses; and was not complete until now in His day, when the covenant was not remade but fulfilled, finally, by the indwelling life of Christ.

This is the power of God poured out upon mankind. It is the reality of all His promises brought to the peak of perfection. This is the unconditional love of God made evident as the heavenly promise of life eternal is planted in the flesh of man. It is the silent onslaught of God's holy Kingdom recruiting its warriors from the inner man.

We are empty shells without the Spirit. Like Adam after his fall, there is no possible salvation if we do not have the Spirit because the seed of new life is not inside us. The changing process cannot take place, and the strange work of conversion cannot go forward. The quickening is not possible.

New birth requires a seed from the ministry of Jesus Christ. He came that we might put on new and abundant life! The old person begins to die the moment the Holy Ghost comes in, which is the reverse of what happened with Adam. Adam's eternal life began to die the moment he received the seed of satan through the rebellious act of taking the fruit of the tree.

However, once we receive the Holy Spirit in a supernatural merger, a child is born on the inside, and just like the child conceived in Mary, it is a product of the Holy Ghost. Slowly He grows in our experiences to replace the old with the new. We begin to show signs of Jesus in our walk, our talk, and our thought. We shed the resemblance we have to the devil and renounce his guidance in our lives; then we pledge our allegiance to the Spirit of Christ.

The seed begins to germinate and put forth shoots, stems, and buds. Before long there are some flowers and eventually a number of new seeds. Soon it produces waves of righteousness like fields of golden wheat. We learn to be more loving, meek, gentle, faithful, humble, joyful, peaceful, and respectful with every passing day. We put on the person of Jesus, the firstfruit of God. We bury the old man, and sprout new buds, new leaves, and new fruit—and with the fruit comes new power.

I am the true vine, and My Father is the husbandman. Every branch in Me that beareth not fruit He taketh away: and every branch that beareth fruit, He purgeth it, that it may bring forth more fruit. Now ye are clean through the word which I have spoken unto you. Abide in Me, and I in you. As the branch cannot bear fruit of itself, except it abide in the vine; no more can ye, except ye abide in Me. I am the vine, ye are the branches: He that abideth in Me, and I in him, the same bringeth forth much fruit: for without Me ye can do nothing. If a man abide not in Me, he is cast forth as a branch, and is withered; and men gather them, and cast them into the fire, and they are burned. If ye abide in Me, and My words abide in you, ye shall ask what ye will, and it shall be done unto you (John 15:1-7).

Jesus fulfilled the promises at Sinai (see Ex. 19:5-6) when He said, "...I have chosen you, and ordained you, that ye should go and bring forth fruit, and that your fruit should remain: that whatsoever ye shall ask of the Father in My name, He may give it you" (Jn. 15:16).

The special relationship promised at Sinai is fulfilled in Jesus Christ by the *indwelling Spirit*. He has empowered us to represent Him before the world. He has promised us access to the Father in His name and authority, so we are expected to overcome the world even as Christ overcame the world. Those who overcome may look forward to His promises:

1. "I will grant that you sit with Me in My throne" (see Rev. 3:21).

2. "I will make of you a pillar in the temple of God" (see Rev. 3:12).

3. "I will clothe you in white raiment. I will confess your name before My Father and before His angels" (see Rev. 3:5).

4. "I will give you the morning star" (see Rev. 2:28).

5. "I will give you power over the nations" (see Rev. 2:26).

6. "I will give you hidden manna and a white stone that carries a new name" (see Rev. 2:17).

7. "I will give you a crown of life" (see Rev. 2:10).

8. "I will give you to eat of the tree of life" (see Rev. 2:7).

In the middle of Paradise beside the River of Life, stands a tree which bears 12 types of fruit and yields its fruit each month. The leaves of this tree are for the healing of nations, and its name is the Tree of Life (see Rev. 2:7; 22:2).

The Holy Ghost is our ticket to Paradise (see Rom. 8:11). He guarantees us a place in the Kingdom of God and a share in the inheritance of Christ (see Eph. 1:13-14). He grants us the opportunity to drink of the Water of Life and to eat from the Tree of Life.

Blessed are they that do His commandments, that they may have right to the tree of life.... And the Spirit and the bride say, Come. And let him that heareth say, Come. And let him that is athirst come. And whosoever will, let him take the water of life freely (Revelation 22:14,17).

Jesus said, "Blessed are they which do hunger and thirst after righteousness: for they shall be filled" (Mt. 5:6). Ever since Christ's ascension and the Day of Pentecost, the hungry have been filled with the Holy Ghost!

So the Spirit saith to the churches:

"The Lord hath need of you,
For works that only you can do.
Can He be sure that you'll endure
A light that is both bright and pure?

"The Lord hath made a plan
That binds the Spirit and the man.
The only thing is that this stream
Must channel through you clear and clean.

"The Lord hath need of you,
A funnel, flowing fully through;
The less assumed, the more of Whom
The Lord appointed to His room.

"The Lord hath need of you,
For works that only you can do.
Can He be sure that you'll endure
A light that is both bright and pure?"

Part VII

Conclusion

Chapter 24

Absolute Power: The Romance of the Spirit

When I was a child, I loved the Lord. He was the only Father that I knew, and I tried to be the best child that I could. I vowed to do whatever He told me to. I tried to be holy from what I understood out of the Scriptures. I could feel the guardian angels all around me, and I knew that God would do miracles if I needed them. I felt a special calling for my life.

When I became a young man, though, I strayed away from God. My curiosity took my eyes off of Him and led me into worldly pursuits. They eventually caused me to fall, and I sank deeply into sin. After a number of years, I began to see demons closing in on me for the first time. Although God's Spirit never left me, and though I could sense Him beckoning my return, my life became dangerous as satan pursued me with deadly temptations. Eventually I reached a point where I could see no way out, and I thought that maybe my life was over.

One desperate night I believe I saw the devil himself. A huge cloak of blackness hovered over me and it seemed to pronounce my doom. As close to death as I might have felt before, I was not prepared for this. With panic in my heart, I began to seek the Lord more earnestly than ever before. I refused to stop praying until the Lord gave me an answer. The answer came very quickly. The Lord heard my cry and said, "Go forward!"

From the moment that He answered me, all my struggles disappeared. At first, I was more shocked than relieved. I could not believe that He had forgiven and delivered me so quickly. I continued to pray for long hours every day until one day something suddenly happened. I began to experience visions and miraculous occurrences. I had prophetic experiences and heard the voice of God. Needless to say, my life has never been the same again.

It has been a few years since then, and my life is richer than ever before. For a long time, I could not understand why God waited 20 years to reveal Himself with such power and in such awesome proportions. After much thought, I have concluded that if He had done it while I was a child, I would not have understood His love or appreciated His great power. In my innocence, I would have thought that I had done something to deserve the miracles. I would not have appreciated His deep concern for my life, thinking instead that God was rewarding my goodness. His power would not have meant much. That is why I walked away from it to begin with. I could not fully see it. I was like Adam and Eve, who did not know the difference between good and evil.

Now that I look back on things, however, I can see the tender romance of the Spirit. The Spirit of God was with me every moment of my life. He played with me. He danced with me. He laughed and ran and cried with me. What I felt, He felt. What I learned, He helped me to see it. While I hoped and dreamed, He fed my every wish with the will and way for its complete fulfillment.

We were tied together from the earliest moment of my existence. His love for me was infinite. It caused my life to leap forward with an extraordinary depth of positive influence that was at my beck and call. Right there at my side was the divine source and basic preparation for entry into absolute and everlasting power. I merely had to see it, recognize it for what it was, and enter into it. So, the question should not have been "Why did God take so long to see me?" It should have been, "Why did I take so long so see Him?" Now I understand that all of my trials led me to where I am now.

This is the romance of the Spirit. It woos and wins the love of God's children. God has chosen to lead us into unholy ground so He can draw us back to Himself with a grand shower of His love and power. He knew full well that we would be tangled in sin, but He planned all along to bring us back again. Without this divine romance, the children of God would all feel a sense of entitlement and believe that God's power was simply deriving from their actions, goodness, or personal merit. They would not appreciate the blessings of God when everything was going well.

God loved all of us from the start. He lavished His affections upon the darlings of His heart, and He had planned from the beginning to make every tie between His people and Himself. He intended to give us His name and create a spiritual line through us that would never end. He would give to us His nature and His image. Nonetheless, He also longed to show His deepest love and matchless power, though He knew from the start that this would require a revelation and transformation.

Satan was raised up for a very specific purpose—to show the absolute power of God. Satan seeks to wrestle us down, weaken us, and then trap us, so he can take away our strength and vision. He craftily puts every evil thing before us, touting the flesh as superior to the Spirit. He wants to glorify that which is sensual and temporal, emphasizing the things we see, touch, and feel with our emotions. He even did this to angels!

The entrapment of satan causes us to lose our faith in the flesh. If we endure and overcome his terrible temptations, then our faith will never again rely upon the self, the flesh, or the world. Satan himself allows God's love and mercy to banish every false hope that pride has given us because satan was raised up to do this exact thing. Despite his best efforts to the contrary, he gives glory to our God. After we have thoroughly examined the enemy, we lose all faith in ourselves and are emptied of our pride. In the end, we turn to God with a solid foundation in faith that is unmovable!

Jesus Christ came out of the Father to remind us how He loved us from the brink of time. In all of our distastefulness, He still called us His own. Although we are stunned by His sweetest advances, He will pour out His power from Heaven above. It is the power of love and faith unto salvation and surrender to the Spirit of God. Only then do we fall to our knees and adore Him. Only then do we exalt Him above every hope. Only then do we come to see Him in His glory and love Him more than ourselves! This is the sweet romance of God for His people. The romance of the Spirit is the wooing and the winning of our hearts!

Dearly beloved, there is so much more that I could say about the matchless power of God's love—the romance of the Spirit. But we must start with the basic elements of understanding

God—unconditional love, undaunted faith, and obedience unto death. They ornament the life of God within us and give full meaning to His Word. With these basic keys, we can open the realm of the Spirit and find our place before the One from whom undiluted power may be drawn.

The "How To" Tapes

Series 1: Background material for understanding the *Power* text, $16 (postage included).

    Tape 1   "Love's Passage Back to the Image of God"
- How to find power from your identity that was hidden in God and revealed through Christ!

    Tape 2   "The Image of Perfection"
- How to understand love, obedience, and faith!
- Three times when God touched man and gave him power

    Tape 3   "Overcoming the World, Recognizing the Enemy"
- How to resist the enemy through vision and courage!
- Know satan's counterfeits of the true power of God

Series 2: Summary of the *Power* message, $22 (postage included).

    Tape 1   "The Power of Love"
- How to claim the power of our birthright!
- Accessing the power of a heavenly citizenship

    Tape 2   "The Power of Faith"
- How to use the most powerful weapon in the universe!
- Eight steps to incredible wonder-working faith

    Tape 3   "The Power of Obedience"
- How to experience healing and wholeness by participating in the divine nature!

    Tape 4   "The Merger of God With Man: Absolute Power"
- How to be a partner and coworker with Jesus through the indwelling of God!

CUT ALONG DOTTED LINE

Please send: ____ Series One: Background for Power $16 value
       ____ Series Two: Power Summary $22 value
       ____ Series One & Two $38 value

Name: _____

Address: _____

City, ST, ZIP: _____ Phone _____

Mail Check or Money Order to:
The Center of Power
P.O. Box 43749
Washington, DC 20010
Or call:
1-800-684-5467
Wait for instructions, and then enter **6493**.
VISA and MasterCard accepted.